OUTSIDERS

OUTSIDERS

American Short Stories for Students of ESL

Jean S. Mullen
Northeastern University

PRENTICE HALL REGENTS
Englewood Cliffs, New Jersey 07632

Library of Congress Cataloging in Publication Data

Mullen, Jean S., (date)
Outsiders.

1. English language—Text-books for foreign speakers.
I. Title.
PE1128.M748 1984 428.2'4 83-22946
ISBN 0-13-645366-X

Editorial/production supervision and
interior design by Lisa A. Domínguez
Cover design by George Cornell
Manufacturing buyer: Harry P. Baisley

Prentice-Hall, Inc.
A Paramount Communications Company
Englewood Cliffs, New Jersey 07632

Printed in the United States of America
20 19 18 17 16 15 14 13

ISBN 0-13-645366-X

Prentice-Hall International (UK) Limited, *London*
Prentice-Hall of Australia Pty. Limited, *Sydney*
Prentice-Hall Canada Inc., *Toronto*
Prentice-Hall Hispanoamericana, S.A., *Mexico*
Prentice-Hall of India Private Limited, *New Delhi*
Prentice-Hall of Japan, Inc., *Tokyo*
Simon & Schuster Asia Pte. Ltd., *Singapore*
Editora Prentice-Hall do Brasil, Ltda., *Rio de Janeiro*

To my mother and father,
who loved the study of language and literature

Copyrights and Acknowledgments

"On the Outside," by August W. Derleth, from *Writers in Revolt: The Anvil Anthology, 1933–1940.* Eds., Jack Conroy and Curt Johnson (New York: Lawrence Hill and Company, 1973). Reprinted by permission of Arkham House Publishers, Inc.

"Sorrow for a Midget," from *Something in Common,* by Langston Hughes. Copyright © 1963 by Langston Hughes. Copyright © 1935, 1944, 1952, 1958, 1960 by Langston Hughes. Copyright © 1933, 1934 by Alfred A. Knopf, Inc. Reprinted by permission of Hill and Wang, a division of Farrar, Straus and Giroux, Inc.

"I Want to Work," from *Puzzled America,* by Sherwood Anderson. Copyright © 1935 by Charles Scribner's Sons. Renewed 1962 by Eleanor Copenhaver Anderson. Reprinted by permission of Harold Ober Associates Incorporated.

"The Loudest Voice," from *The Little Disturbances of Man,* by Grace Paley. Copyright 1959 by Grace Paley. Reprinted by permission of Viking Penguin, Inc.

"The Test," by Angelica Gibbs. Reprinted by permission; © 1940, 1978 *The New Yorker Magazine.*

"Señor Payroll," by William E. Barrett, from the *Southwest Review.* Copyright © 1943 by University Press in Dallas. Reprinted by permission of Harold Ober Associates Incorporated.

"Going Home," from *Inhale and Exhale*, by William Saroyan (New York: Random House, 1936). Reprinted by permission of the Estate of William Saroyan.

"Mr. K*A*P*L*A*N and Vocabulary," from *The Education of Hyman Kaplan,* by Leonard Q. Ross; copyright 1937 by Harcourt Brace Jovanovich, Inc.; renewed 1965 by Leo Rosten. Reprinted by permission of the publisher.

"Hawsmoot," by Peter Lars Sandberg. Reprinted by permission of the author.

"Rope," by Katherine Anne Porter. Copyright 1930, 1958 by Katherine Anne Porter. Reprinted from her volume, *Flowering Judas and Other Stories,* by permission of Harcourt Brace Jovanovich, Inc.

"His Secret Garden," by Blanche McNamara, from "The Poet's Workshop," *The Writer,* May 1970. Reprinted by permission of *The Writer.*

"A Plea," by John Ciardi, from *In the Stoneworks,* 1961. Reprinted by permission of the poet.

"Soldier's Home," by Ernest Hemingway, from *In Our Time.* Copyright 1925, 1930 by Charles Scribner's Sons; copyright renewed 1953, 1958 by Ernest Hemingway (New York: Charles Scribner's Sons, 1925, 1930). Reprinted with the permission of Charles Scribner's Sons.

Contents

XII

Preface

During the classes we were not just reading the story itself but we were also discussing about the facts, learning new words and idioms, colloquialisms, and getting information about the setting and the background.

Ece Onay, Turkey

At first used my own ethical education to think about the stories, and they seems ridiculous to me then. And also it was very hard for me to understand what the author trying to tell us. . . . When I began to get used to western ideas and cultures, I didn't feel the stories were queer any more . . . studying English by reading short stories helps you a lot while you are in this country. Sometimes I enjoyed the stories so much that I couldn't wait till I finish it, I would read the last two pages for get to know the result.

Harriet Hui-Hua Lin, Taiwan

Like native English-speaking Americans, the many thousands of foreign students in degree programs in the United States are still required, even in this age of emphasis on technology, to study literature. They also share with native English speakers the need to develop and polish their *writing skills* to a level of competency acceptable in college work. The purpose of *Outsiders* is to help address this twofold obligation to nonnative English users in our colleges and universities by offering the following:

Short stories carefully chosen for their quality, diversity, and appeal, so that they can provide a sound, structural basis for studying fiction as a literary genre in a *college credit course.*

A glimpse of American lifestyles, cultural variations, and social issues as portrayed in fictional settings by first-class American writers.

The unifying motif of "the outsider in the U.S.A.," a theme that recent arrivals can understand and appreciate and then recognize as broader in scope than they had at first supposed.

An objective ("scientific") approach to literature, using the skills of observation and inference to develop reading techniques appropriate for a college-level study of literature and adaptable also for the intensive reading required in other disciplines.

Extensive vocabulary support provided in a unique format, which not only makes unfamiliar words conveniently accessible but lends itself to special study of different American cultural backgrounds and colloquial speech patterns.

Exercises, discussion topics, writing assignments, and group projects that are clearly derived from the stories themselves and that aim to cultivate college-level thinking and writing skills.

The order in which the *Outsiders* stories appear pertains, in general, to their sophistication of style and content. Since the "outsiders" theme, if left undiluted, could become somewhat intensive, an effort was made to intersperse the stories having more serious themes with lighter, more humorous pieces such as "The Loudest Voice," "Señor Payroll," "Mr. K*A*P*L*A*N and Vocabulary," and "Rope." However, because the study of short fiction as literature is of paramount concern in *Outsiders,* the length and complexity of the stories increase toward the end of the book.

The study questions and other activities that accompany each story are closely related to the story itself. Since the nature and type of the study materials vary from one chapter to another, a descriptive label has been assigned to each activity and can be found as a numbered heading where that activity begins, as well as in the contents. The instructor should feel free to omit whole chapters or parts thereof, or to shift the order for studying them, should teaching purposes so require.

A discussion of the Vocabulary Aids and how to use them appears in Chapter I. The rationale for providing such a prominent and thoroughgoing treatment of vocabulary is, in short, to facilitate the student's ready grasp of precisely what the author is saying. Undergraduates are generally expected to study literature in their own native language, and even then they find sufficient challenge in the artistic subtleties of a great writer. Meanwhile, the real meaning and drive of a literary work can be lost in the complicated process of hunting down many unfamiliar words in the dictionary, as Phil Scholfield points out in his article entitled, "Using the English Dictionary for Comprehension."* A conscientious student may, in fact, follow the seven intricate steps that Scholfield outlines for choosing the right meaning to fit the context. One gifted Taiwanese student in a Harvard summer school class described the unfortunate result of his applying such a method:

> Yes, by investing a lot of time looking up different sorts of special purpose dictionaries, one can eventually find answers to most of his questions. But, by then, he might be so tired and have lost his interest on the work he was reading. I went

*Phil Scholfield, "Using the English Dictionary for Comprehension," *TESOL Quarterly,* 16, No. 2 (June 1982), 185–194.

> through this kind of experience and was most discouraged when I, after having spent a lot of time going through several dictionaries, still failed to find an answer.
>
> Joseph Peng, Taiwan

The Vocabulary Aids in *Outsiders* are a response to this student and to the others quoted in the beginning of the Preface.

Much of the material in the book has been used (in its initially crude and unrevised form) in teaching ESL freshman English to over 400 students at Northeastern University. Most of the students were majoring in engineering and had TOEFL scores of 450–500; moreover, their English instructors were used to teaching grammar and composition, not literature. Yet both students and faculty responded favorably to the unaccustomed experience of studying and writing about the stories in *Outsiders.*

The author has endeavored to furnish enough basic tools for the instructor new to the teaching of literature, and also to offer a wide choice of alternate approaches to instructors already comfortable with teaching complex literary themes. As everyone who stands before an ESL class has discovered, the teacher can immeasurably extend the students' cultural awareness simply by drawing upon her or his own personal history and familiarity with the language.

The stories and activities in *Outsiders* are intended to reinforce that process and to further enhance the special creative interaction so well known to be a welcome feature of the ESL classroom.

I would like to express my thanks to Lynn Stevens and to William Biddle, whose advice and encouragement helped to launch this book, and to the colleagues who tested out much of the material in their classes and gave me the benefit of their students' reactions and their own opinions: Mary Lynn Cramer, Faye Firnhaber, Janet Littell, Linda Moussouris, Melanie Schneider, and Valerie Warrior.

A special word of appreciation is due Timothy D. DiPace, reference librarian at Roxbury Community College, who searched diligently on my behalf for information concerning Angelica Gibbs, author of "The Test."

I am particularly grateful for the interest and understanding of friends, colleagues, and family at different stages in the book's preparation. John F. Smith gave me continuing encouragement and very much practical help, while Dianne Frederickson and the English Department secretarial staff at Northeastern University tirelessly typed and retyped the manuscript. Of invaluable assistance in the revision process were editorial reviews and comments from my fellow professionals across the country as well as the perceptive comments and suggestions of my editors at Prentice-Hall.

My son Richard W. Mullen supplied useful feedback from Mexico on the story, "Señor Payroll." And finally, my daughter Meredy Amyx provided timely editorial advice along with her experienced proofreader's eye.

My warm thanks to these and to many others for their aid and support.

Jean S. Mullen

Northeastern University
January 1984

OUTSIDERS

I

Introduction and Guide to the Readings

You have now reached a more advanced level in your study of English as a second language. You can speak and write English well enough to make yourself understood, and you are working every day to improve your skills in these areas. Although you may find it difficult to keep up with a literature course as it is usually offered to American students, you are probably ready to read the work of some first-class writers with appreciation and enjoyment.

Fiction is a familiar genre in all cultures. Moreover, the best stories and tales have a universal quality of appeal for everyone, because they emphasize human needs, feelings, and the problems experienced by people in all times and in all places.

Since the stories in this collection are short, you will have time to read them carefully and study them in depth. Much of your study can be done in class, sometimes in projects in which you can work together with your classmates. Other activities will help you individually to develop your vocabulary and your analytical skills, as well as to improve your writing.

Each story is by a highly recognized American author and has an American setting. Some of the stories are about actual "outsiders" trying to cope with life in the United States, while others are about Americans who feel in some way alienated from their own society.

As you encounter American ideas and folkways in your reading, you will broaden your cultural base by relating what you read to what you are personally familiar with at home. Best of all, in sharing others' insights not only will you enrich your own, but you will learn to express them better.

1. A "SCIENTIFIC" APPROACH TO LITERATURE

FICTION IN THREE DIMENSIONS

The greatest advances of technology depend on:

- the observation of facts;
- the recognition of problems and needs inferred from those facts;
- the search for imaginative and workable solutions.

The engineer lays out plans for an underwater tunnel across a harbor. The city planner blueprints a combined residential, shopping, and recreational area. The medical team researches a new and more effective treatment for leukemia. In every case, as with all scientific achievement, the three-dimensional approach is the key.

Observation: The scientist tries to observe and to accurately record the processes of nature;

Inference: The scientist must interpret the data, or learn to understand and evaluate what those facts mean;

Imagination: The scientist then forms a hypothesis (an "educated guess") based on these facts, about other possibilities as yet undiscovered. It is like making a calculated leap from the known to the unknown.

It is this last step that is the basis for the discovery of hitherto unknown facts about the universe, such as the quantum theory, black holes in space, and many more. The greatest scientists have been, and still are, the ones who have brilliantly combined the techniques of *experimental observation* and *inference* with their own *imagination*. In so doing, they have carried mankind another technological leap away from his primitive past.

That may be the way scientists operate, but what does all this have to do with literature?

First of all, since both the scientist and the fiction writer are creative, they have some important things in common. They both use the same three dimensions of *observation, inference,* and *imagination*. Their results, however, are different because they work in quite different media: The scientist is concerned with tangible, measurable data; the fiction writer deals with intangible, human qualities such as values, attitudes, ideas, and feelings.

In other words, then, the scientist deals with facts, while the writer makes up stories that aren't really true.

It may seem like that, but there is another way of looking at it. Although fiction is not "true" in the sense that each story actually happened as recounted, it is based in some way on the writer's own experience and his observations about life. Like the scientist, the writer must try to write honestly about human beings and happenings as he has seen them.

But he does more than that. Because his "seeing eye" has made him discern meanings beyond the events themselves, the author wants us to share his insights and be stirred, as he himself has been, by the failures and the victories, the frailties, the follies, and above all, the ultimate courage of the human spirit. Like the engineer, the architect, and the medical research team, the writer uses the same sort of three-dimensional technique:

Observation: The writer employs all his senses to learn about people, events, and life and then describes them as precisely as he can.

Inference: The writer reinforces and amplifies his perceptions by relating them to his own prior knowledge and experience. He will not spell out all his inferences for us; he will only *imply* some of them, leaving the reader free to seek and find others of his own.

Imagination: The writer's close observations of his world and his response to it become authentic materials for creating the mental and emotional images and fantasies that we call stories.

As you can see, *truth* for a fiction writer is not quite the same as it is for the news writer or the historian. For them *truth* means giving the facts that really happened and reporting them as accurately as possible. The story writer, on the other hand, creates a world or a society of characters that never has existed in real life. His obligation to truth—and to his art—is to make his story *seem* so real that we are convinced that, had it actually happened, it would all have taken place just as he has told us.

As an example, here is a very short story based on one of the most familiar of Aesop's Fables:

THE ANT AND THE GRASSHOPPER

On a clear, breezy day late in the summer, a grasshopper was singing happily as he swung on a stalk of wheat. The sun was warm and bright, and around him were acres of grain, ripe and ready to eat.

The grasshopper looked down and saw an ant rushing along, dragging a large kernel of wheat bigger than she was. She did not even stop to rest, but if she lost her grip, she would shift the grain about until she had a firm hold. Then she would hurry on her way.

"Where are you going with such a heavy load?" asked the grasshopper.

"Home," she said. "I have a big family to feed."

"What's the hurry?" he asked. "It's too hot to work so hard. And besides, there's plenty of grain right here."

"Harvest time is coming soon, and then all the grain will be gone," the ant said, running even faster.

She was right. After the wheat was cut and gathered, the cold winds came, and the grasshopper was soon very hungry. He went to the ant's house and saw that she had a great pile of many kinds of grain.

"Can you spare a few kernels for an old friend?" he asked her.

"No, I cannot," said the ant. "This is our whole winter's supply of food. But don't worry—you will have plenty to eat next summer!"

And she sent the grasshopper away hungry.

The three dimensions are at work here as they are in all fiction: First, the author based the story on his *observations:* what summer is like on a farm; how ants behave; and how seasons and situations change. Then the author drew some *inferences* from what he had observed: Some take it easy when times are good; others are prudent and work hard, even when they don't feel like it.

Finally, the author used his *imagination* to express his ideas by letting insects represent two types of people: those who plan ahead and work toward a goal, and those who do only what they feel like doing or what they can do easily.

Although the writer had insects talking like human beings, he showed them also acting as ants and grasshoppers do, the way we all have observed that they behave. Because we can see that his observations are valid and since we enjoy the story, we are willing to temporarily take it seriously and look for some implications in it:

Those who plan ahead and work hard will live in comfort and plenty;

OR

Those who will not work do not deserve to eat.

In the following space write down another idea that you thought of when you read this story.

____

____

____

____

By now you may be anticipating that the three-dimensional formula might work for the reader as well. It does:

Observation: The reader examines the text to see precisely what the author has written: who the main characters are, what they say, what choices they make, etc.

Inference: The reader tries to think what additional information, along with possible meanings, may be *implied*—though not stated—by the writer. *This is the key to knowing how to read, understand, interpret, and enjoy literature.*

Imagination: The reader allows the story material to come alive as he or she creates mental images of the characters and their struggles. The reader may even experience the wonder and excitement of feeling drawn into the story itself, so that the characters seem like real people.

You don't have to be an English major to reap the benefits of studying fiction. A university student from Lebanon commented at the end of his literature course: "I wish I hadn't waited until my senior year to take this course. We squeezed so much out of those stories we read that I even found it helped me to get more out of my courses in business and computer science!"

Taking a literature course can do some other good things for you, if you are willing to take it seriously. It can teach you to notice things, to observe, to see more clearly, more accurately, and more honestly. It will encourage you to think about what you see: to make reasonable inferences or deductions, to try to make connections with what you already know, to find meanings and to discover your own values. Literature can help you to become more human.

Everyone's experience is necessarily limited, but we can extend it by projecting ourselves into the experience of others. We can even begin to bridge the gap between ourselves and them by trying to imagine how they feel. Developing our literary imagination can be liberating for us, and it can also be beneficial to our relationships with other people.

In this sense, then, literature—like science and technology—can be a means of civilizing us. Not only in the physical world, where so much progress has been made, but also in the area of human experience, where so much remains to be discovered—here, too, we can stretch our minds through the experience of reading and begin to grow farther beyond our primitive, historical past.

Some of the stories in this collection will be easier to read than others, and some have more complicated activities connected with them. But for each story we can use the three-dimensional approach described earlier:

- We'll first *observe* the story carefully to see exactly what is there,
- While we are reading it and again afterward we'll think about the material the author has given us and decide what else we can reasonably *infer* from it,
- We'll let our feelings become involved through our *imagination* as we ask ourselves, "What if *I* had been. . . ?"

The purpose of this first chapter is to help you become acquainted with some of the terms and the methods you will be using in your study of literature. The next section of this chapter will introduce you to the most commonly used literary terms and will explain what they mean. You will be referring to them often as you study the stories.

Sections 3 and 4 will describe the Vocabulary Aids and explain their use. They are an important tool for helping you to *really know what each story is all about,* rather than skipping over or guessing at the words you do not understand. Section 5 gives you a list of abbreviations (with definitions) you will be seeing in the Vocabulary Aids and the Activities. It is not necessary for you to *learn* these terms; just read them through once and remember where to look them up later, if you should need to.

Last of all, Section 6 will show you how you can use the *present tense* to talk about the past, as students of literature are accustomed to doing when they discuss or write about fiction.

2. LITERARY TERMS

LITERARY TERMS USED IN DISCUSSING FICTION

In this brief list of some of the more common literary terms the arrangement is according to close association of ideas rather than to the alphabet. As you use these conventional labels in class discussion and in your writing, you will gradually become familiar with both the terminology of fiction and the basic method used in analyzing it. Although some of these expressions have been mentioned earlier and you may be familiar with them already, they are defined here for future reference and also for the purpose of showing the precise distinctions between one term and another.

1. ***Fiction:*** A story that has not really happened, but is told as though it had. It is not *history*, which is a record of actual events, but it must be "true to life," or seem like a real happening.
2. ***Tale:*** A story that is so old that the original author is usually unknown. Since tales are told over and over again, they are often recounted in a variety of ways. The one telling the story tells it in his own words and may even add to it.
3. ***Short story:*** A story that is written by an author as his own creation, like a painting or a piece of music. In reproducing the short story, the author's exact words are never changed. If we copy even a small part of the story, we enclose that part in quotation marks. The short story is complete in itself and not part of a longer work, such as a novel. It generally portrays a single, important experience in someone's life, such as a time of decision or a choice that changed the person forever.
4. ***Setting:*** The combination of *place* and *time* (situation) in which a story takes place. It may be simply a background for the story, as in "The Test" or "Soldier's Home," or it may be a very important part of the plot and/or the theme, as in "Going Home."
5. ***Flashback:*** A short interruption in the chronological arrangement of the story to tell about or explain an earlier episode. An author uses this technique to slip in necessary or useful information without delaying the action or the pace of the story.
6. ***Point of view:*** The particular angle from which the story is being told. It may be from the viewpoint of a certain character (who is called the "persona"), written either in the *third* person or in the *first* person, as though that character were actually telling the story. Sometimes, however, it is told from the "omniscient" view of the author, who knows what each one is thinking and feeling.
7. ***Characters:*** The individuals who are the focus of the story. More important ones are known as *major* characters; less important ones are called *minor* characters. The chief character is the "protagonist" (see Plot); opposing him is the "antagonist." The author himself is *never* a character in a story, even when the story is told in the first person.

Two Types of Characters

"Flat" Characters:

A. Show only one side of themselves; seem to represent a single trait (a mean boss, a nagging wife, etc.)

"Round" Characters:

A. Can be seen from several sides; have many qualities, not all good and not all bad, like real people.

B. Are seen only from the outside, never from within.	B. Are often portrayed from within, so that their motivation is easily seen, as well as their inner conflicts and feelings.
C. Seem to have a special purpose or function in the story, such as acting as a contrast or a "foil" to other characters.	C. Are not there simply to relate to others or to serve as a "foil," but are part of the conflict or plot because of their own acts or decisions.
D. Behave in a rather predictable way.	D. Are never altogether predictable, although they must be "in character," or behave in a way consistent with what we know about them.
E. Often appear in stories that seem to support a social cause or in stories with a lot of action or violence. In both types of stories, there is little character development.	E. Do not remain the same, but *change* and develop in some way. Often the change is a moral one, leaving the person "better" or "worse" as a result of his decision or choice.

8. ***Motivation:*** The reasons why the characters do and say what they do. They are said to be "in character" when they behave in ways the author has led us to expect. The writer's challenge is to portray characters so realistically that their actions seem natural for them, even inevitable. *Note:* Sometimes a character tries to rationalize—make his behavior look better than it actually was, perhaps by arguing that this was the best thing to do under the circumstances. The reader must then look carefully for his *real* motivation.
9. ***Dialogue:*** Conversation between characters. It is deliberately designed to do one or more of the following:
   a. Move the plot forward by exposing the underlying conflict;
   b. Show what the characters are like—*reveal* them for what they are;
   c. Help to convey the setting or to reveal background events important to the story (flashbacks).
10. ***Plot:*** The main conflict within the story. It usually comes about because someone (the protagonist) very much *wants something,* but one or more obstacles stand in the way of the person's obtaining what he or she wants. *It is the protagonist's struggle to achieve his goal that makes the plot.* Sometimes the obstacle in one's way is another person (the antagonist). The struggle may be between characters, between a character and outside circumstances (the law, danger, etc.), or even between two choices within oneself. This last type, while sometimes very quiet, may be especially dramatic because it is such a difficult decision and has such an impact on that person's life or on someone else's.

11. ***Climax:*** The point of highest dramatic tension in the story. Each small episode, the dialogue, and the thoughts/feelings of the characters all contribute to the process called the *rising action,* as the protagonist struggles toward his or her goal. At some point near the end of the story, the struggle is at last in some way "resolved," and the leading character knows (so does the reader) whether or not the desired goal has been reached. *This turning point in the story is the climax.* The concluding part, or *falling action,* simply finishes the story or hints what might come afterward.
12. ***Theme:*** The *underlying idea* (or ideas) illustrated by the story itself, but expressed in general terms that could apply to other stories with quite different plots and characters.
13. ***Symbol:*** An object or act in the story that seems to represent a deeper or larger meaning, usually one closely associated with the theme. Sometimes we can recognize a symbol as having universal meaning: The ocean may represent "the sea of life."
14. ***Tone:*** The emotional feeling conveyed by the author to the reader; also, the reader's sense of the way the author feels about his characters and what happens to them. The tone may be both serious and satirical, as in "On the Outside," or it may be light and friendly, as in "Señor Payroll." An important clue to the tone of a story can be found in the connotation of the words used. (*Connotation* is explained in Chapter VI, Activity 2.)

3. VOCABULARY: AN INTRODUCTION

THE VOCABULARY AIDS

What They Are For and How to Use Them

If you are like many other ESL students, you have found that the greatest obstacle you encounter when you read anything in English is the vocabulary.

You can often guess the meaning of a word from its context (how it is used in a sentence); however, that only works part of the time, and you probably often come across words that you simply can't figure out on your own. You just have to look them up. If there are very many of them, you could spend a large part of your time searching through the dictionary.

There is another factor involved in the reading process that we sometimes fail to recognize: Whenever you are reading something, you are drawing upon your prior knowledge and experience. You use this background to help you figure out and interpret this new information, which you then *incorporate* (build) into your own body of knowledge.

As you can see, then, the more you already know about a subject, the more easily and quickly you can grasp new, sometimes very difficult material. For instance, if you are well into your major concentration in business, you can read and understand your American textbook's discussion of marketing techniques about as well as an American can. Or if you are specializing in computer science, you can comprehend information about programming from an English language textbook that would seem like a foreign language to most Americans. *It is your familiarity with the material that enables you to know what to expect.* As it happens, that simple advantage is a basic psychological part of the process of understanding anything at all.

You can see why it may be easier for you to read scientific or technological material than to read American literature. You may already be familiar with the first type, but you lack the native cultural background needed for understanding the second. In reading stories written by and for Americans, you soon find that you cannot safely assume that what you might *expect* to be the meaning is certain to accurately reflect what the author intended.

This is where the Vocabulary Aids can help to fill the gap for you. Whether the word is one you think you know or one you have never heard before, you can usually find *a simple definition that fits the text* right at the bottom of the page. If you use the Vocabulary Aids often, you will extend your own vocabulary even as you discover that you can better understand and enjoy what you are reading.

A good way to begin each story is to read the introductory material (the setting, main idea, information about the author). Then read the story through quickly once, without taking time to *look for* any meanings, but pausing only to underline each word you are not sure of. After the first reading, look for the words you didn't know and see if they are defined or explained in the Vocabulary Aids. (Don't forget, you can find much *more* information about the words by looking them up in your English dictionary.) Now you are ready to read the story once again, this time slowly and carefully.

The following two sections will provide explanations and a guide to help you use the Vocabulary Aids to your own best advantage.

4. VOCABULARY: EXPLANATION AND GUIDE

AN EXPLANATION OF THE VOCABULARY AIDS

At the bottom of each page of text, you will find a three-column list of the Vocabulary Aids. The number to the left of each word or phrase refers to its original location in the text. All the words are given in the form in which they have appeared in the text, and their definitions are aimed to fit that context as accurately and simply as possible.

Glossary

The Glossary contains words and expressions that are important for helping you to understand the story, but that would not be particularly useful additions to your own active vocabulary. There may be occasional exceptions to this, such as *capitalism,* from "On the Outside" or *ecstasy,* from "Mr. Kaplan and Vocabulary." Often you will find that the Glossary can give you many clues to the *setting* of a story.

The following types of explanation are most often found in the Glossary:

- Proper names of people, places, and institutions,
- Longer phrases containing several difficult or unfamiliar words,
- Certain nonstandard forms or dialect, such as the phonetically spelled words in "Mr. Kaplan and Vocabulary."

Informal Speech

Like people in most other countries, Americans *speak* differently from the way they *write.* For that reason, the words and expressions used in dialogue may be less familiar to ESL students than the vocabulary used in their textbooks. The middle column of the Vocabulary Aids lists many expressions that are very often heard in conversation but are not always to be found in the dictionary.

Obviously, the best way for international students to become exposed to more idiomatic, colloquial English is to talk with Americans and *listen* to them. Where such experiences are limited, reading stories with American settings is one way for international students to "get inside the U.S.A." and "hear" native American speakers in their own surroundings.

Standard Vocabulary

Words listed in the right-hand column of the Vocabulary Aids are the ones you are most likely to encounter in your reading and to find the most practical to learn and use. Although the definitions have been kept very simple, remember that even a *synonym* cannot be interchanged with another word in all situations. Before you try to use the words, then, learn more about them.

For many students of ESL, an effective method of doing this is to acquaint themselves with other forms of the same word and list that word according to its parts of speech. If your teacher recommends that you follow this method, you might set up a word chart like the following one, which has examples taken from the Standard Vocabulary of the first story, "On the Outside." *The form found in the text is in capital letters.*

5. ABBREVIATIONS AND DEFINITIONS

ABBREVIATION	STANDING FOR	MEANING	EXAMPLE ON PAGE:
cf	*conferre,* Latin for *compare*	Compare with a similar or a slightly different usage.	22: pa, ma
cli	cliché	A trite or hackneyed expression that has been used so often it has become stale. Not acceptable in formal writing, but natural and acceptable in everyday speech.	188: get things straightened out
coll	colloquial	Very informal or conversational in style.	55: kids
dial	dialect	A form of language used in a particular part of the country or by a certain group of people.	39: were not right bright
emph	emphatic	Spoken to sound very strong or forceful.	38: where on earth
exag	exaggeration	Making something sound bigger, better, worse, etc., than it really is. See also *humorous exaggeration.*	104: practically dying
euph	euphemism	A way of saying something unacceptable in a more polite or pleasant way than it would sound in plain, factual language.	37: morticians; 208: apocryphal
fig	figurative	Not meant to be taken as the exact or *literal* meaning; imaginative or poetic.	70: chilly shadow
fig sp	figure of speech	A poetic way of describing or making a comparison. See also *metaphor, personification, simile.*	66: every window is a mother's mouth
frml	formal	Referring to a serious or ceremonious type of word, usually of Latin or Greek origin; used when wanting to sound dignified or educated.	21: theorize; 37: morticians
hist	historical	Referring or alluding to a	55: after the war

The abbreviations listed here will be referred to from time to time in the Vocabulary Aids. Even where the terms are not abbreviated, you may occasionally want to refer to this section in order to understand or to review the definition.

ABBREVIATIONS AND DEFINITIONS

ABBREVIATION	STANDING FOR	MEANING	EXAMPLE ON PAGE:
		historical event connected with the story or its background.	
hum	humorous	Funny or comic, or meant to sound that way.	69: strawberry blonde wig
hum exag	humorous exaggeration	An overstatement of the situation beyond the facts in order to produce a comic effect; sometimes done in conversation to make someone laugh while you still make your point.	139: worked havoc with
hum frml	humorously formal	Using formal language in place of simple language, either deliberately or unintentionally, producing a comic effect.	104: favored us with
hyperb	hyperbole (pronounced *hy-PER-bo-lee*)	Intentional exaggeration, not expected to be taken literally.	141: had suffered a deep hurt
id	idiom	An expression in common use that cannot be translated word-for-word.	168: hard to make out
indef	indefinite	Having no clear or specific meaning; often found in dialogue, where precise meanings are usually avoided.	184: wait and see
inf	informal	Referring to everyday language, sometimes incorrect in grammar, although accepted in ordinary speech.	120: you sure was thirsty
iron	irony or ironic	Word or words used to express the opposite of what one really means; to amuse, lighten a serious subject, express irritation or criticism, or for other reasons.	105: skilled virtuosos; 24: starve healthily
iron euph	ironic euphemism	Something made to sound much better than it really is, but done to complain or criticize in a humorous or friendly way.	105: condemned coal

ABBREVIATIONS AND DEFINITIONS

ABBREVIATION	STANDING FOR	MEANING	EXAMPLE ON PAGE:
lit	literal or literally	Referring to the exact meaning, in contrast to the way the word is used in the context of the story; often contrasted with *fig* meaning.	164: rock pile of the cannery; 210: the politics
met	metaphor	A poetic way of making a comparison, as: "My heart is a singing bird." See also *fig sp.*	66: the happy chorus of my inside self
obsc	obscene	Considered socially offensive because it refers to bodily functions (includes so-called "four-letter words").	No example in these stories
OD	outdated	Referring to an expression no longer commonly used, except perhaps in certain regions or by older people.	213: beau
OD sl	outdated slang	An expression that used to be familiar as slang but is not used anymore.	37: spunk
onomat	onomatopoeia	A word whose meaning is indicated mainly by the *sound* of the word as it is pronounced, as: "rattle," "roar," "buzz," etc.	117: splash; 138: muttered
pejor	pejorative	Disparaging, or intended to make a person or a situation look bad; meant as a "putdown."	162: crazy bastard
person	personification	Presentation of an object or a quality as though it were a human being. See also *fig sp.*	104: Downtown
sarc	sarcasm or sarcastic	A cutting form of irony, intended to hurt another person. Sarcasm is *spoken*, not written, its force depending on the tone of voice used.	187: she was sure she begged his pardon
sim	simile (pronounced SIM-ill-ee)	A poetic form of imagery in which "like" or "as" is used to compare two dissimilar things. See also *fig sp.*	161: like a circle of possums
sl	slang	Very informal expression used in everyday con-	121: playing hookey

ABBREVIATIONS AND DEFINITIONS

ABBREVIATION	STANDING FOR	MEANING	EXAMPLE ON PAGE:
		versation and considered to be nonstandard English, or "street" language, found in the dictionary only when it becomes acceptable usage.	
So dial	Southern dialect	A way of speaking (both in the expression used and in pronunciation) found in the Southern part of the United States east of the Mississippi River. See also *dialect.*	88: you-all . . . down yondah
spec	special term	An expression used in a particular context or discipline, as "leading indicators," in economics.	105: sit on the hiring line
sw	swear word	A word showing disrespect to religion or deity (often spoken to express strong negative feelings).	90: Damn you!
tech	technical term	A word relating to specialized knowledge, generally scientific or mechanical. See also *special term.*	190: hopeless melancholiac

WORD FORMS CHART

VOCABULARY PAGE	NOUN	VERB	PRESENT/PAST PARTICIPLE	ADJECTIVE	ADVERB
21	extreme (extremism)	——— (no form)	——— (no form)	EXTREME	extremely
21	EXPRESSION	express expressed	expressing expressed	expressive	expressively
24	avoidance	avoid avoided	AVOIDING avoided	avoidable	avoidably

These, like the starred words (*) in the Standard Vocabulary for each story, are ones for which word forms can readily be found in the dictionary. Among the activities that follow the stories are occasional practice exercises using word forms and other types of vocabulary study.

6. LANGUAGE CONVERSION: THE HISTORICAL PRESENT

A NEW USE FOR THE PRESENT TENSE

Why do we use the present continuous form of the main verb in the following two sentences?

The teacher is writing on the blackboard.
Car #49, driven by A. J. Foyt, is pulling out in front of the rest.

The present continuous tense tells us that these events are happening *right now,* even as they are being described.

Stories, of course, are generally written in the *past* tense, but when we talk about them we like to imagine that we are right there with the action, watching and describing what we "see." For instance, in telling about the movie we saw last night we might say:

It's after midnight when Nora wakes up with the smell of smoke in her hotel room. She jumps out of bed—

We often discuss a story in class the same way. It is a way of projecting oneself into the scene of the story so that it seems to be taking place anew; we are *there,* so to speak. Obviously, the events are *not* happening right now, so instead of the present continuous, we use the *regular* present, now called the "historical present":

Original text, direct speech	Historical present, direct speech
Squeezing past a young man with a large backpack, George reached the girl with the gorgeous dark eyes and said,	Squeezing past a young man with a large backpack, George reaches the girl with the gorgeous dark eyes and says,
"Haven't we met before?"	"Haven't we met before?"
"I don't think so," said the girl coolly, and turned her back to him.	"I don't think so," says the girl coolly, and turns her back to him.

But when we are talking about a much longer story, it begins to sound awkward (and it could be rather difficult) to keep on repeating the *exact words* of each speaker, so we simply *report* what each speaker says. This means we have to make other changes:

Historical present, reported (indirect) speech

Squeezing past a young man with a large backpack, George reaches the girl with the gorgeous dark eyes and asks her if they haven't met before. She says coolly that she doesn't think so, and turns her back to him.

What words were changed? How was the punctuation changed? *When direct speech or dialogue is reported by a third person,* you must:

Change the pronouns to the third person;
Make the verbs agree with their new subjects.

In order to experiment with this process yourself, try the language conversion exercise below.

A. Practice Exercise

Rewrite "The Ant and the Grasshopper" (p. 3), changing it to the *historical present* by means of the following steps:

1. Change all the main verbs to the (regular) present tense, third person.
2. Change the pronouns to the third person, so that the story will be "reported."
3. When the quotation is a *question,* report it as: He asks if. . .
4. For all other types of statements, begin with the speaker as the subject and use *that:* The ant says that. . .
5. Be careful to punctuate correctly.

Begin with: On a clear, breezy day late in the summer, a grasshopper is singing happily as. . . .

When you have finished writing the exercise, reread it to see if you have stayed with the *present tense* consistently.

B. For Additional Practice

Convert your reported version of the *dialogue only* from the *historical present* to the *simple past* tense. To do this:

1. Change the present tense verbs to the simple past.
2. Change the present perfect to the past perfect.
3. Think about what to do with *contractions* and also with any *adverbs* that might need to be changed.

Begin the past tense of the reported dialogue with: The grasshopper asked her where. . . .

When you have finished writing this exercise, check it also to see if you have kept the tense consistent.

August W. Derleth (1909–1972)

The stock market crash of 1929 occurred during August Derleth's senior year at the University of Wisconsin. His graduation in 1930 thrust him and his classmates out into a severely depressed job market. Although times were hard, he started at once to do what he liked best: write fiction. In fact, he was so successful that he averaged nearly three published books a year throughout most of his life.

Best known for his many novels with settings in his home state of Wisconsin, he wrote a whole series of them about one particular community which he named Sac Prairie, but which was actually modeled on Sauk City, Wisconsin. Derleth's many works include poetry, short stories, a biography, science fiction, and detective stories. A few of his better-known works are: Still Is the Summer Night *(1937);* Wind Over Wisconsin *(1938);* Bright Journey *(1940);* The Hills Stand Watch *(1960); and* Sac Prairie People *(1948), a collection of short stories.*

II

On the Outside

Story Setting: *Written in the early 1930s, this story describes an episode that takes place on a train traveling from Detroit to New York. At that time, trains were still the major means of travel in the United States for both rich and poor people.*

Background and Main Idea: *It took this country ten years to recover economically from the stock market crash of 1929, which led to the Great Depression. During those years, millions of Americans lost their jobs and many also lost all their savings.*

Not everyone was affected equally, however. A few continued to prosper and even to become rich, although many suffered from great poverty. "On the Outside" shows us these extremes.

I can't remember when the boy got on the train. Perhaps he'd been there already when I boarded it and I hadn't seen him, or perhaps he'd changed coaches while I was reading.

I can't even remember what it was that made me see him at last. A thin little fellow, looked to be under twelve. He had sharp black eyes, intelligent eyes, and when I saw him

GLOSSARY

2 **changed coaches:** went from one car to another on a train.

INFORMAL SPEECH

3 **fellow:** an informal term for a man or boy.
4 **looked to be:** appeared to be.

STANDARD VOCABULARY

2 **boarded:** got on (used for buses, ships, and trains).
4 **intelligent:** having a good mind.

they were fixed on a prosperous-looking businessman, sunk deep in a fur coat. The boy had turned in his seat to look at the businessman and to listen to him.

I had noticed the businessman when I passed him to go to my seat, just a glance, no more. He had been talking for the past half hour with two university students who sat across the aisle from him.

When I looked at the boy and watched him, I began to listen to the conversation. The businessman was talking.

"You fellows," he was saying, "are on the outside. You theorize. That's all very well. But you don't know anything about it. . ."

GLOSSARY

5 **prosperous-looking businessman:** a well-dressed man whose clothes made him appear to be successful.
5 **sunk deep . . . fur coat:** wearing a large, luxurious coat made of thick fur.

INFORMAL SPEECH

12 **on the outside:** not in the mainstream of society, not one of the important, successful people.
12 **That's all very well:** actually a negative response meaning, "That sounds good, but I don't believe it."

STANDARD VOCABULARY

5 **fixed on:** fastened on, unmoving.
7 **glance:** a quick look.
9 **aisle:** passageway between rows of seats.
12 ***theorize:** talk about ideas without having had experience with the reality.

*These are words that are especially appropriate to add to your word chart, as explained in Chapter I, Activity 4: Vocabulary Explanation and Guide. Each chapter's vocabulary activities refer to and make use of the starred words in the Standard Vocabulary.

"Capitalism," interrupted one of the students.

"Catchwords," cut in the businessman. "I know, I'm on the inside. I have to go through these things. You know nothing but what you read in the newspapers—and God knows what they don't all print."

"Capitalism," said the student patiently, "is bound to collapse within a few decades."

The businessman smiled but said nothing.

"This massacre at Detroit, now," cut in the second student. "What do you think of that?"

"It serves those men right. The only thing I'm sorry about is that it gives them a chance to be martyrs for the martyr-worshipping hoodlums who cause riots and disturbances."

"Riots and disturbances," murmured the first student. "Riots and disturbances. If a man wants bread and goes to get it, that's a riot. If a woman wants milk for her children, it's a disturbance, and dangerous to the peace. Hunger is a crime against society."

"Bosh," said the businessman. "That's an extreme view."

"Hunger," said the second student, "is always extreme."

There was an expression of satisfaction on the businessman's face, and it was not dispelled by the student's bitter words. The man looked away from the students. Suddenly his eyes met the boy's. "You," he said smiling, "what do you think about it?"

The boy looked at him for a moment without answering. "Detroit," he said slowly, "was a hungry place."

GLOSSARY

14 **capitalism:** an economic system characterized by private or corporate ownership of goods and open competition for business.
16 **go through these things:** endure them, try to keep on with business as usual.
19 **decades:** periods of ten years.
21 **Detroit:** a Michigan city that is the center of the American automobile industry.
24 **martyr-worshiping:** making heroes of victims they believe to have been persecuted.
24 **riots and disturbances:** noisy public demonstrations, sometimes violent.
28 **dangerous to the peace:** a legal term referring to anything that may cause noise and unrest in a community.

INFORMAL SPEECH

15 **catchwords:** slogans or terms meant to attract attention (cf. "catchy").
15 **cut in:** interrupted.
15 **on the inside:** having power or influence, knowing other important people who understand and largely control events.
18 **is bound to:** is certain to, definitely will.
23 **It serves those men right:** they deserve whatever happens to them ("they asked for it," "they got what was coming to them").
24 **hoodlums:** those who do criminal acts such as stealing, destroying property, attacking people, etc.
29 **Bosh:** expression of contempt, disbelief, and disdain (but not a form of swearing).

STANDARD VOCABULARY

14 ***interrupted:** broke into the conversation.
17 **print:** publish (literature set in type for publication).
18 **patiently:** without haste or irritation.
18 ***collapse:** fall apart, break down.
21 **massacre:** episode in which people are killed without mercy.
24 ***martyrs:** those who suffer and die for a cause, victims of persecution.
26 **murmured:** (onomat) spoken very softly ("under his breath").
28 **hunger:** a need for food.
28 **crime:** serious offense punishable by a fine (money) or jail, or both.
29 ***extreme:** very far to one side or the other. (Here used with two meanings; check dictionary.)
31 ***expression:** the look on a person's face.
31 ***satisfaction:** pleasure.
32 **dispelled:** drove away, banished.
32 **bitter:** angry and despairing.

Everyone looked at the boy.

"I'm glad we're going away from it."

"Oh, you're not alone, then?" asked the businessman.

"No, pa's along. We're both going. We're going to New York where ma is."

Silence fell. The clicking of the drivers edged into the coach, sounding louder and louder.

"I didn't see your father," said the businessman. "I didn't see him come in. Where's he at?"

The boy made a vague gesture in the direction of the smoking car.

"Oh, I see," said the businessman. He looked speculatively at the boy and asked, "What are you going to do in New York, you and your dad?"

"I don't know."

Silence crept into the coach again and presently the businessman turned away. But the boy continued to look at him, staring at him rather, without once blinking his eyes or shifting his stare. The businessman was conscious of the boy's scrutiny, for he looked up again, fixed the boy with his eyes, and said, "Your dad's been gone some time. He must have a whole box of cigars."

At that, the boy's stare wavered for the first time. He closed his eyes for a moment. "A big box," he murmured. "A big box."

The businessman got up suddenly and stretched himself. "I'm getting old," he muttered.

GLOSSARY

40 **Silence fell:** idiom meaning "Everything became quiet."
40 **clicking of the drivers:** the sound of the train's driving wheels on the tracks.
44 **smoking car:** one car (the "smoker") was often reserved for people, usually men, who smoked.
49 **rather:** usually means "somewhat," but here it means "instead" as a self-correction (rather than). Ex.: "He thought the letter might contain a large check, or *rather* he hoped it would."
52 **a whole box of cigars:** (exag) usually about two dozen, or 24, cigars.

INFORMAL SPEECH

39 **pa('s):** a familiar term for one's father (cf. papa, pop, dad, daddy).
39 **ma:** a similar term for one's mother (cf. mama or mamma, mom, mum, mummy).
42 **where's he at?:** where is he?
45 **I see:** a vague reply supposed to mean "I understand," often a meaningless response.
51 **gone some time:** gone for a noticeable length of time ("quite a while," "a good while," "quite some time").

STANDARD VOCABULARY

40 **edged into:** moved slowly into (began to be noticed).
44 **vague:** indefinite, not clear or specific.
44 **gesture:** body movement, usually with head or hand, to indicate something.
45 ***speculatively:** thoughtful.
48 **crept (in, into):** moved in slowly and quietly.
48 **presently:** soon, a moment later ("in a minute").
49 **staring at:** steadily fixing one's eyes on.
49 **blinking:** quick closing or winking of the eyes.
50 **shifting:** changing position.
50 **was conscious of:** was aware of, distinctly felt.
50 ***scrutiny:** very careful, searching look.
53 **wavered:** became uncertain or unsteady.
55 **stretched:** extended his arms to tighten the muscles.
56 **muttered:** (onomat) spoken in a low voice.

"No, I'm stiff, too," said one of the students, and came to his feet.

"I tell you what," said the businessman abruptly, looking toward the boy. "Let's go find your dad."

The boy nodded eagerly and jumped from his seat. He went quickly along the aisle, pausing only once to look back to see whether the others were following. On an impulse, I got up, too.

We passed through another coach, in which three men were sleeping, one with a newspaper spread over his face. Then we came to the smoker, but there was no one in it. The businessman, who was directly behind the boy, stopped, but the boy apparently did not notice, for he kept on going.

"This is the smoker," he called to the boy. Then he turned, said, "Diner ahead, perhaps," and went on.

But there was no one in the dining car either. The boy kept on, and we followed him.

We came to the baggage car. Two men were sitting in it; they looked curiously at us.

The boy stopped and pointed. "There's my pa," he said.

He was pointing at a long box.

The students stared. The businessman drew a sharp gasping breath, and his face coloured.

"They shot him in Detroit," the boy said, his voice sounding loud in the sudden silence.

"Listen," said the businessman jerkily, turning to the boy, "have you had dinner?"

The boy shook his head. "I'm hungry," he said in a slow, dispassionate voice, as if despair of ever getting food had saturated his thin body. "I was always hungry in Detroit. All of us. It used to be better—before they put oil on the stuff in the garbage cans. They wanted to save our health."

GLOSSARY

60 **nodded eagerly:** indicated an emphatic "yes" by moving his head up and down.
61 **on an impulse:** without a reason, just suddenly feeling like doing something ("on the spur of the moment").
67 **diner:** the dining car, set up like a restaurant, with covered tables and waiters to serve.
70 **baggage car:** the car in which luggage is stored. It is also the place on a train for a traveling pet or for a coffin containing a body.
77 **jerkily:** in a stilted, somewhat shaky manner.
80 **garbage cans:** containers of food scraps and waste materials, placed on the street to be taken away and disposed of.

INFORMAL SPEECH

58 **I tell you what (usually I'll tell you what):** I have a good idea for what we can or should do.
66 **kept on going:** did not stop.
77 **listen:** informal way of drawing attention to a point one wants to make.

STANDARD VOCABULARY

57 ***stiff:** rigid, not easy to move.
58 **abruptly:** suddenly, without warning.
61 **pausing:** slowing down or briefly waiting.
65 **directly:** immediately, closely.
65 ***apparently:** seemingly, judging by appearances.
68 **perhaps:** maybe.
70 **curiously:** with an inquiring expression.
71 **pointed:** extended the index finger to show or direct attention to something.
74 **coloured (usually spelled colored in the U.S.):** reddened, became flushed.
78 **dispassionate:** without feeling.
79 ***despair of:** (noun) complete hopelessness about.
79 ***saturated:** entirely soaked through (fig).

One of the students smiled bitterly. "They wanted them to starve healthily," he said.

The businessman said, "We'll fix that in a jiffy," avoiding the eyes of the students. "You come right along and see what Rastus can find for you in the dining car."

He took the boy by the hand and led him quickly out of the car.

One of the students began to laugh harshly. "Using an eyedropper on a burning skyscraper. My God! what about the millions?"

GLOSSARY

82 **starve healthily:** (iron) die from lack of food, but not get sick from eating garbage.
84 **Rastus:** a common name in slave times (stereotype name) for a black servant or waiter.
86 **eyedropper:** a small instrument that allows one drop at a time (usually of medicine) to flow out.
87 **the millions:** At that time (the Depression), the population in the United States was about 120 million people, of whom a large number were poor and unemployed.

INFORMAL SPEECH

83 **in a jiffy:** right away, right now, immediately.
87 **what about:** idiom for "What is to be done about. . .?"

STANDARD VOCABULARY

83 ***avoiding:** keeping away from, evading.
86 **harshly:** roughly, unpleasantly.
87 **skyscraper:** very tall buildings, originally referring to those in New York City.

1. READING: MAKING THE RIGHT INFERENCES

THE "ART" OF READING

Good readers learn to "read between the lines." That is an idiomatic way of saying that they learn to squeeze additional information out of the data they are given or the words that they read.

For instance, this story, like most stories, starts right in the middle of the happenings, with no introduction. It is up to the reader to figure out further details, or the particulars, of what the author has *implied* in his very first paragraph.

From the writer's implications, or hints, in the opening sentence alone we can *infer* the following facts:

1. One of the characters is telling the story and must be the narrator.
2. The narrator is traveling on a train.
3. A boy who gets on the train must be important, because he is called "*the* boy."

On the other hand, *from that opening sentence* we cannot safely infer that the narrator can't remember because he is getting old or that the boy is going away to school. We may notice that the boy seems to be traveling alone—then watch to see if that proves to be true.

The more reading we do, the more we learn to draw inferences—almost unconsciously—from the words that are actually written there. *The art of reading involves our recognizing the author's implications and being able to see for ourselves what they may mean.*

The following exercise is designed to encourage you to reread passages in the story more closely and decide what can be inferred from them. You may find it especially helpful to work on each short passage first by yourself or with a partner, and then to discuss your answers with the rest of the class.

Which Inferences Are Valid?

Each one of the quoted passages below is followed by a group of inferences. Some of them are logically sound (valid), thus probably true; others could be possible, although we are not sure; and certain inferences are either very unlikely or we simply do not have enough information to take them seriously.

After you have read the short passage, think about each of the inferences and indicate how valid it seems to you by checking one of the three columns. Base your decision on what has been written in the story *up to that point*, including the passage itself. Be ready to explain the reasons for your choices.

	PROBABLY TRUE	*POSSIBLE*	*UNLIKELY OR NO INFOR-MATION*
1. "The boy had turned in his seat. . ." (p. 20, line 6).			
a. The boy was uncomfortable.			
b. The boy was curious about the businessman.			
c. The boy was the businessman's son.			
d. The boy had been listening to what the businessman was saying.			
2. "I began to listen to the conversation" (p. 20, line 10).			
a. The narrator was annoyed at their talking while he was trying to read.			
b. The narrator was tired of reading.			
c. The narrator was interested in the boy.			
d. The narrator wondered what they were saying.			
3. "'Capitalism,' said the student patiently, 'is bound to collapse. . .'" (p. 21, line 18).			
a. The student disagreed with the businessman, but he was trying to be polite.			
b. The student was a Communist.			
c. The student liked to argue about politics.			
d. The student had been taking courses about government or politics.			
4. "I didn't see your father,'" said the businessman. . .' 'Where's he at?'" (p. 22, line 42).			
a. The businessman was worried about the boy's father.			
b. The businessman was somewhat curious about the boy's father.			
c. The businessman was trying to sound important.			
d. The businessman didn't believe the father was really on the train.			
5. "'This is the smoker,' he called to the boy." (p. 23, line 67).			
a. The businessman wanted to sit down there and have a smoke.			
b. The businessman thought the boy didn't know which car was the smoker.			

	PROBABLY TRUE	*POSSIBLE*	*UNLIKELY OR NO INFORMATION*
c. The businessman was older and couldn't go as fast as the boy.			
d. The businessman was wondering why the boy's father wasn't there.			
6. "'They shot him in Detroit,' the boy said." (p. 23, line 75). a. The boy was angry and said that to embarrass the businessman.			
b. The father must have been one of those people the students were talking about.			
c. The father preferred to be shot rather than to go hungry.			
d. The businessman felt ashamed of what he had said about the rioters.			

2. STUDY QUESTIONS

DISCOVERING THE STORY THROUGH OBSERVATION AND INFERENCE

1. ***Observation:*** The story is told by a "narrator," an unknown character whom the author has included just for the purpose of telling the story. Where is the narrator as the story opens, and what is he doing? What other four characters are introduced to us early in the story?
   Inference: What does the businessman mean when he tells the students that they "theorize"? Do you think he is correct, or not?
2. ***Observation:*** According to the businessman, who is "on the outside" and who is "on the inside"? Inside or outside of *what?*
   Inference: "The businessman smiled and said nothing" in answer to what comment? What do you think his "answer" shows about his attitude?
3. ***Observation:*** When the businessman says, "It serves those men right," who and what he is talking about?
   Inference: Can you explain the irony in the student's reply, beginning with line 26, p. 21 ("Riots and . . .") Why does he talk like this?
4. ***Observation:*** Note the repetition of the word "extreme." What *political* meaning would this have for the businessman? What meaning does the word have as the students use it?
   Inference: Why does the businessman have an "expression of satisfaction" on his face? What kind of answer do you think he is expecting to receive from the boy?
5. ***Observation:*** What information does the businessman learn about the boy from their conversation? What does he assume about the boy's father?

Inference: Now that you have finished reading the story, can you say what double meaning is implied by the words, "a big box"?

6. ***Observation:*** Who suggests going to find the boy's father? Who goes along with the boy to look for him?
   Inference: On page 23, line 67, we read: "'This is the smoker,' he called to the boy. Then he turned, said, 'Diner ahead, perhaps,' and went on." What *other* words that he does not say are actually implied here?
7. ***Observation:*** At what point do you realize that the boy's father is dead? (Point out the statement in the story.) What earlier clues did we have about his death?
   Inference: Why do you think that the boy did not mention it earlier?
8. ***Observation:*** How does the businessman's *first* reaction to the news differ from that of the students?
   Inference: Why does he suddenly ask the boy if he has had dinner?
9. ***Observation:*** Complete the following statement in your own words: According to the boy, in Detroit they all were so hungry that ________________.
   Inference: Look up the meaning of the word "sarcasm," and explain the meaning and the *tone* of the student's reply. (You can find "Tone" in the Literary Terms, item 14.)
10. ***Observation:*** What does the businessman expect to "fix . . . in a jiffy"? How?
    Inference: Paraphrase the figure of speech in the student's last remark by filling in the blanks of the following statement:
    ______________ for one small, hungry boy is supposed to ______________.

3. DISCUSSION: REVIEW/REPORT

TAKING A CLOSER LOOK AT THE STORY

Group Reports for Discussion

A. ***The Setting*** (Reference: "Setting," Literary Terms, item 4.)
   One of the first things we notice about any story that we read is its setting. You can find the information for the first question in the story itself, while the second question can be answered by reviewing the Vocabulary Aids.
   1. In the story:
      a. What is the *immediate* setting of "On the Outside"?
      b. What is its *general* setting?
      c. How important is the setting in this story? (Explain your answer.)

2. The Glossary:
   a. Look through the Glossary and point out every expression you can find that is connected with the setting.
   b. Pick out 6–7 examples of such expressions, and explain their particular significance for the reader's understanding of the story.
   c. Which of these words and phrases were not very familiar to you before reading this story? Did others in your group or in the class find the same ones to be unfamiliar to them?

B. ***The Narrator*** (Reference: "Point of View," Literary Terms, item 6.) Review the story carefully to see what part is played by the narrator. Then report your answers to the following questions:

1. Can you find all the places where the narrator mentions himself?
2. Would you call him an *active participant* or a *passive bystander?* Explain why, using some examples.
3. How can you tell that the narrator is not the author himself?

C. ***The Climax*** (Reference: "Climax," Literary Terms, item 11.) In the beginning of the story, the businessman is so sure he is right that he wants to convince all his listeners of the "truth" as he sees it. At the end we find that his attitude has changed from certainty to uncertainty. How did the author achieve this effect?

1. What are some of the things he is sure about in the beginning?
2. Each of his contacts with the boy seems to help undermine or reduce his certainty about things. Trace the small episodes or steps by which this happens.
3. Where or when does the climax happen in the story? Why is this the "climax"?
   a. What would you say are the most obvious "certainties," at this point?
   b. What uncertainties are the various characters left with at the end of the story?

D. ***The Theme*** (Reference: "Theme," Literary Terms, item 12, and "Symbol," item 13.)

Authors usually claim that they are not trying to communicate a "message" to their readers—just tell a story. However, it is often possible to find underlying themes and symbols in the story such as "On the Outside." What double meanings, or symbolism, can you see in the following expressions?

1. ". . . businessman sunk deep in a fur coat" (p. 20, line 5).
2. "'I'm getting old,' he muttered" (p. 22, line 55). Hint: Can you relate this to p. 21, line 18?
3. ". . . no one in the dining car either" (p. 23, line 69).
4. Tie title itself.

4. VOCABULARY PRACTICE: WORD FORMS

FIND THE RIGHT WORD FORMS

Twelve of the starred words from the Standard Vocabulary appear below. Each word is in the same form in which it first appeared in the story. Here is a chance to practice using that word in *other* forms.

Each blank in every numbered sentence represents a different form of the word given ahead of it. Find the form that *most accurately expresses the meaning* by using the *correct word form,* or part of speech.

The first two blanks have already been filled in for you with the past tense of the verb, *theorize,* and the noun form. The third blank is the adjective form. Can you find it and fill it in? (Although the businessman's words were in the present tense, when they are "reported" as indirect speech, they must be changed to the past tense.)

Use your word forms chart or consult a dictionary as you fill in the rest of the blanks. (How many additional forms for these same words can you find in your dictionary?)

1. theorize (verb)
   When the businessman told the students that they ___theorized___ , he meant that they had studied many ___theories___ but had little experience, so their knowledge of life was only ______________.
2. collapse (verb)
   The students thought that capitalism would be in a state of ______________ within a few decades, and in fact it might already be ______________.
3. extreme (adjective)
   In Detroit there were ______________ poor people whose hunger had driven them to the ______________ of rioting.
4. expression (noun)
   The views which the students were ______________ were very strongly against the ______________ opinion of the businessman.
5. satisfaction (noun)
   To the businessman, capitalism was an entirely ______________ economic system, but the students were not ______________ with his arguments.
6. speculatively (adverb)
   Following the boy through the train, they ______________ whether his father would be in the smoking car or in the diner, but their ______________ turned out to be wrong on both counts.

7. scrutiny (noun)
The boy was ______________ the businessman throughout the conversation, until finally the businessman turned and ______________ the boy.
8. stiff (adjective)
Sitting still for a long while can have a ______________ effect, so that the businessman and the student both complained of ______________.
9. apparently (adverb)
The businessman expected the boy's father to be ______________ shortly, but in a while it became ______________ that he was not going to make his ______________ very soon.
10. despair (noun)
The boy knew so well what it was like to be ______________ hungry that he had ______________ of ever getting enough to eat.
11. saturated (past participle)
______________ the garbage with oil may have increased the poor people's discouragement to the point of ______________.
12. avoiding (present participle)
The businessman's ______________ of responsibility for the problem was shown when he ______________ the eyes of the students, who believed that great poverty and hunger were ______________.

5. COMPOSITION:
A. USING TRANSITIONS

WHO IS REALLY "ON THE OUTSIDE"?

The short essay that follows develops an idea or proposition, which we call the *thesis*. The thesis of this essay is that, in a sense, all of the characters in this story are outsiders. After you have read the essay, filled in the blanks, and studied how it is organized, you can use it as a model for compositions that you will later be writing about the stories.

Directions for Studying and Completing the Model Essay

1. First, read the essay quickly all the way through, in order to get a general idea of what it is about and where it is going. You will notice that the blanks in the first part can be completed with information that you will find right in the story. The rest of the blanks will need connecting words and phrases, which you can take from the list provided. (After you have done this, go on to 2.)

2. As you write the title and the author's name in the blanks, notice where the quotation marks are placed, and remember to use capital letters when needed.
3. The introductory paragraph contains general information about the story. Which sentence states the *thesis of the essay?* (Remember that the "thesis" is *a statement of the main idea* of the essay.) Fill in its blanks, and then be ready to explain how you know it is the thesis.
4. Fill in the remaining blanks in the first paragraph, and then in the *first sentence only* of the second paragraph.
5. All the rest of the blanks are for *connecting* words or phrases, expressions that provide *transitions* (bridge words) between one idea and the next. Transitional expressions must be used carefully, for they give the reader important clues about your meaning, particularly about the relationship of ideas and information to each other.

   Each of the words or phrases in the list is intended for one of the blanks, although some can be interchanged since they mean almost the same thing. In order to be sure that the expression you use clearly and logically relates one idea to the next one, *read the whole sentence first.* Then choose the word or phrase that best completes the sentence:

after all	in fact	too
also	in other words	until
although	last of all	where
because	nevertheless	whereas
consequently	so	while
however	then	yet

6. After you have filled in the blanks, discuss your choices with others in the class and with your teacher. Consider what other possibilities could have been used, and take note whether they would have changed the meaning in any way.

(Questions 7 and 8 can be found following the essay.)

5. COMPOSITION: B. ANALYZING THE MODEL COMPOSITION

OUTSIDERS OR INSIDERS?

The story, "__________ __________ __________," by __________ W. __________, is about an episode that takes place on a __________ traveling from __________ to __________back during the time of the __________ __________. There are __________ characters in the story, including the one who tells the story (called the __________,) and all of them can be seen, in some way, to be "__________."

The main character is a __________, who argues with two __________

__________, about the value and the benefits of __________. He says they are "on the outside," __________ he himself is "on the inside" __________ he knows all about what is really happening in the business world. __________, he does not know or care about the hard realities of the working world, __________ many people have been rioting because they were unemployed and hungry, __________ the students consider him to be the *real* "outsider."

__________ the businessman turns to a little boy nearby and confidently asks him what he thinks about it. He is expecting the boy to agree with him, __________ he learns that the boy's father was one of the rioters who was killed. Now the businessman feels guilty about having defended wealth and capitalism. __________, he offers to treat this young "outsider" to a luxurious meal in the dining car. __________ __________ __________, __________ he is a capitalist, he has a heart __________.

__________ __________ __________, there is the narrator, the first character who appeared in "On the Outside." He __________ is an "outsider," a person who has only been observing what has been happening, __________ the other characters have taken an active part in the story.

As readers, we are __________ "outsiders," to begin with. __________, like the narrator, we get more interested as the story unfolds and we find ourselves understanding more and more about each of the characters. __________ __________, it could be said that both the narrator and we, the readers, have become "insiders," __________ __________ __________.

7. When you feel satisfied that your completions make the essay clear and readable, read it through again and answer the following questions:
   a. You probably discovered that the thesis statement was the last sentence in paragraph one. What are its *key words*—the words that give you clues about the *subject matter* and the *controlling idea* of the essay?
   b. Check each one of the sentences that follow the thesis. How is each sentence related, in some way, to the topic sentence? Does any sentence spoil the unity?
   c. What is the *conclusion* about? In what way does it repeat the idea of the thesis? What additional point or idea does it offer? Do you feel that the addition is justified (allowable), or does it seem to be changing the subject?
8. Begin your own list of ***Transitional Expressions,*** with their definitions. Use the ones given in question 5, adding your own meanings. Watch for other connecting words and expressions (you can include words like *when, therefore, since* meaning *because, while, as,* etc.) and add these to your list. Be sure to note whether a period, semicolon, or comma must come *before* the expression, and also whether a comma should appear *after* it.

   Try to use these transitional expressions to make your own compositions read more smoothly and easily.

Langston Hughes (1902–1967)

Langston Hughes began his writing career at a time when it was considered unacceptable, as well as financially ruinous, for any black person to protest against racism or mention the difficulties of black people in the United States. These themes were prominent in his poetry; yet Hughes was the first American black writer to make his living from his art.

Hughes is one of our finest poets of what has been called "The Harlem Renaissance," a period during the 1920s that is outstanding for the quantity and quality of its black American literature. Employing the rhythms of Negro folk music, Hughes's poetry expresses the bittersweet theme of sorrow interwoven with sardonic humor. As with all great writers, his best work reaches beyond his own community and race to convey universal truth about human beings.

Although it was for his poetry that Langston Hughes achieved his highest reputation, he also wrote several plays, a novel, many short stories, and two autobiographical works. His writings include:

Four volumes of poetry: The Weary Blues *(1926),* The Negro Mother *(1931),* Shakespeare in Harlem *(1942), and* Montage of a Dream Deferred *(1951);*

Mulatto *(1935): A tragic play about a young man with a black mother and a white father;*

Simple Speaks His Mind *(1950): humorous sketches written originally for a Negro newspaper.*

Four works of fiction dealing with the problems of black people in the United States: Not Without Laughter *(1930), a novel;* The Ways of White Folks *(1934);* Something in Common and Other Stories *(1935), from which "Sorrow for a Midget" was taken; and* Laughing to Keep from Crying *(1952).*

Two volumes of autobiography written sixteen years apart: The Big Sea *(1940) and* I Wonder as I Wander *(1956).*

III

Sorrow for a Midget

Story setting: *A hospital in Harlem, a predominantly black neighborhood in uptown New York City; the time is probably in the early 1930s, during the Depression.*

In the story: *The narrator is a black orderly (male general helper in a hospital), who tells the story in the first person, as though he were recounting his experience to one of his friends.*

Use of dialect: *Being an artist, the author does not create characters who speak exactly like Harlem dwellers, because many readers would not understand what they say. Instead, Hughes introduces us to a modified form of "Black English," which departs somewhat from the grammar of standard English, but is generally understandable to most readers. (Expressions that might give you trouble are listed under Informal Speech and marked "dial.")*

About "Black English": *The language of the street, especially among black speakers, is constantly contributing variety and color to American slang. Words like "jazz," "rap," "jive," "soul," "soul food," and many others, invented or given special meanings by black speakers, have circulated widely, especially among the young, and many now are accepted at all levels of English usage.*

Exposure to Black English will enlarge and enrich your experience with American English. As you become more familiar with the vernacular (everyday, popular usage), you will more easily take in and appreciate its rhythms and its many shades of meaning. In the process, you will be more attuned to its users, who have a knack of conveying their true feelings in few words.

Listen to Black English whenever you hear it being spoken—in the classroom, around the campus, in the subway, or on the street. You will be catching a glimpse of the language "at the grass roots," the down-to-earth, human level from which ever-changing American English grows.

No grown man works in a hospital if he can help it—the pay is too low. But I was broke, jobs hard to find, and the employment office sent me there that winter.

Right in the middle of Harlem.

Work wasn't hard, just cleaning up the wards, serving meals off a rolling table, bulling around, pushing a mop. I didn't mind. I got plenty to eat.

It was a little special kind of hospital; there was three private rooms on my floor, and in one of them was a female midget. Miss Midget—a little lady who looked like a dried-up child to me. But they told me (so I wouldn't get scared of her) that she was a midget. She had a pocketbook bigger than she was. It laid on a chair beside her bed. Generous, too—nice, that little midget lady. She gave me a tip the first day I was there.

But she was dying.

The nurses told me Countess Midget was booked to die. And I had never seen nobody die. Anyhow, I hung around her. It was profitable.

"Take care of me good," she said. "I pay as I go. I always did know how to get service." She opened her big fat pocketbook, as big as she was, and showed me a thick wad of bills. "This gets it anytime, anywhere," she said.

It got it with me, all right. I stuck by. Tips count up. That's how I know so much about what happened in them few days she was in that hospital room, game as she could be, but booked to die.

"Not even penicillin can save her," the day nurse said, "not her." That was when penicillin was new.

GLOSSARY

2 **employment office:** a place where a person can go to get help in finding a job.
3 **Harlem:** uptown New York City where many black people live.
4 **wards:** hospital areas usually containing four or more patients' beds.
7 **midget:** abnormally small adult, sometimes no more than 3–4 feet tall, but well-proportioned. (A *dwarf* has adult-sized head and trunk, half-size limbs.)
9 **pocketbook:** a woman's handbag or purse.
10 **tip:** a gratuity, extra money in appreciation for good service.
12 **Countess Midget:** Midgets often earn money by being displayed and dressed up as sideshow attractions. Americans do not have titles, but "Countess" was supposed to add glamor.
20 **penicillin:** one of the first antibiotics, and still very useful.

INFORMAL SPEECH

1 **if he can help it:** if he can avoid it or do anything else.
1 **broke:** out of money.
5 **bulling around:** (sl) fooling around, doing nothing in particular.
5 **pushing a mop:** cleaning floors.
13 **hung around (someone):** stayed close by. (To *hang around*, in general, means to linger with no purpose.)
14 **pay as . . . go:** pay immediately instead of using credit.
15 **wad:** collection of papers or money folded together.
17 **stuck by:** faithfully served or stayed with (stood by).
17 **count up:** add up.
18 **game:** courageous, brave ("a good sport" who does not whine about defeat).

STANDARD VOCABULARY

6 **private:** separate, arranged for an individual to be alone.
9 ***generous:** liberal and open-handed with money.
12 ***booked:** had a ticket or reservation.
13 ***profitable:** gainful, bringing in money.

Of course, the undertakers that year was all complaining about pencillin. They used to come to the hospital looking for corpses.

"Business is bad," one undertaker told me. "People don't die like they used to since this pencillin come in. Un-huh! Springtime, in the old days, you could always count on plenty of folks dying of pneumonia and such, going outdoors catching cold before it was warm enough, and all. Funerals every other day then. Not no more. The doctors stick 'em with penicillin now—and they get well. Damn if they don't! Business is bad for morticians."

But that midget did not have pneumonia, neither a cold. She had went without an operation she needed too long. Now operations could do her no good. And what they put in the needle for her arm was not penicillin. It was something that did her no good either, just eased down the pain. It were kept locked up so young orderlies like me would not steal it and sell it to junkies. The nurses would not even tell me where it was locked up at.

You know, I did not look too straight when I come in that hospital. Short-handed—not having much help—they would hire almost anybody for an orderly in a hospital in Harlem, even me. So I got the job.

Right off, after that first day, I loved that midget. I said, "Little Bits, you're a game kiddie. I admire your spunk."

Midget said, "I dig this hospital jive. Them nurses ain't understandable. Nice, but

GLOSSARY

22 **undertakers:** those in the business of embalming bodies and conducting funerals.
23 **corpses:** dead bodies.
26 **pneumonia:** serious illness from a virus in the lungs.
27 **every other day:** (lit) every second day, often.
28 **Damn if they don't!** (short for "Damn me if they don't"): I swear it's true, even though it seems impossible that so many could recover from pneumonia.
29 **morticians:** (frml, euph) undertakers. (Note other euph terms used at funerals: *pass on* or *pass away, the remains, the deceased,* etc.)
38 **Little Bits:** a term of affection.
39 **spunk:** (OD sl) courage or fortitude ("gameness").

INFORMAL SPEECH

25 **Un-huh!:** Yes, indeed!
25 **in the old days:** a nostalgic way of referring to the past.
25 **count on:** rely on.
26 **and such:** and other similar causes.
26 **catching cold:** getting a virus infection from being chilled.
27 **and all:** a vague term, like "etc."
27 **stick 'em:** give them shots (injections).
31 **could do . . . no good:** could not help.
34 **junkies:** street people addicted to drugs.
35 ***straight:** reliable, respectable (and neat-looking).
38 **right off:** immediately.
39 **kiddie:** (sl) friendly term for "child."
39 **spunk:** (coll) courage.
40 **I dig . . . jive:** (dial, no literal explanation) "it's crazy here, but nice."
dig: often means to like.
jive: special terms used in a line of work, jargon.

STANDARD VOCABULARY

22 ***complaining:** making negative or critical remarks.
31 ***operation:** surgery, in a hospital; also means a performance of work.
33 **eased (down):** somewhat relieved, made a little less severe.
35 **short-handed:** lacking the regular number of workers necessary.
39 ***admire:** look up to, have high respect for.
40 ***understandable:** (lit) can be understood (she may mean *understanding:* able to understand).

don't understand. You're the only one in here, boy, I would ask to do me a favor. Find my son."

"You look like a baby to me, Countess. Where and when on earth did you get a son?" I asked.

"Don't worry about that," said Countess Midget. "I got him—and he's mine. I want him *right now.* He do not know I am in here sick—if he did, he would come—even were he ashamed of the way he looked. You find my son." She gave me twenty bucks for subway fare and taxi to go looking.

I went and searched and found her son. Just like she had said he might be, he were ashamed to come to the hospital. He was not doing so well. Fact is, her son was ragged as a buzzard feeding on a Lenox Avenue carcass. But when I told him his mama was sick in the Maggie Butler Pavilion of the Sadie Henderson Hospital, he come. He got right up out of bed and left his old lady and come.

"My mama has not called for me for a long, long time," he said. "If she calls me now, like this boy says," he told his girl, "wild horses could not hold me. Baby, I am going to see my mama," he said.

"I did not even know you had a mama," whined the sleepy old broad in the bed, looking as if she did not much care.

"Lots of things you do not know about this Joe," said the cat to the broad. He got up and dressed and went with me, quick.

"That little bitty woman," I asked him in the street, "she is your mama?"

GLOSSARY

41 **do . . . a favor:** do a kind deed, at someone's request.
51 **buzzard:** a scavenger bird that eats dead animals.
51 **Lenox Ave.:** the main street of Harlem.
52 **Maggie Butler Pavilion . . . Hospital:** a section or wing of a hospital is often named for someone who donated a large sum of money.

INFORMAL SPEECH

41 **boy:** here, a friendly term. "Boy" has long been used by whites toward black men of all ages, thus has been resented as derogatory. A black person may call another "boy" or even "nigger," but a white person may not.
43 **where . . . on earth:** emphatic for "where?" (also "where in the world").
47 **twenty bucks:** (sl) 20 dollars.
50 **fact is:** the truth is.
53 **his old lady:** (sl) vague term that could mean girlfriend, mistress, wife, or mother.
55 **Baby:** affectionate term for a girlfriend.
57 **broad:** (sl) derogatory term for a woman.
59 **this Joe:** (sl) this "guy," meaning himself.
59 **cat:** (dial) may simply be a "guy," or may mean especially one who is proud of his way with women. (Can also mean a "jazz freak".)
61 **little bitty:** (sl) very tiny.

STANDARD VOCABULARY

47 ***ashamed of:** embarrassed by.
50 **ragged:** having torn or worn-out clothes.
51 **feeding on:** eating (used for animals only).
51 **carcass:** dead body or corpse of an animal.
57 **whined:** spoke in a complaining tone of voice.

"Damn right, she's my mama," said the guy, who was near six feet, big, heavy-set, black, and ragged. No warm coat on. I thought I was beat, but he was the most. I could tell he had *been* gone to the dogs, long gone. Still, he was a young man. From him I took a lesson.

"I will never get this far down," to myself I said. "No, *not never!*"

"Is she very low sick?" he asked about his mama. "Real sick?"

"Man, I don't know," I said. "She is sunk way down in bed. And the sign on the door says NO VISITORS."

"Then how am I gonna get in?"

"Relatives is not visitors," I said. "Besides, I know the nurses. Right now is not even visiting hours. Too early. But come with me. You'll get in."

I felt sorry for a guy with a mama who was a midget who was dying. A midget laying dying! Had she been my mama, I guess I would have wanted to be there, though, in spite of the fact she was a midget. I couldn't help wondering how could she be so small and have this great big son? Who were his papa? And how could his papa have had her?

Well, anyhow, I took him in to see the little Countess in that big high hospital bed, so dark and small, in that white, white room, in that white bed.

They had just given his mama a needle, so she were not right bright. But when she saw her son, her little old wrinkled face lighted up. Her little old tiny matchstick arms went almost around his neck. And she hollered, "My baby!" real loud. "My precious baby son!"

"Mama," he almost cried, "I have not been a good son to you."

"You have been my *only* son," she cried.

GLOSSARY

62 **heavy-set:** having a large, thick body.
75 **how could she . . . have:** how would she have been able to give birth to.
76 **how could . . . had her:** had sexual relations with such a small woman.
80 **match-stick:** (exag) very thin.

INFORMAL SPEECH

62 **damn right:** (sw) emphatic assertion.
63 **beat:** beaten, defeated.
63 **the most:** (sl) vague way of saying "nobody could be worse off than this."
64 **gone to the dogs:** (cli) made a complete failure of his life.
64 **took a lesson:** learned something important.
68 **man:** here, an expletive similar to "good grief!" or "good Lord!" Also (dial) a casual term of address used among black males.
79 **were not right bright:** (dial) was not clear in her mind or mentally competent just then.
80 **little old (wrinkled face):** (dial) an affectionate term, but probably literal here also.
80 **lighted up:** became very happy-looking.
81 **hollered:** shouted, yelled.

STANDARD VOCABULARY

71 ***relatives:** kinfolk, persons related by blood.
81 **precious:** (lit) very valuable. Here, a term of great endearment and love.

The nurse hipped me, "Let's get out of here and leave 'em alone." So we went. And we left them alone for a long time, until he left.

That afternoon the midget died. Her son couldn't hardly have more than gotten home when I had to go after him again. I asked him on the way back to the hospital was he honest-to-God sure enough her son.

He shook his head. "No."

That is when I felt most sorry for that midget, when I heard him say No. He explained to me that he was just a took-in son, one she had sort of adopted when he was near-about a

GLOSSARY

89 **shook. . . head:** made a negative motion.

INFORMAL SPEECH

84 **hipped:** (dial) made me aware of what was happening ("clued me in," "made me get wise," "gave me the scoop"). Here it may also mean that she literally nudged him with her hip to get his attention.
86 **couldn't . . . home:** would have just had time to get home.
88 **honest-to-God:** absolutely the whole truth.
88 **sure enough:** (dial) adjective meaning "real true."
91 **a took-in son:** (dial) one who is "taken into" someone's home and unofficially adopted.
91 **sort of:** in a way, but not exactly.
91 **near-about a baby:** (dial) little more than a baby; probably a young child (toddler).

STANDARD VOCABULARY

91 ***adopted:** of a child, assuming all responsibility for, as though a natural parent.

baby—because he had no father and no mother and she had no son. But she wanted people to *think* she had a son.

She was just his midget mama, that's all. He never had no real mama that he knew. But this little tiny midget raised him as best she could. Being mostly off in sideshows and carnivals the biggest part of the time, she boarded him out somewhere in school in the country. When he got teen-age and came back to Harlem, he went straight to the dogs. But she loved him and he loved her.

When he found out, about 5:30 P.M., that she had died, that big old ragged no-good make-believe son of hers cried like a child.

GLOSSARY

95 **sideshows and carnivals:** working as a circus attraction.

INFORMAL SPEECH

95 ***raised:** reared, "brought up" to adulthood.
95 **as best she could:** as well as she could manage.
95 **off in sideshows:** away working in sideshows of the circus.
99 **no-good:** worthless, useless.
100 **make-believe:** pretended in the way children do.

STANDARD VOCABULARY

1. STUDY QUESTIONS

UNDERSTANDING THE STORY THROUGH OBSERVATION AND INFERENCE

1. ***Observation:*** Like the first story "On the Outside," this one is told by a narrator. What information do we learn about him in the first part of the story (through line 5)? Is his role as narrator similar to that of the first story? Explain.
   Inference: What does Miss Midget mean when she says, "I always did know how to get service?" What do you think about her keeping so much money with her there in the hospital?
2. ***Observation:*** What do the following phrases tell us about Countess Midget?

   "female midget"   "generous, too"
   "dried-up child"   "booked to die"
   "pocketbook bigger than she was"

   Inference: Can you paraphrase the undertaker's remarks (express each of his statements in your own words), beginning: "Business is bad . . ."?
3. ***Observation and inference:*** Taking note of the information given in the paragraph that begins on line 30, p. 37, answer the questions below:
   a. What do you suppose that "they put in the needle for her arm . . ."?
   b. In your opinion, what is wrong with Countess Midget?
   c. What can you infer from the narrator's comment: "I did not look too straight"?
4. ***Observation:*** As the young orderly (the narrator) gets to know Miss Midget better, what does he think of her? In what ways does he try to help her?
   Inference: What do you think Miss Midget means when she says the "nurses ain't understandable" and the orderly is "the only one in here"?
5. ***Observation:*** When the narrator finds her son and sees that he is "not doing so well," what is he talking about (line 50, p. 38)? What is the "lesson" that he takes from this young man?
   Inference: Point out some possible similarities and differences between the son and the narrator.
6. ***Observation:*** The narrator is clearly puzzled at the possibility of the midget's having a son this large. What is the real explanation, and how does he learn the facts?
   Inference: After he understands the truth he comments, "She was just his midget mama, that's all." Is this remark intended as a "put-down," suggesting that she was not a good mother? What kind of mother do you think she was?

2. DISCUSSION: GROUP REPORTS

TAKING A CLOSER LOOK

A. There is a famous story in the Bible called "The Prodigal Son." It is found in the New Testament, Luke 15: 11–32. Since some may not know the story, have someone look it up and tell or read it to the class. Then answer the following questions:

1. How is the homecoming of the Prodigal Son similar in circumstances to the midget's son's return to his mother?
2. How are the two situations different?
3. What symbolic meaning(s) can you see in each of the stories?

B. Most Americans come from a mixture of national and often of racial origins. In recent years, many people have been eagerly searching for their "roots"—or the national, racial, and cultural heritage of their own ancestry.

1. In "Sorrow for a Midget," who is searching for whom? In what way might this be a *reversal* of "searching for one's roots"?
2. What are some of the reasons why people want so very much to have children? Do you feel that adopting, or "taking in," a child who is not one's own can be a satisfactory substitute for having a biological child?
3. Many people have adopted newborn infants and raised them as their own. The children were never told who their biological parents were, and laws even prohibited agencies from revealing the real parents. Now the laws in some states have been changed, and many adopted children are seeking out their biological parents. Do you agree with this practice? Why or why not?

C. The word "mourn" means to grieve or to feel very sorrowful when someone dies. "Mournful" is the adjective, meaning "sad" or "sorrowful," and "mourners" are the people who attend a funeral honoring one who has just died.

With these definitions in mind, look again at the undertaker's speech on p. 37, lines 24–29:

1. Experiment with oral interpretation: Let several members of the class take their turns reading this passage aloud, trying to sound as *mournful* as they can. Vote on who sounds the most mournful. Then, as a class, decide what is the effect of hearing that passage read in this way.
2. A "pun" is a word with a clever double meaning, such as: The mortician in the story made a *mournful* complaint. Can you explain the double meaning here? Can you think of any other expressions that have double meanings?

3. What makes the speech of the undertaker both *ironic* and *comic*? Why do you think that Hughes would include a passage intended as humorous in this otherwise sad story?

D. A midget is a human being who is very small, but is normal in other respects. The word "miniature" refers to very tiny, but perfect imitations of any objects. For instance, a *midget* is a child-sized adult whose home would need to be equipped with *miniature* furniture.
   1. Why do you think that normal-sized people have always been so fascinated by these tiny, adult human beings?
   2. Even children have loved fairy tales and folk stories about a character named Tom Thumb, as well as elves and other small beings. In your own language and culture, have there been any similar stories that you can remember hearing or reading about? Why do you think children enjoy them so much?
   3. Do you think there are any moral issues (questions of right or wrong) about the practice of charging or paying money to view someone with physical deformities (including midgets):
      a. On the part of the showman who exhibits them?
      b. From the standpoint of the deformed person who allows himself or herself to be a public exhibit?
      c. On the part of the public who pay money to look at other people because of their deformities?

3. GRAMMAR: A. STANDARD ENGLISH

HOW GOOD IS YOUR STANDARD ENGLISH?

"Black English" is a recognized dialect spoken by many people in the United States. It follows definite rules of syntax, which are understood among those who use it but are not accepted in conventional academic or social settings.

How many of the following expressions, which are entirely appropriate for *Black English,* can you "translate" into *standard English?*

BLACK ENGLISH	PAGE	LINE	STANDARD ENGLISH
1. . . . there *was* three private rooms . . .	36	6	________________
2. It *laid* on a chair. . . .	36	9	________________
3. . . . had never seen *nobody* die.	36	12–13	________________
4. Not *no* more.	37	27	________________
5. She had *went* without. . . .	37	30	________________
6. It *were* kept locked up. . . .	37	33	________________
7. *Them* nurses *ain't* understandable.	37	40	________________
8. He *do* not know I am. . . .	38	46	________________
9. . . . *were* he ashamed to come. . . .	38	46	________________

BLACK ENGLISH	PAGE	LINE	STANDARD ENGLISH
10. He got right up . . and *come.*	38	52–53	______________
11. Who *were* his papa?	39	76	______________
12. . . . .she *were* not *right* bright . . .	39	79	______________
13. . . . *couldn't* hardly have more than gotten home. . . .	40	86	______________
14. He never had *no* real mama. . . .	41	94	______________

3. GRAMMAR: B. PRONOUNS

USE THE RIGHT PRONOUNS!

In English, a personal pronoun must "agree" in *gender* and *number* with the word it stands for. In addition, it must be in the right *case,* according to its use in the sentence.

In order to find out whether you can remember and use the rules on personal pronouns correctly, try the following completion exercise. As you fill in each of the blanks, be sure to choose the pronoun that:

- Agrees with the *antecedent* (the noun it stands for), and
- Is in the right *case* (nominative, possessive, or objective).

MORE ABOUT MIDGETS

The most famous midget in the United States was Charles Sherwood Stratton (General Tom Thumb, 1838–1883), who made ______________ living as a sideshow attraction traveling with P. T. Barnum's circus. In 1862 ______________ married another midget named Mercy Lavinia Warren Bump, who was 32 inches tall and weighed 29 pounds. Barnum, who was famous for ______________ showmanship, gave ______________ an extravagant (costly) wedding and kept ______________ busy for many years as a popular exhibit in ______________ traveling circus.

Although Lavinia outlived ______________ husband, ______________ dedicated ______________ life to being on tour for the public right up to the time of ______________ death in 1919. Having been married a second time, this time to Count Primo Magri, ______________ became known as Countess Lavinia, a name which may have inspired Langston Hughes's choice of ______________ character's name, "Countess Midget."

For many years, midgets were such well-known and popular attractions as entertainers that ______________ were widely imitated in local small-town shows. Churches and schools would put on "Tom Thumb Weddings," for which parents would dress

______________ children in elaborate, small-sized wedding outfits. Besides the bride and groom, there would be many other children in the wedding party, including a flower girl who scattered ______________ rose petals in front of the bride and a small boy as ring-bearer, who carefully carried ______________ little pillow holding the mock wedding ring. At the proper moment in the ceremony, ______________ would hand the ring to the best man, who would give ______________ to the groom, standing next to ______________. The groom then would turn to ______________ bride and place the ring on ______________ finger.

Although midgets are no longer the outstanding attractions ______________ used to be in the entertainment world, some movies and television shows continue to feature ______________ because of the irresistible fascination that ______________ will always hold for the public. If you would like to read more about what ______________ like to live as a child-sized adult, Countess Lavinia has left us ______________ own life story. ______________ somewhat lengthy title is: *The Autobiography of Mrs. Tom Thumb (Some of My Life Experiences),* by Countess M. Lavinia Magri, formerly Mrs. General Tom Thumb.*

4. COMPOSITION: THE TOPIC SENTENCE

MAKING THE MOST OF THE TOPIC SENTENCE

A topic sentence is not simply a topic or the subject. It *includes* the subject, but it does something more: It gives the reader *definite clues* about what the writer plans to *do* with the subject.

Like every complete sentence, a topic sentence contains a subject and a predicate—a noun (phrase) and a verb (phrase)—along with other modifying words. Your topic sentence can work best if:

- It mentions the topic or subject of your paragraph;
- It states something definite and specific about your subject.

The words that provide these "definite clues" are called *key words.* If the topic sentence has more than one clause, the key words may be found in one of them, or they may be partly in one and partly in the other.

*A. H. Saxon, Editor, Archon Books on Popular Entertainments Series (Hamden, Conn.: The Shoe String Press, Inc., 1979).

A. Can you find the key words in each of the topic sentences below?

1. Countess Midget was a tiny human being, but she had a big heart.
2. Although the young orderly gave the midget special attention at first because of her tips, later he was kind to her for other reasons.
3. The son was not all bad, since he really loved his midget mama.
4. Tipping people is one way to get good service.
5. A midget is/is not really like other people.
6. In my opinion, "Sorrow for a Midget" was/was not a sad story.

B. After you have underlined the key words and discussed them with others in the class, choose one to write about. Jot down notes (or make a list) of 3–5 points that could be used to support that statement. If the topic sentence you select is #5 or #6, decide whether you agree with the *positive* or the *negative* statement.

C. Write a paragraph of six or seven sentences, including and beginning with the topic sentence you used in Part B. Include all your supporting points in your paragraph, and try to finish up with a strong, concluding statement.

D. For a longer composition: First of all, think about these questions: What are *your* roots, or your own national, racial, or cultural background? In what ways do they influence you and help you to establish your own sense of identity: knowing who you are, developing your own code of behavior and your lifestyle, and defining your purpose in life?

1. Compose a thesis. A "topic sentence," such as those in Part B, states the main idea of a paragraph. A "thesis statement" (sometimes called just a "thesis") states the main idea of a full-length essay. Like the topic sentence, it also mentions the subject and then states something definite about it—gives a controlling idea for developing the subject.

   Example: My roots are partly in East Africa and partly in Pakistan, so I come from two cultures and speak three languages.

   How would you make an outline based on this thesis? Your own thesis, stating what you consider to be your roots, should also suggest a possible outline.

2. Write a brief outline. Sketch out the main points your essay would cover. A more detailed outline would also add notes or information to go under each main point.
3. Write your composition. Include your thesis in the first paragraph, and use your outline as a guide for writing a composition of about two pages.

5. SPECIAL PROJECT: A. READING

SEEING THE POLARITIES OR OPPOSING IDEAS

As a writer who is primarily a poet, Langston Hughes makes rich use of colorful imagery, such as the one on p. 38, lines 50–51: ". . . ragged as a buzzard. . . ." The story is also full of ironic contrasts, or opposites with an underlying, symbolic meaning. Some of those contrasting pairs of ideas are given below:

Point out the *contrasting elements* that you see in each pair.
Comment on the larger implications, or the *symbolic meaning,* that each pair seems to suggest.

1. I was broke	thick wad of bills
2. business is bad	people don't die
3. game kiddie	booked to die
4. her son . . . ragged as a buzzard	generous . . . little midget
5. the little Countess . . . so dark and small	white, white room . . . white bed
6. my precious baby son	the guy . . . near six feet, big, heavy-set
7. big old ragged . . . son	cried like a child

5. SPECIAL PROJECT: B. VOCABULARY

ENRICHING YOUR VOCABULARY THROUGH SYNONYMS AND ANTONYMS

Synonyms

A *synonym* is a word whose meaning is very close to that of another word, although it does not always work as an exact substitute.

Each of the following words is a synonym for a word taken from the vocabulary lists of the first two stories. Most of them are found in the Standard Vocabulary columns. You may need to use your English dictionary for words you are not familiar with.

	SYNONYM		SYNONYM
1. rigid	______	5. maybe	______
2. pleasure	______	6. mentally alert	______
3. reared	______	7. shun	______
4. corpse	______		

	SYNONYM		SYNONYM
8. kinfolk	________	12. pretended	________
9. tattered	________	13. beneficial	________
10. unfeeling	________	14. seeming	________
11. gaze	________	15. valuable	________

Antonyms

An *antonym* is a word that is opposite to another word in meaning. Finding antonyms is a good way to sharpen, as well as to enlarge, your vocabulary.

Each of the words below is an antonym for a word taken from the vocabulary lists of the same two stories. Using your dictionary, see how many you can find.

	ANTONYM		ANTONYM
1. stingy	________	9. gaze	________
2. crooked	________	10. gentle	________
3. certainly	________	11. disdain	________
4. stupid	________	12. shouted	________
5. proud	________	13. clear	________
6. wasteful	________	14. flexible	________
7. discontent	________	15. worthless	________
8. giant	________		

Sherwood Anderson (1876–1941)

Sherwood Anderson was what Americans call a "self-made man." With little formal education, he began to work when he was 14 and for years drifted from one job to another, until at last he settled down and began to write.

His greatest literary reputation came from his third book, Winesburg, Ohio *(1919), a collection of stories that were penetrating in their psychological insights. Anderson's favorite subjects for his short stories, poems, and novels were the small Midwestern towns he knew, the mindless materialism of the machine age, the disappearing values of individualism and craftsmanship, and the drab, routine lives of ordinary working-class people.*

"I Want to Work" comes from the book, Puzzled America *(1935), which contained stories concerned with the Great Depression. In this "slice of life" story there is little action or plot; however, there is something very real and timeless in its dialogue, which conveys the typical Midwestern attitudes and speech patterns for which Sherwood Anderson is famous. With only a very few changes, such an incident and conversation could take place today in that same region of the country.*

Anderson's writings also include Poor White *(1920), a novel in which the "hero" is a Midwestern town;* The Triumph of the Egg *(1921), stories and poems depicting the frustration some people feel in American small-town life; and* Perhaps Women *(1931), in which he advanced the hope that women would some day lead modern society away from the dehumanizing effects of mechanization.*

IV

I Want to Work

Story Setting: *In "a small Southern industrial town" rather than in Anderson's usual Midwestern setting. The story takes place during the early Depression days, when the South was still a very rural and agricultural region.*

Main Idea: *A middle-aged man, who has been out of work for two years, has a chance meeting with a man whom he invites into his home for conversation over a beer.*

I went home with a workman from a meeting of unemployed. He had come in there, out of curiosity, as I had. We happened to come out of the meeting at the same time and stopped outside to talk.

The preliminary talk led to another and the next day we met. "Yes, I'm out of work. I'm fifty-two, you see." He was a sturdily-built, clear-eyed man. "I used to make big wages. I should have got fixed for this. I didn't. I was proud, sure of myself. I thought things would always go on as they were. When I did make good money I spent it."

He had been a machinist as a young man and later had become a machine-tender in a factory. He had been out of work for two years. I asked him to come with me to my hotel but he didn't like the idea.

"No," he said, "I'm not dressed for it. You come on home with me."

GLOSSARY

1 **meeting of unemployed:** a meeting of people who had lost their jobs and were out of work.
5 **sturdily-built:** solid, strong-looking, stocky.
8 **machinist . . . machine-tender:** one who works with machinery or runs a machine.

INFORMAL SPEECH

6 **should have got fixed for:** should have prepared or planned for.
6 **sure of myself:** full of confidence.
7 **good money:** reasonably high salary or wages.
10 **didn't like the idea:** didn't want to.
11 **not dressed for it:** not wearing proper or appropriate clothes.

STANDARD VOCABULARY

2 ***curiosity:** desire to know something.
2 **happened to** (id): without plan or intention, by luck.
4 **preliminary:** preparing the way for, introducing.
6 **wages:** money earned by working at a job, a salary.

This was in the early afternoon of a cold day. He was in blue overalls and wore a shabby coat. His thick, stiff gray hair was only half concealed by his cap. He wore the cap tilted a bit to one side—as though to say—"O.K.—after all I'm as good as the next man."

We went down to where he lived, stopping at a corner grocer's on the way. "I'll get a few bottles of beer," I said.

"All right. I wouldn't mind having a bottle with you."

I got his story, going down and as we sat in his house. It was an every-day, common enough story.

He had got married as a young man and had one daughter who married a young workman, a machine-fixer like himself. When he was forty his wife died and two years later he got a new wife. He got a young one, nearly twenty years younger than himself, but they had no children.

"They are all at work," he said, "my wife, my daughter, and her husband."

His daughter and her husband had no children. The three of them, his own wife, his daughter, and her husband, had bought a house—it was a small, neat frame house on a little hill beyond a district of huge factories in a Southern industrial town and when we got there we climbed a flight of stairs to a bedroom on the second floor. "You wait and I'll go stir up the furnace and get some glasses for the beer, " he said, and when he returned he began to talk—"You see," he said, "I tend to the furnace. I do what I can around here."

He said something, speaking a little bitterly about what he couldn't do, "I should have been born a woman. If I could cook for the others now. If I could do the family wash, it would save money for them."

You could see that he had been lifted, by circumstances, outside the life of the house in which he had once been the head man.

The point is the way he was taking it. It was obviously the old story of a man whose civilization had got through with him before he was through with it. He had got laid off,

GLOSSARY

12 **overalls:** loose, heavy trousers worn by workmen to protect their clothes.
26 **frame house:** a house that is built of wood.
27 **Southern industrial town:** a town in one of the Southern states, near the East Coast, where the business is mostly manufacturing, rather than farming.

INFORMAL SPEECH

17 **wouldn't mind having:** an indirect way of saying, "I'd like to have one," without sounding too eager.
29 **stir up the furnace:** put more coal on the fire to get more heat.
32 **do the family wash:** launder or wash the clothes for the whole family.
35 **head man:** the man in charge.
36 **the way he was taking it:** the attitude he was showing.
37 **got through with:** finished with, no longer wished to have around.
37 **laid off:** dismissed from a job because of lack of work.

STANDARD VOCABULARY

13 **shabby:** faded and worn-looking.
13 ***concealed:** hidden.
14 **tilted:** slanting, not straight.
14 **after all:** anyhow.
18 **common:** ordinary, usual, everyday.
27 **district:** special area or division of a larger area.
27 **huge:** very large.
27 **factories:** buildings where workers operate machines in order to make (manufacture) things for sale.
30 **tend to:** take care of, keeping in good working order.
31 ***bitterly:** sadly, hopelessly.
34 **lifted:** carried above.
34 **circumstances:** events that affect a person.
36 **obviously:** easily seen as.
37 ***civilization:** social environment, society.

when the Depression hit the town, and then, later, when his shop started up again, a younger man got his place. "I'm not as fast as I once was," he said, "but I'm a careful man, a good workman yet."

He said he didn't want to offer to work for less wages than the younger man, who had been taken back. "If you begin that," he said, "you cut the standard of a whole shop."

We sat in two chairs by a window that looked down on the factories while we drank our beer and talked. An old feeling, so common in American men, concerned with modern industry—pride in the very thing that has apparently thrown life out of gear.

I have talked to many manufacturers and factory superintendents, and rarely, I think never, have I gone into a shop without being shown some new machine.

Here, in a tin can factory, is a machine that makes can tops. It is the superintendent of

GLOSSARY

45 **thrown life out of gear** (fig): suddenly forced one to shift or change his direction in life.
46 **manufacturers and factory superintendents:** owners and managers of companies that make (manufacture) goods to sell.
48 **can tops:** small, round tins cut out to fit the tops of cans and seal them shut.

INFORMAL SPEECH

38 **hit:** arrived very suddenly and unexpectedly.
42 **cut:** reduce, lower.

STANDARD VOCABULARY

42 ***standard:** accepted rule or level of excellence.
42 **shop:** (as used here) place of work.
44 ***concerned (with):** involved.
45 **apparently:** seemingly, evidently.
46 ***rarely:** very seldom.

the shop showing me through. "When I first came to work here, when I first became a foreman, we had a machine that turned out forty can tops a minute. There was a man at work on every machine. Now you see this long battery of machines. The two men you see walking up and down take care of them all. They don't work so hard. There isn't any heavy work in any modern shop.

"When I was a young man here, a young foreman, I used to go home at night, having seen a new machine installed that would knock out forty can tops a minute. I used to think: 'Are there people enough in the world to use so many tin cans?'" He laughed. "Look at these machines," he said, with pride in his voice. "Every machine in this long row of machines is knocking out three hundred and sixty can tops a minute."

"And you have laid off many men who can never get back into this shop?"

"Yes."

"I do not see many older men."

"No. The younger ones have the call. They are quicker, you see, less likely to get hurt."

I asked him what I have asked many men in positions of control in industry. "When you are all doing it, laying off so many men who can never get back, aren't you laying off your own customers, users of goods you make here?"

"Yes, we are, all right."

"Well, what are you going to do?"

"I don't know."

That attitude on the part of most of the men in control of the shops. What about the workmen?

Those who say that American workmen, so often now thrown out of their place in our social and economic scheme by the modern machine, so often robbed of something peculiarly vital to their feeling of manhood—this I kept thinking the most important thing of all, the thing I keep hoping that we may come more and more to understand and appreciate—

GLOSSARY

51 **long battery of machines:** a long row or series of machines.
64 **positions of control:** jobs where important decisions are made, places of power.
72 **thrown out of their place:** replaced, pushed aside.
73 **social and economic scheme:** the system by which a person works and earns money, which he can then spend on things he needs and wants.
74 **feeling of manhood:** a sense of one's masculinity, or of having a man's role in society.

INFORMAL SPEECH

50 **turned out:** made or produced, manufactured.
55 **knock out:** turn out or make.
62 **have the call:** are called in to work, get the opportunity to work.
67 **all right:** (as used here) for sure, for certain, indeed.
70 **what about:** what will happen to.

STANDARD VOCABULARY

50 **foreman:** the "boss" or supervisor over a group of workmen.
55 ***installed:** set up and connected so it would work.
64 ***industry:** the business of manufacturing, in general.
66 **customers:** clients, people who pay for goods or services.
73 ***robbed of:** loses something because it is forcibly taken.
73 **peculiarly:** in a very special and unusual way.
74 ***vital:** valuable and important to life itself.
75 ***appreciate:** recognize and value.

The machines themselves apparently becoming always faster and faster, more and more efficient—the man in the street can see it with his own eyes in the increased beauty, speed, and efficiency of the automobile——

As though there were actually a kind of devil sleeping down in these so-gorgeously beautiful masses of steel in action——

Those who hold that American workmen do not want to work with the machines, that they do not want to be in the factories, simply do not know what they are talking about.

In the greater majority of American workmen, and now in American workwomen, is an actual love of the machine and—yes, I am sure of it—in spite of everything—love of the factories. There are, to be sure, always the stupid ones, the dull ones, but the numbers of the other constantly amazes.

The workman, past his prime, who knew what had happened to him and with whom I drank the beer, had got into the habit of going into the public library of the town. As I have said, we were in a Southern town. "I was born a Yank," he said.

"So was I," I said.

His father, a carriage blacksmith, had come South after the war when he was a young boy.

"The kids here used to dog me a lot about being a Yank.

"So I thought, sometime, I thought, when I have time, I'm going to read up on the war.

"I'd never been much to read."

He had got on to one of my own hobbies. "Well," I said.

"Now there was Grant," he said. "I've got to liking that man, at least to liking what

GLOSSARY

79 **so-gorgeously beautiful masses of steel:** machines that are spectacular in their ability to work effectively and well.
90 **Yank:** someone from the Northeast region of the United States.
92 **carriage blacksmith:** a builder of iron frames for horsedrawn vehicles.
92**after the war:** the American Civil War between the North and the South, 1861–1865.
99 **Grant** (Ulysses S.): General Grant was appointed by President Lincoln to lead the Union Army against the South during the Civil War. He won great military victories and was later elected President (1869–1877). However, he was unable to stop the dishonest activities of government officials he had appointed.

INFORMAL SPEECH

81 **hold that:** have the opinion, believe.
82 **not know what they are talking about:** are both ignorant and foolish.
88 **past his prime:** no longer able to perform as well as he once did.
94 **kids:** children (a friendly, informal term).
94 **dog:** tease, make fun of, ridicule.
95 **read up on:** read a lot about something for information.
97 **never been much to read:** didn't like reading very much, or didn't do it very well.
98 **got on to:** happened to mention.
99 **I've got to liking:** I've begun to like.

STANDARD VOCABULARY

77 ***efficient:** effective, working very well.
79 **devil:** demon, spirit of evil.
84 **majority:** more than half the total number.
86 **stupid:** ignorant.
86 **dull:** indifferent, uncaring, bored and probably boring.
87 ***amazes:** causes great surprise or astonishment.
98 **hobbies:** activities or interests a person follows for his own pleasure.

he was when he was just a general, before he got to be President. He wasn't such a smart man, but I figure he had the big idea all right."

"Yes? And how?"

"I've been figuring it out. I've got plenty of time to figure things out. A lot of the Northern generals during the war couldn't see the war as a whole. That's what made it last so long."

"You mean?"

"You see, I figure, they thought of a battle as a battle. I think he saw the war as a war."

"He and Lincoln, eh?"

"Yes," he said.

"I've been thinking," he said, "that some day, maybe——

"We may see it as a whole, what we are up against."

I left him sitting in the room and went down the stairs and into the street and on the next day I got into the factory where he had been employed. It was a good one, very modern, very big, light, and efficient.

On the day when I left him and got into the street I wasn't thinking of that.

"They were O.K. They can sure take it," was what I was thinking. And I was thinking that the most pathetic thing of all—in the workman who had been put to one side by his civilization—was his undying so-American optimism.

GLOSSARY

101 **the big idea:** a broad understanding of reality and the truth.
109 **Lincoln:** President Abraham Lincoln, who supported Grant's strong military actions with the Union Army because he was determined to keep the South from becoming a separate country.
118 **put to one side:** (lit) moved away from the center; (fig) left out of reach of the opportunities and advantages most people want and expect to have.

INFORMAL SPEECH

100 **got to be:** became.
100 **smart:** intelligent, clever.
103 **figuring it out:** trying to find the answer by thinking about a problem.
112 **what we are up against:** what obstacles or problems we face.
117 **they can sure take it:** they certainly have the courage and the strength to face difficulties and hardships.

STANDARD VOCABULARY

104 **as a whole:** entirely, all at once.
107 **battle:** a single military action, part of a longer military struggle or war.
118 **pathetic:** moving a person to feel pity and compassion.
119 **undying:** unfailing, going on forever.
119 ***optimism:** confidence that things will turn out well in the end.

1. STUDY QUESTIONS

DISCOVERING THE STORY THROUGH OBSERVATION AND INFERENCE

1. ***Observation:*** There are two characters in the story, the workman and the narrator. What do we learn about the workman in the first three paragraphs? How do we know that the narrator is a visitor?
   Inference: The workman says that he "was proud." What do you think he means? In the first part of the story, what do you find that indicates he is still a proud man, even though he is unemployed?
2. ***Observation:*** How would you describe the workman's home and his lifestyle?
   Inference: His comments on p. 52, lines 28–33, reflect the outlook or point of view held by most people in the United States in the 1930s and earlier. How have people's attitudes changed about these things in recent years?
3. ***Observation:*** In your own words, explain why this capable, experienced workman does not have a job.
   Inference: What does he mean by his statement in lines 41–42, p. 53? Do you agree with him?
4. ***Observation:*** What attitude do the factory managers have toward the machines? What are the positive and the negative effects of machines, as shown in this story?
   Inference: What is meant by the following expressions on pp. 54–55?
   p. 54, lines 73–74: ". . . something peculiarly vital to their feeling of manhood."
   p. 55, line 77: ". . . the man in the street. . . ."
   p. 55, line 79: "As though there were actually a kind of devil sleeping. . . ."
5. ***Observation:*** The workman says he was "born a Yank" (a "Yankee"). What other information does he give about his background and childhood?
   Inference: Can you explain in your own words the idea or principle that the workman here discovered from reading about Grant and Lincoln? How did this idea support his "so-American optimism"?

2. VOCABULARY: WORD FORMS

ACTIVATE YOUR VOCABULARY

Reading helps to enlarge your vocabulary because you learn to recognize words that were previously unfamiliar to you. When you can actually use those words yourself, they become part of your "active" vocabulary. You can expand your active vocabulary still more by using the same words in *different forms.*

Try doing this with the words below, all of which can be found among the starred words in the Standard Vocabulary for this story:

1. In the parentheses beside the word write the part of speech of that word.
2. In the blank next to the part of speech you are to supply, write the word in the designated word form.
3. In the space following, use the new word form in a sentence of 8–10 words, or more.

Example:
Curiosity (noun); *adjective* curious

My sister was curious to know who was talking to me on the phone.

1. **bitterly** ( ); *adjective* __________
2. **civilization** ( ); *present or past participle* __________
3. **concerned** ( ); *noun* __________
4. **standard** ( ); *verb, present or past* __________
5. **rarely** ( ); *adjective* __________
6. **installed** ( ); *noun* __________
7. **industry** ( ); *verb, present or past* __________
8. **vital** ( ); *noun* __________
9. **appreciate** ( ); *noun* __________
10. **optimism** ( ); *adverb* __________
11. **amazes** ( ); *present or past participle* __________
12. **efficient** ( ); *noun* __________

3. READING: IDENTIFYING FORMAL AND INFORMAL STYLES

TWO LEVELS OF ENGLISH USAGE

You may have noticed that *spoken* English is very often different from the *written* language. The English we use in conversation is usually very informal, sometimes called "colloquial." It is like the "everyday clothes" which we use for ordinary work or play, while we save our "dress-up" clothes for more important or special occasions.

Although more formal, or standard, English may mean about the same thing as colloquial English, it will be said in a different way:

FORMAL, STANDARD ENGLISH HAS:	COLLOQUIAL, INFORMAL SPEECH HAS:
complete sentences	fragmentary sentences
longer sentences	rather short, simple sentences
dependent (subordinate) clauses	coordination (and, but, for, so)
the third person (he, she, one, they)	first, second, or third person
longer words, often with Greek or Latin roots, prefixes, and suffixes	shorter and simpler words, often with Anglo-Saxon roots
fewer idioms	many idioms
very few (or no) contractions	many contractions (don't, isn't, etc.)
no slang, dialect, or swear words	slang and swear words, if they are appropriate
complete, proper names of people, places, or institutions	nicknames, shortened, casual forms, or abbreviations

If you look closely, you will see that the stories told as though by a narrator (such as the first four stories in this book) are expressed in a more informal style than are the stories in which events are described in the third person. (You will find examples of the omniscient—all-knowing—style of the author in the stories "The Test," "Hawsmoot," and "Soldier's Home.")

Compositions and other papers written in college generally follow a somewhat formal style and use standard English. However, the *degree* of formality may vary rather widely according to the purpose, the circumstances, and the audience for whom the writer intends the work. As a rule, the more serious or important the purpose, the more you "dress up" the language.

The writer of fiction wishes to create an imaginary world where people talk in a natural, realistic way, so that the readers can feel or imagine that the characters and events in the story are "real." For this reason, the story which you have just read, "I Want to Work," contains many colloquial or informal expressions. Can you recognize those same ideas when they have been "dressed up" for a more formal occasion?

Use the informal speech column to help you with this. Read the standard English sentence at the left; then fill in the blanks in the right-hand column with an equivalent or similar expression, expressed in "everyday," informal style.

MORE FORMAL, STANDARD ENGLISH	INFORMAL, EVERYDAY USAGE
1. When the city's budget was reduced, many teachers lost their positions.	1. . . . many teachers were _______ _______.
2. Congressional representatives are not usually in favor of raising taxes before an election.	2. . . . representatives usually don't _______ _______ _______ _______.
3. Several thousand people ran in the Boston Marathon this year. They certainly have a great deal of stamina.	3. They sure _______ _______ _______.
4. While living down South, Kwok-On was served so much hominy, fried chicken, and sweet potato pie that he developed a taste for them.	4. . . . he _______ _______ _______ _______.
5. Most Americans realize that they must plan for an adequate income in their old age.	5. . . . they must get _______ _______ their old age.
6. A refrigerator's doors must be removed when the owner no longer is using it.	6. . . . when the owner gets _______ _______ it.
7. When a young couple claims that two can live as cheaply as one, they are displaying their ignorance.	7. . . . they don't know _______ _______ _______ _______ _______.
8. Intellectual parents often have highly intelligent children.	8. . . .often have _______ _______.
9. Alvaro knew that his writing skills were poor, but when it came to conversational English, he was confident.	9. . . . he was _______ _______ _______.
10. When Sanjay decided to go through college in three years, he did not realize what problems he would meet.	10. . . . did not realize what he _______ _______ _______.

11. Although María had never liked studying mathematics, she found that she loved working with computers.

11. . . . Although María had never been __________ __________ study mathematics. . . .

12. The furniture company produced more dining room sets than it could sell.

12. . . . company __________ __________ more. . . .

13. Even though he was not the great fighter he had been, Mohammed Ali continued to draw enthusiastic crowds.

13. Even though he was __________ __________ __________ Mohammed. . . .

14. Before Mustafa went away to college in Canada, he decided to study about the history of the country.

14. . . . he decided to __________ __________ __________ the history. . . .

15. Christina wrote her parents that she was making a high salary in her new job in electronics.

15. . . . that she was making __________ __________ in her new job. . . .

4. LANGUAGE CONVERSION: PARAPHRASE

SAY IT ANOTHER WAY

The best writing is writing that does *effectively* what it is meant to do. A casual, informal style is the most appropriate way of telling a story and of reproducing natural-sounding dialogue. On the other hand, standard English is more accurate and exact; thus it is the best to use when you need to present information clearly.

The language of the narrator and other characters in "Sorrow for a Midget" is an example of very colloquial usage. It seems exactly right for them to talk that way. What do you think would be the result if the same information or ideas were expressed in a more formal style of English? In doing the following exercise, you will be demonstrating the difference between informal, conversational English and the more formal level used in newspapers, textbooks, and most college writing.

To do this exercise, simply rewrite each of the passages below in conventional, standard English. Use the description of both levels given in Activity 3 for your guide.

As you paraphrase the colloquial speech created by Langston Hughes, keep as close as you can to the original meaning and ideas, but work to make them sound very formal and proper.

A. "'Take care of me good,' she said . . . She opened her fat pocketbook, as big as she was, and showed me a thick wad of bills. 'This gets it anytime, anywhere,' she said."

B. "It got it with me, all right. I stuck by. Tips count up. That's how I know so much about what happened in them few days she was in that hospital room, game as she could be, but booked to die."

C. "He was not doing so well. Fact is, her son was ragged as a buzzard feeding on a Lenox Avenue carcass. But when I told him his mama was sick in the Maggie Butler Pavilion of the Sadie Henderson Hospital, he come." Note: "Maggie" is a nickname for Margaret, and "Sadie" is a nickname for Sarah.

D. "'Damn right, she's my mama,' said the guy, who was near six feet, big, heavy-set, black, and ragged. No warm coat on. I thought I was beat, but he was the most. I could tell he had *been* gone to the dogs, long gone."

E. "They had just given his mama a needle, so she were not right bright. But when she saw her son, her little old wrinkled face lighted up. Her little old tiny matchstick arms went almost around his neck. And she hollered, 'My baby!' real loud."

5. COMPOSITION: WRITING FORMALLY AND INFORMALLY

TRY IT BOTH WAYS

You have seen how natural it can be to use informal or colloquial style in everyday speech situations, and you have tried your hand at converting it into a more formal style. Have you noticed the differences in *emotional tone* that seem to appear at each level?

Generally speaking, the more informal the speech situation, the more we are free to "let out" our feelings—happy, sad, angry, complaining, or whatever. At times like that, we know it's all right to use slang or swear words to talk about what happened: "It all happened down at the corner by Tony's pizza joint this morning. I had a green light and I was just getting going when this goddamned Corvette charged through a red light and plowed right into my front end. The guy must've been doing at least 65!"

There are also circumstances where we are expected to give just the "straight facts," or it may be an occasion for being respectful to an official or to an older person. We are more cautious about "getting emotional" and more careful about giving exact information: "The accident took place at the intersection of Main Street and Rutledge, in front of Tony's Pizza Parlor. My car was proceeding through a green light when it was struck on the front right fender by a black Corvette, apparently speeding through a red light."

Both accounts are of the same happening, but the language is different.

In writing this composition exercise, you will be demonstrating two levels of English usage by writing two different types of paragraphs about the same thing. You may either *describe* something (or someone) or *tell about something that happened:*

First, write about your subject very informally. In this paragraph it is not necessary to be so specific, because your feelings and impressions are what count. Don't be afraid to use slang, or even a mild swear word or two.

Next, write another paragraph dealing with the same subject in a much more formal way. This time, stay away from emotional language and stick to the facts. Try to sound serious and dignified by including some features of formal style.

Some Subject Possibilities

What my first job was like
A party I attended recently
When my apartment was broken into
A teacher I won't forget
A terrible/really great movie I saw recently
What my landlord is like
Getting a parking ticket (or a ticket for speeding)
An American custom I like or don't like
Getting lost in Boston (or New York, or another city)

Grace Paley (1922–   )

Grace Paley has for years been a controversial figure in American academic life. She was active in many peace rallies during the 1960s and once was jailed as a result of her protests against the war in Vietnam. Even in her short stories, she is known for her outspokenness and her fearless habit of writing honestly, yet sensitively, about unpopular issues. "The Loudest Voice" is a blend of several of her strongest qualities as a writer and a human being: a keen ear for natural dialogue (especially reflecting the Jewish community); warm appreciation for everyday, human relations; and the skill to offset her own sharp-tongued frankness with lively touches of humor.

Born in the Bronx, New York, she attended Hunter College and New York University and has taught literature at Columbia, Sarah Lawrence, and Syracuse University. This story comes from an early work, The Little Disturbances of Man *(1959); a more recent collection,* Enormous Changes at the Last Minute *(1974), contains stories that originally appeared in several magazines, including* Atlantic *and* Esquire.

V

The Loudest Voice

Story Setting: *A lower middle-class neighborhood in New York City, possibly the Bronx. The time is post-World War II, around the 1950s.*

Main Idea: *In this cross-cultural story, Jewish public school children are asked to help put on a Christmas program, and their parents are not sure whether to feel pleased or insulted. The question at issue becomes focused on one little Jewish girl, who has been given the leading part in the play.*

Cultural Background of the Story: *Christmas Day (December 25) is such a favorite among all the holidays celebrated in the United States that it has, in the minds of many people, practically universal appeal. In one sense, it has become a largely secular, or nonreligious, festival here in the United States. Christmas entertainments, parties, and other holiday activities are a common occurrence in schools and places of work throughout the month of December.*

However, although Christmas trees and Santa Claus are widely enjoyed and associated with this day, the holiday's original significance (still very real to many people) was a religious one, the purpose being to celebrate the birth of Jesus, whom Christians worship as the son of God. In their enthusiasm for this joyous holiday, many Americans, including the public school teachers in this particular story, become quite insensitive to the religious views of others around them and simply assume that everyone *likes to sing Christmas carols and participate in or attend Christmas programs.*

The play that the teachers devise is actually more than the usual production that simply retells through songs, Bible readings, and stage scenes the story of the birth of the infant Jesus. Instead, the teachers become carried away with their own enthusiasm and have the children present the whole life of Jesus: his years of preaching, his choice of twelve disciples or followers, and his betrayal by one of them to the Roman rulers, who executed him by hanging him on a cross.

All this is alluded to in "The Loudest Voice," where the artistry and benevolence of the writer become evident in her mildly humorous description of the Christmas play that the children present to a religiously mixed audience.

There is a certain place where dumb-waiters boom, doors slam, dishes crash; every window is a mother's mouth bidding the street to shut up, go skate somewhere else, come home. My voice is the loudest.

There, my own mother is still as full of breathing as me and the grocer stands up to speak to her. "Mrs. Abramowitz," he says, "people should not be afraid of their children."

"Ah, Mr. Bialik," my mother replies, "if you say to her or her father, 'Ssh,' they say, 'In the grave it will be quiet.'"

"From Coney Island to the cemetery," says my papa. "It's the same subway; it's the same fare."

I am right next to the pickle barrel. My pinky is making tiny whirlpools in the brine. I stop a moment to announce: "Campbell's Tomato Soup. Campbell's Vegetable Beef Soup. Campbell's S-c-otch Broth. . . ."

"Be quiet," the grocer says, "the labels are coming off."

"Please, Shirley, be a little quiet," my mother begs me.

In that place the whole street groans: Be quiet! Be quiet! but steals from the happy chorus of my inside self not a tittle or a jot.

GLOSSARY

1 **dumb-waiters:** small elevators used in restaurants to move food and dishes up and down to different floors.
1 **every window** (fig): Mothers call out to all the children to stop making so much noise.
2 **skate:** Children's roller-skating makes a loud noise on city sidewalks.
5 **Mrs. Abramowitz:** a Russian Jewish surname. (Watch for other ethnic names indicating this is a Jewish neighborhood.)
8 **Coney Island:** a famous New York outdoor entertainment place for families.
10 **whirlpools:** water moving about in circles.
15 **the happy chorus of my inside self** (fig): the happy thoughts and feelings within her.
16 **not a tittle or a jot:** not the least bit, none at all.

INFORMAL SPEECH

2 **shut up** (impolite slang): be quiet.
10 **pinky:** the smallest finger (little finger).

STANDARD VOCABULARY

2 **bidding:** ordering, commanding.
4 ***breathing:** drawing one's breath in and out, inhaling and exhaling (thus alive).
7 **grave:** a hole dug in the ground where a body is buried.
8 **cemetery:** area of land (not a churchyard) set aside for burials.
10 **pickle:** preserved cucumber with a sour and salty taste.
10 **barrel:** a large, round, deep container.
11 ***announce:** speak out publicly, proclaim.
13 **labels:** paper signs stuck on to indicate the contents of a jar or bottle.
14 **begs:** tries to persuade, coaxes.
15 **groans:** makes a deep sound of pain.
15 **steals:** robs, takes what belongs to another person.

There, too, but just around the corner, is a red brick building that has been old for many years. Every morning the children stand before it in double lines which must be straight. They are not insulted. They are waiting anyway.

I am usually among them. I am, in fact, the first, since I begin with "A."

One cold morning the monitor tapped me on the shoulder. "Go to Room 409, Shirley Abramowitz," he said. I did as I was told. I went in a hurry up a down staircase to Room 409, which contained sixth-graders. I had to wait at the desk without wiggling until Mr. Hilton, their teacher, had time to speak.

After five minutes he said, "Shirley?"

"What?" I whispered.

He said, "My! My! Shirley Abramowitz! They told me you had a particularly loud, clear voice and read with lots of expression. Could that be true?"

"Oh, yes," I whispered.

"In that case, don't be silly; I might very well be your teacher someday. Speak up, speak up."

"Yes," I shouted.

"More like it," he said. "Now, Shirley, can you put a ribbon in your hair or a bobby pin? It's too messy."

"Yes!" I bawled.

"Now, now, calm down." He turned to the class. "Children, not a sound. Open at page 39. Read till 52. When you finish, start again." He looked me over once more. "Now, Shirley, you know, I suppose, that Christmas is coming. We are preparing a beautiful play. Most of the parts have been given out. But I still need a child with a strong voice, lots of stamina. Do you know what stamina is? You do? Smart kid. You know, I heard you read 'The Lord is my shepherd' in Assembly yesterday. I was very impressed. Wonderful delivery. Mrs. Jordan, your teacher, speaks highly of you. Now listen to me, Shirley

GLOSSARY

22 **down staircase:** stairway meant for one-way traffic or students going down.
23 **sixth-graders:** the highest grade in an elementary school for children 11–12 years old.
33 **bobby pin** small, tight metal clip for holding the hair in place.
41 **'The Lord is my shepherd':** the first line of the Twenty-third Psalm, in the Old Testament—one of the most familiar passages in the Bible.
41 **wonderful delivery:** clear, impressive way of speaking.

INFORMAL SPEECH

22 **did as I was told:** obeyed the order.
22 **in a hurry:** as fast as possible.
23 **wiggling:** moving about or twisting.
27 **My! My!:** expression of surprise.
28 **with lots of expression:** in a way that sounded full of feeling.
30 **don't be silly:** be sensible.
30 **might very well be:** am likely to become (could very easily be some day).
34 **messy:** disorderly, untidy.
35 **bawled:** shouted in a loud, uncontrolled way. (See also the definition of "screaming at," Informal Speech, below, for another meaning.)
36 **calm down:** don't be so excited, relax.
37 **looked me over:** gave me a general, somewhat careful inspection.

STANDARD VOCABULARY

19 ***insulted:** offended, disturbed.
26 **whispered** (onomat): spoke in a soft, breathy way.
27 **particularly:** exactly, especially.
40 **stamina:** endurance, ability to use a lot of physical energy without getting tired.
42 **speaks highly** (of): praises, commends.

Abramowitz, if you want to take the part and be in the play repeat after me, 'I swear to work harder than I ever did before.'"

I looked to heaven and said at once, "Oh, I swear." I kissed my pinky and looked at God.

"That is an actor's life, my dear," he explained. "Like a soldier's, never tardy or disobedient to his general, the director. Everything," he said, "absolutely everything will depend on you."

That afternoon, all over the building, children scraped and scrubbed the turkeys and the sheaves of corn off the schoolroom windows. Goodbye Thanksgiving. The next morning a monitor brought red paper and green paper from the office. We made new shapes and hung them on the walls and glued them to the doors.

The teachers became happier and happier. Their heads were ringing like the bells of childhood. My best friend Evie was prone to evil, but she did not get a single demerit for whispering. We learned "Holy Night" without an error. "How wonderful!" said Miss Glace, the student teacher. "To think that some of you don't even speak the language!" We learned "Deck the Halls" and "Hark! The Herald Angels." . . . They weren't ashamed and we weren't embarrassed.

Oh, but when my mother heard about it all, she said to my father: "Misha, you don't know what's going on there. Cramer is the head of the Tickets Committee."

"Who?" asked my father. "Cramer? Oh yes, an active woman."

"Active? Active has to have a reason. Listen," she said sadly, "I'm surprised to see my neighbors making tra-la-la for Christmas."

GLOSSARY

50 **the turkeys and the sheaves of corn:** symbols of Thanksgiving Day, a time for feasting and for family gatherings.
52 **red . . . and green paper:** red and green are traditionally the colors used for Christmas decorations.
54 **ringing like the bells of childhood:** bells are associated with Christmas, which parents try to make a very special, happy time for children.
55 **prone to evil:** a phrase from the Bible meaning "inclined or likely to commit sin." Used here for its comic effect due to exaggeration.
56 **"Holy Night," "Deck the Halls," "Hark! The Herald Angels Sing":** Christmas carols or songs celebrating the birth of the Christ child.
64 **making tra-la-la:** joining in the singing to celebrate a Christian holiday.

INFORMAL SPEECH

45 **kissed my pinky:** a ritual children often used for making a serious promise or commitment.
61 **what's going on there:** what sort of thing is happening.
61 **The head of:** the person in charge.

STANDARD VOCABULARY

43 **swear** (to): make a solemn promise or vow (take an oath that).
47 **tardy:** late.
48 ***disobedient:** refusing to obey.
50 **scraped:** used a sharp, flat tool to make a surface clean and smooth.
50 **scrubbed:** rubbed hard with a brush to make clean.
55 **demerit:** a mark indicating a fault or an offense.
58 **ashamed:** feeling a sense of shame or guilt.
59 ***embarrassed:** feeling self-conscious and uncomfortable.

My father couldn't think of what to say to that. Then he decided: "You're in America! Clara, you wanted to come here. In Palestine the Arabs would be eating you alive. Europe you had pogroms. Argentina is full of Indians. Here you got Christmas. . . . Some joke, ha?"

"Very funny, Misha. What is becoming of you? If we came to a new country a long time ago to run away from tyrants, and instead we fall into a creeping pogrom, that our children learn a lot of lies, so what's the joke? Ach, Misha, your idealism is going away."

"So is your sense of humor."

"That I never had, but idealism you had a lot of."

"I'm the same Misha Abramovitch, I didn't change an iota. Ask anyone."

"Only ask me," says my mama, may she rest in peace. "I got the answer."

Meanwhile the neighbors had to think of what to say too.

Marty's father said: "You know, he has a very important part, my boy."

"Mine also," said Mr. Sauerfeld.

"Not my boy!" said Mrs. Klieg. "I said to him no. The answer is no. When I say no! I mean no!"

The rabbi's wife said, "It's disgusting!" But no one listened to her. Under the narrow sky of God's great wisdom she wore a strawberry-blond wig.

Every day was noisy and full of experience. I was Right-hand Man. Mr. Hilton said: "How could I get along without you, Shirley?"

He said: "Your mother and father ought to get down on their knees every night and thank God for giving them a child like you."

He also said: "You're absolutely a pleasure to work with, my dear, dear child."

Sometimes he said: "For God's sakes, what did I do with the script? Shirley! Shirley! Find it."

Then I answered quietly: "Here it is, Mr. Hilton."

Once in a while, when he was very tired, he would cry out: "Shirley, I'm just tired of screaming at those kids. Will you tell Ira Pushkov not to come in till Lester points to that star the second time?"

GLOSSARY

66 **In Palestine . . . :** many Jewish people have experienced terror and destruction at various times and places, but very few are able to make jokes about it as Mr. Abramovitch is trying to do here.
75 **may she rest in peace:** an expression of respect used when one speaks of someone who has died.
81 **narrow sky of God's great wisdom:** ironic reference to the strict beliefs of orthodox religion.
82 **strawberry-blonde wig:** false reddish-blonde hair.
92 **points to that star:** the "star of Bethlehem," which showed the Wise Men where the Christ child was to be found.

INFORMAL SPEECH

74 **I didn't change an iota:** I haven't changed at all or the least bit.
83 **Right-hand Man:** the most reliable and important helper to the person in charge.
84 **get along without:** manage to survive or to live without.
92 **screaming** (at): very loudly giving orders and directions; also scolding ("bawling out").

STANDARD VOCABULARY

67 **pogroms:** massacres of groups of innocent people.
70 **tyrants:** cruel dictators.
70 ***creeping:** (lit) crawling, approaching very slowly.
71 ***idealism:** living or being guided by one's highest beliefs or purposes (ideals).
72 **sense of humor:** the ability to see the comical or funny side of things.
81 ***disgusting:** loathsome, making one feel terribly disturbed or upset.
87 **absolutely:** utterly, completely.
88 **script:** text of a play being performed.
90 **quietly:** softly and calmly.

Then I roared: "Ira Pushkov, what's the matter with you? Dope! Mr. Hilton told you five times already, don't come in till Lester points to that star the second time."

"Ach, Clara," my father asked, "what does she do there till six o'clock she can't even put the plates on the table?"

"Christmas," said my mother coldly.

"Ho! Ho!" my father said, "Christmas. What's the harm? After all, history teaches everyone. We learn from reading this is a holiday from pagan times also, candles, lights, even Chanukah. So we learn it's not altogether Christian. So if they think it's a private holiday, they're only ignorant, not patriotic. What belongs to history, belongs to all men. You want to go back to the Middle Ages? Is it better to shave your head with a secondhand razor? Does it hurt Shirley to learn to speak up? It does not. So maybe someday she won't live between the kitchen and the shop. She's not a fool."

I thank you, Papa, for your kindness. It is true about me to this day. I am foolish but I am not a fool.

That night my father kissed me and said with great interest in my career, "Shirley, tomorrow's your big day. Congrats."

"Save it," my mother said. Then she shut all the windows in order to prevent tonsillitis.

In the morning it snowed. On the street corner a tree had been decorated for us by a kind city administration. In order to miss its chilly shadow our neighbors walked three blocks east to buy a loaf of bread. The butcher pulled down black window shades to keep

GLOSSARY

101 **Chanukah:** Hanukkah, the Jewish holiday in December when lit candles are displayed in the window, to commemorate the burning of the oil lamps for eight days.
103 **the Middle Ages:** the period between the 11th and the 13th centuries in Europe when there was great hatred and persecution of Jewish people.
105 **between the kitchen and the shop:** referring to a family business, where the store is in front and the family lives at the back of the building or upstairs.
110 **to prevent tonsillitis:** People used to think that a severe throat infection such as tonsillitis came from a person's breathing "night air."
112 **tree had been decorated:** an evergreen tree had been hung with colored lights as a public Christmas tree.
113 **chilly shadow:** (lit) small dark, cold place shaded from the sun; (fig) a somewhat ominous or threatening spot, suggesting an evil influence.

INFORMAL SPEECH

94 **what's the matter with you?:** (usually said rudely) Why are you acting so stupid? When said quietly, "What's the matter?" can mean, "Where do you feel bad?" or "Has something bad happened?"
94 **Dope!:** You stupid fool!
103 **secondhand:** already used by someone else and therefore worn, perhaps also of poor quality.
104 **speak up:** (lit) speak loudly and distinctly; (fig) express an opinion freely, especially regarding one's rights.
109 **big day:** important, very special day.
109 **congrats:** short for "congratulations," an expression of recognition and praise for someone's achievement.
110 **save it:** never mind, I don't want to hear it.

STANDARD VOCABULARY

94 **roared:** shouted with full force, in a somewhat frightening way.
98 **coldly:** without any friendly feeling.
99 **harm:** danger, damage.
100 **pagan:** heathen, without any conventional religion.
101 **altogether:** entirely.
101 ***private:** restricted to a particular group, exclusive.
102 ***ignorant:** lacking in knowledge.
102 **patriotic:** taking pride in one's own country.
103 **shave:** cut hair off closely, leaving the skin smooth.
105 **fool:** a person without much intelligence or good sense.
106 **foolish:** not very sensible or wise.
108 **career:** one's chosen lifework or profession.
113 **miss:** avoid, be without.

the colored lights from shining on his chickens. Oh, not me. On the way to school, with both hands I tossed it a kiss of tolerance. Poor thing, it was a stranger in Egypt.

I walked straight into the auditorium past the staring children. "Go ahead, Shirley!" said the monitors. Four boys, big for their age, had already started work as propmen and stagehands.

Mr. Hilton was very nervous. He was not even happy. Whatever he started to say ended in a sideward look of sadness. He sat slumped in the middle of the first row and asked me to help Miss Glace. I did this, although she thought my voice too resonant and said, "Show-off!"

Parents began to arrive long before we were ready. They wanted to make a good impression. From among the yards of drapes I peeked out at the audience. I saw my embarrassed mother.

Ira, Lester, and Meyer were pasted to their beards by Miss Glace. She almost forgot to thread the star on its wire, but I reminded her. I coughed a few times to clear my throat. Miss Glace looked around and saw that everyone was in costume and on line waiting to play his part. She whispered, "All right . . . " Then:

Jackie Sauerfeld, the prettiest boy in the first grade, parted the curtains with his skinny elbow and in a high voice sang out:

"Parents dear
We are here
To make a Christmas play in time.
It we give
In narrative
And illustrate with pantomime."

GLOSSARY

116 **stranger in Egypt:** (fig) an allusion to the Christ child, whose parents took him to Egypt when they feared he would be killed.
118 **propmen and stagehands:** helpers who set up the stage for the actors.
125 **yards of drapes:** large curtains hung in front of the stage.
128 **thread the star on its wire:** fasten a thin, metal wire to a star cut out of foil or paper, to be hung high above the stage.

INFORMAL SPEECH

116 **poor thing:** an expression of pity and compassion.
117 **go ahead:** you're expected, so it's okay for you to go in.
123 **show-off:** one who tries to get attention by loud or conspicuous behavior.
124 **make a good impression** (on): win the approval of someone.
125 **peeked:** gave a quick look while trying not to be seen by anyone.
132 **skinny:** thin.
132 **sang out:** spoke loudly, as though singing or chanting.

STANDARD VOCABULARY

116 ***tolerance:** acceptance of something one does not happen to agree with.
117 **staring:** gazing with wide-open eyes.
120 **nervous:** anxious, restless, ill at ease.
121 **slumped:** with shoulders bent over and head down.
122 **resonant:** deep and vibrant, like a man's voice.
125 **audience:** those who are there to listen and to watch a performance.
127 **pasted:** stuck together with a smooth, creamy substance (paste).
129 **costume:** special clothes that actors wear for their part in a play.
137 **narrative:** story form.
138 **illustrate:** make an event or story more interesting by showing pictures.
138 **pantomime:** the acting out of a drama without making any sound.

He disappeared.

My voice burst immediately from the wings to the great shock of Ira, Lester, and Meyer, who were waiting for it but were surprised all the same.

"I remember, I remember, the house where I was born . . . "

Miss Glace yanked the curtain open and there it was, the house—an old hayloft, where Celia Kornbluh lay in the straw with Cindy Lou, her favorite doll. Ira, Lester, and Meyer moved slowly from the wings toward her, sometimes pointing to a moving star and sometimes ahead to Cindy Lou.

It was a long story and it was a sad story. I carefully pronounced all the words about my lonesome childhood, while little Eddie Braunstein wandered upstage and down with his shepherd's stick, looking for sheep. I brought up lonesomeness again, and not being understood at all except by some women everybody hated. Eddie was too small for that and Marty Groff took his place, wearing his father's prayer shawl. I announced twelve friends, and half the boys in the fourth grade gathered round Marty, who stood on an orange crate while my voice harangued. Sorrowful and loud, I declaimed about love and God and Man, but because of the terrible deceit of Abie Stock we came suddenly to a famous moment. Marty, whose remembering tongue I was, waited at the foot of the cross. He stared desperately at the audience. I groaned, "My God, my God why hast thou forsaken me?" The soldiers who were sheiks grabbed poor Marty to pin him up to die, but he wrenched free, turned again to the audience, and spread his arms aloft to show despair and the end. I murmured at the top of my voice, "The rest is silence, but as everyone in this room, in this city—in this world—now know, I shall have life eternal."

GLOSSARY

140 **the wings:** both sides of the stage, out of view of the audience.
143 **hayloft:** place in a barn where hay is piled for the cows. (The Christ child was born in a stable.)
147 **It was a long story . . . :** see p. 65 for explanatory notes.
148 **upstage and down:** back and forth across the stage.
151 **prayer shawl:** special cloth worn by Jewish men when they pray.
153 **orange crate:** wooden box used for shipping oranges.
153 **harangued . . . declaimed:** lectured in a loud, pompous tone, trying to sound like a prophet.
155 **whose remembering tongue I was:** a reference to Shirley's role as the narrator for the play.
156 **"My God . . .":** the last words spoken by Jesus before he died on the cross.
157 **sheiks:** the boys' costumes made them look like Arab chiefs.
160 **life eternal:** everlasting life, meaning that he would never die. This expression is taken from the

INFORMAL SPEECH

141 **all the same:** anyhow.
143 **yanked:** pulled quickly and forcefully.
148 **lonesome:** lonely and forlorn.
157 **grabbed:** seized in a rude, awkward way.
159 **at the top of my voice:** as loudly as I can.

STANDARD VOCABULARY

139 **disappeared:** went out of sight.
140 **burst:** came forth like an explosion.
140 **immediately:** without any delay.
140 ***shock:** disturbance caused by sudden surprise.
144 ***favorite:** one's first choice, preferred above any others.
154 ***deceit:** falsehood, trickery done in order to mislead someone.
156 **desperately:** anxiously, but hopelessly.
158 **wrenched:** forcibly pulled away.
158 **aloft:** on high.

That night Mrs. Kornbluh visited our kitchen for a glass of tea.

"How's the virgin?" asked my father with a look of concern.

"For a man with a daughter, you got a fresh mouth, Abramovitch."

"Here," said my father kindly, "have some lemon, it'll sweeten your disposition."

GLOSSARY

life eternal (*cont.*):
King James Version of the Bible, a translation from the original Hebrew and Greek in 1611. Even though the language sounds rather strange and quaint today, it is the most familiar translation of "the Scriptures," or the Bible, to English-speaking people everywhere.

162 **virgin:** girl or woman who has never had sexual relations with a man (an allusion to the Virgin Mary, who is highly revered among Christians).

INFORMAL SPEECH

163 **a fresh mouth:** an impolite, sassy way of talking.

STANDARD VOCABULARY

162 **concern:** interest and consideration.

164 **disposition:** one's usual mood, attitude, or temperament.

They debated a little in Yiddish, then fell in a puddle of Russian and Polish. What I understood next was my father, who said, "Still and all, it was certainly a beautiful affair, you have to admit, introducing us to the beliefs of a different culture."

"Well, yes," said Mrs. Kornbluh. "The only thing . . . you know Charlie Turner—that cute boy in Celia's class—a couple others? They got very small parts or no part at all. In very bad taste, it seemed to me. After all, it's their religion."

"Ach," explained my mother, "what could Mr. Hilton do? They got very small voices; after all, why should they holler? The English language they know from the beginning by heart. They're blond like angels. You think it's so important they should get in the play? Christmas . . . the whole piece of goods . . . they own it."

I listened and listened until I couldn't listen any more. Too sleepy, I climbed out of bed and kneeled. I made a little church of my hands and said, "Hear, O Israel. . . ." Then I called out in Yiddish, "Please, good night, good night. Ssh." My father said, "Ssh yourself," and slammed the kitchen door.

I was happy. I fell asleep at once. I had prayed for everybody: my talking family, cousins far away, passersby, and all the lonesome Christians. I expected to be heard. My voice was certainly the loudest.

GLOSSARY

165 **Yiddish:** language used by many Eastern European Jews, many of whom settled in New York.
165 **fell in a puddle:** (fig): slipped into a mixture of the two languages.
170 **in very bad taste:** improper, very inappropriate.
173 **blond like angels:** Light or blond hair and fair skin have been popularly associated with goodness.
176 **made a little church:** put her hands together, pointing upward, as Christians do when praying.

INFORMAL SPEECH

166 **still and all:** anyway, after all, anyhow.
169 **cute:** attractive.
172 **holler:** shout or yell loudly.
172 **by heart:** from memory.
174 **the whole piece of goods:** everything about it.
175 **sleepy:** drowsy, finding it very hard to stay awake.
177 **Ssh:** a hissing sound meaning "Be quiet."
178 **slammed:** gave the door a hard push so it would close with a loud noise. (This is sometimes done to emphasize a point.)

STANDARD VOCABULARY

165 **debated:** argued.
166 **affair:** occasion, event.
167 ***admit:** concede or allow some truth in the opposite viewpoint.
180 **passersby:** people who happened to be walking along the street.

1. STUDY QUESTIONS

DISCOVERING THE STORY THROUGH OBSERVATION AND INFERENCE

1. ***Observation:*** The setting for this story is a New York City neighborhood. Point out all the places in the beginning of the story where either *noise* or *quietness* is mentioned or suggested.
   Inference: What is meant by "the happy chorus of my inside self"? Can you explain lines 15 and 16, p. 66?
2. ***Observation:*** How many details show that Shirley is a child who tries to obey the rules and please the authorities?
   Inference: Do any of these details help to explain her immediate willingness to "swear to work harder" than ever before? What other reason(s) might be involved?
3. ***Observation:*** What preparations does the school make for Christmas? Which details suggest a mood of joy—"the Christmas spirit"?
   Inference: What is meant by the ironic statement: "They weren't ashamed and we weren't embarrassed"?
4. ***Observation:*** Shirley's mother takes this Christmas affair very seriously. What are some of the things about it that bother her?
   Inference: Why does Shirley's father make such wildly exaggerated remarks in response to her mother? Where can you find some comic elements in their conversation?
5. ***Observation:*** The writer is mostly "poking fun" at the Christians and their one-sided view of their favorite holiday, Christmas. However, some of the humor comes from the inconsistencies in the Jewish community also. How many of them can you find so far?
   Inference: What is Shirley getting out of all this?
6. ***Observation:*** In the father's speech on p. 70, he makes a more reasoned defense of Shirley's part in the Christmas play. In your own words explain the points he makes about history.
   Inference: The last three lines of this argument are more practical, but they are difficult to understand. What do you think he means?
7. ***Observation:*** What different attitudes and viewpoints (p. 70–71) are shown by: The decorated tree? The actions of the neighbors and the butcher? Shirley's kiss of tolerance?
   Inference: Why is Shirley's mother "embarrassed" at the play? Considering her disapproval of the whole occasion, why do you think she came to see the play?
8. ***Observation:*** In a play, the actors try to make it seem more real by using items or articles called "properties," or "stage props." What stage props are used by the children in the Christmas play, and what does each one represent?
   Inference: The long paragraph beginning, "It was a long story . . ." deals with matters that many people take very seriously. How does the author manage to avoid offending such people, yet still convey gentle humor in that paragraph?

9. ***Observation:*** What part did Mrs. Kornbluh's little girl have in the play?
Inference: Do you think that Mr. Abramovitch really means what he says to Mrs. Kornbluh? Explain your answer.
10. ***Observation:*** What were those improprieties (improper actions) that Mrs. Kornbluh considers to be "in bad taste"?
Inference: Why do you think these things bother her? Why don't they bother Mrs. Abramovitch?
11. ***Observation:*** Paraphrase the answer that Shirley's mother makes in response to Mrs. Kornbluh's comments.
Inference: How has Mrs. Abramovitch's attitude changed from what it was earlier?
12. ***Observation:*** The belief that it would be good for the major religions to unite with each other is called *ecumenism.* What *ecumenical* aspects do you see in Shirley's prayer? How does she feel at this point?
Inference: In what way or ways has this whole experience changed her life?

2. READING: RECOGNIZING ARTISTIC STRUCTURE

TRY YOUR HAND AT LITERARY ANALYSIS

The more carefully you scrutinize a well-written story, the more interesting it becomes. *Analysis* simply means taking a close-up look at each part separately, then seeing how they all fit together.

Literary terminology gives you some convenient "handles," or terms, to use when you are exploring the meaning and the make-up of a story such as this one of Grace Paley's. Refer freely to the list of Literary Terms and their definitions as you examine each component. Then discuss or write down what you have found.

1. Look at the setting and its relation to the story:
   a. The physical environment.
   b. The neighborhood and its people.
   c. The larger community.
2. Observe the three characters central to the story:
   a. Their full names, including variations or nicknames. (Leave a line after each one of their names.)
   b. Beside each character, a brief description in your own words (three or four adjectives or phrases).
   c. "Flat" or "round" characteristics of each of those three.
3. Explain the point of view from which the story is told:
   a. The narrator as a bystander or as participant.
   b. The narrator's role here as compared with the narrator in stories read earlier.
   c. Significance and effect of having a child as narrator.

4. Identify the main elements of the plot:
   a. The protagonist and the antagonist.
   b. What the protagonist wants and is trying to do.
   c. The climax: when and how the protagonist's struggle is "resolved."
5. Trace the development of the plot by showing the probable effects of the following episodes on both the protagonist and the antagonist:
   a. The selection of Shirley as narrator for the Christmas play.
   b. The first talk between Shirley's parents.
   c. Disagreement among the neighbors over the play.
   d. The father's second argument (with her mother).
   e. Mrs. Abramovitch's attendance at the performance of the play.
   f. Mrs. Kornbluh's worries over the "improprieties" (see Study Questions, item 10).
6. Determine the theme, or themes, of the story by searching out some of the underlying meanings:

Theme A

a. Take note of the clues provided by the title and the last sentence.
b. Find and make a list of all the words that describe or refer to Shirley's voice, and comment on what you notice about them.
c. Try to express this theme in one sentence.

Theme B

d. Although the subject is treated both humorously and kindly, there is a basic conflict between the Christian and the Jewish communities. Explain what that conflict is all about.
e. In ancient times, the Hebrew prophet Isaiah spoke of a future day when even traditional enemies of the animal world will live together in peace, "and a little child shall lead them" (Isaiah 11:6). Think about this and see if such an idealistic prophecy can be applied to the story you have just read.
f. Compromise or confrontation? (Look up the meanings of those two words.) In this story, the school authorities are all in agreement: They see Christmas as a universal holiday that *everyone* should want to celebrate.

   The Jewish community, on the other hand, is divided. Some of the parents are more pragmatic, or practical; they think it is best to *cooperate* with the teachers. Why?

   Other Jewish parents believe that their fundamental religious beliefs are being disregarded by the school authorities. They may even question whether their religious liberty is being threatened. Which side would you agree with?

   Can you state the problem as *another* underlying theme?
g. In what way or ways does Mr. Abramovitch's humor help the Jewish community through this crisis? Try stating this idea as a theme by completing the following statement:
   Sometimes humor can be used to *defuse* a conflict because it ____________
   ____ .

3. LANGUAGE USAGE: PRESENT AND PAST PARTICIPLES

CHOOSE THE VERB FORM THAT SAYS WHAT YOU MEAN

Participles are very useful verb forms, since they may serve either as adjectives or as main verbs, together with some form of the helping verbs, *be* or *have.*

For regular verbs, the present participle ends in –ing, while the past participle ends with –ed. *They are not interchangeable,* so be careful which one you use. While the main part of the word *looks* the same, the endings can change the meaning completely.

Each of the verbs in the following exercise came from the vocabulary for the first four stories. The verb is to be used twice in each sentence, as a *present* participle and as a *past* participle. Fill in the blanks with the correct verb forms. Be sure you are also spelling each word correctly.

1. disgust
   When Michel saw the way his apartment looked after the party, he was ____________. "I'm going to clean up this ____________ mess right now!" he said.
2. amaze
   I was ____________ when I saw the Grand Canyon. It was the most ____________ sight I had ever seen.
3. insult
   Helen said that she had resigned from her job because her boss was ____________; moreover, she was ____________ by the low salary.
4. rob
   The bank that they were ____________ has been ____________ many times before.
5. count on
   Although Andrea knew she was ____________ on to give her report in class, she was ____________ on the other members of the group to do most of the work.
6. conceal
   I saw that he was ____________ drugs, so I reported that drugs were ____________ in his car.
7. adopt
   ____________ parents love their ____________ children as much as parents love their biological children.
8. ignore
   Since my brother felt he was ____________ by his classmates, he was ____________ them also.

9. complain
   Although ______________ about by more and more students, the food did not improve. Instead, the cook simply grumbled about "those ______________ kids."
10. tolerate
    Reyad was ______________ the weekend parties that went on upstairs, but he felt that the constant practicing of the band in the next room could not be ______________.
11. embarrass
    John and Amy were ______________ when their two-year-old son snatched the wig off the head of the man sitting in front of them. In fact, it was an ______________ moment for them all.
12. deceive
    When Boonsong first arrived, he was easily ______________ by friendly strangers, until he learned that looks could be ______________.
13. admire
    A greatly ______________ pianist in his younger days, Rubenstein still played for ______________ audiences when he was in his eighties.
14. satisfy
    "We had a really ______________ meal at the Union Oyster House," said Fawaz as he loosened his belt. "I feel very ______________."

For Additional Practice

Make up your own sentences to illustrate correct use of the present and past participles for the following verbs:

bore	amuse	drive
excite	break	nauseate
interest	horrify	rise
depress	tire	cheer
shock	thrill	irritate

4. GRAMMAR REVIEW: DEFINITE AND INDEFINITE ARTICLES

LISTEN TO WHAT YOU WRITE

Native speakers learn to use "a," "an," and "the" naturally, simply by hearing them spoken by other people. There are rules regarding definite and indefinite articles, and it may help you to refer to them or to review them from time to time.

Another way to learn about their correct usage is to train your ear to identify them by sound. *Listen to Americans.* Notice when and how they use "a" or "the," and also when they *omit* them. Make a practice of reading your own work aloud so that you can "hear" your mistakes and correct them.

Filling in the blanks in the passage below will give you an opportunity to try this approach. You don't have to shout it, like Shirley reading her script. But try murmuring each sentence to yourself, listening to catch the *right sound* for the sentence as you write in articles where they are needed. (Mark X if there should be *no* article.)

__________ story we have just read, "__________ Loudest Voice," is __________ example of humor that results from seeing __________ absurdities and __________ inconsistencies in __________ human nature. Mr. Hilton is __________ educated and intelligent man, __________ schoolteacher who clearly is dedicated to __________ task of educating all __________ children. He would not consider himself to be __________ prejudiced man; yet he is totally unaware of __________ fact that he is disregarding __________ religious traditions of __________ substantial section of __________ community in order to enthusiastically promote his own.

On __________ other hand, __________ Jewish parents also behave in __________ inconsistent manner, for they cannot agree among themselves whether to support __________ Christmas program or not. __________ few of __________ parents are proud that their children have __________ part in __________ play, but Shirley's mother expresses __________ worries of some of __________ parents that their children are being taught "__________ lot of __________ lies."

Of all __________ adults, only Mr. Abramovitch, who happens to have __________ sense of humor, is able to recognize all __________ issues involved and to have __________ clear appreciation of what they mean. He is __________ only one who sees __________ comic aspects of __________ situation and understands that it really represents __________ conflict between __________ cultures and __________ traditions rather than __________ violation of __________ Jewish religious values.

But while he sees __________ absurdity in __________ whole affair, Mr. Abramovitch is __________ person who can sympathize with Shirley's longing to play __________ leading role in __________ show. As __________ proud father, he seems to "get ____________ kick out of" ____________ fact that ____________ teacher considers his little girl to be ____________ most reliable of all ____________ children in ____________ school.

And finally, like Shirley herself, he is both relieved and happy to discover, for ____________ first time, that having ____________ loudest voice can be ____________ asset as well as ____________ liability.

After you have completed this exercise, discuss your results with others in the class. Remember that the use of definite and indefinite articles is largely determined by the meaning, which occasionally is subject to slightly different interpretations. Your teacher is the best one to help you to determine what is typical American usage.

5. COMPOSITION: WRITING A THESIS (*Group Project*)

COMPOSE YOUR OWN THESIS: PRELIMINARY DISCUSSION

Some people find it relatively simple to write a topic sentence and to develop it into a paragraph, but when asked to state their thesis for a composition or a longer paper, they get worried and back off. If you can write a good topic sentence, you can compose a good thesis. (Remember that the *thesis* is the statement of your main idea. For a quick review, look again at the model composition exercise in Chapter II, Activity 5.) Not only does a well-stated thesis help you to focus your ideas so that you know what you want to say, but it suggests the direction you can take and your organization plan.

What the topic sentence does for a paragraph the thesis statement should do for the whole essay: It mentions the subject you are discussing, and it makes a definite and specific statement or assertion about it. Another way of putting it is to say that the thesis states a *premise,* or a point of view that you believe and can logically defend.

Since you will need to have a firm basis for your thesis (at least three strong points), look for an angle or an aspect of the subject that you can support with some *observations* (facts) and some *inferences* (further information that can reasonably be assumed to be true).

Which of these statements could you defend, as a thesis?

1. I am going to write about my country.
2. Anyone who really wants to can become an opera singer.

3. A student should never be late to class, if he or she wants to get a good grade.
4. A large part of my education in the United States has been taking place outside the classroom.

From the examples above, can you say what are some of the things that *don't* work in a thesis and some of the things that *do?*

One method of composing a thesis that often does work is to ask questions about your subject. Sometimes you have to keep on asking them until you happen to hit on a good idea that can be stated as a thesis, one you feel you can develop and support. The important thing is to ask yourself "seed questions"—questions that lead on to other questions, until you have new ideas "sprouting" (literally, shooting up out of the earth) that you had not thought of before. Another word for this is "brainstorming," a process that works best when done in a small group.

FROM QUESTION TO THESIS: A PROJECT FOR SMALL GROUPS

The seed questions below are concerned with the four stories you have read so far, and they are designed to start your thoughts sprouting. Some of the ideas that come out of discussion are the kinds that can be developed as short compositions. These are the ones that can best be formed into thesis statements.

Seed Questions

1. All the four stories are told by narrators, but why do you feel that you know *two* of the narrators so much better than the *other* two?
2. At first glance, the main character in "On the Outside" and the main character in "I Want to Work" seem altogether different. But is that really so?
3. How do you feel about the characters who have no names? What is the effect, if any, of not giving a name to a character?
4. Do the titles tell you what the story is about? What do they do?
5. What can be learned about each story from its first sentence? What do you think the first sentence of a story should do?
6. What do you notice about the *last* sentence of each story?
7. Do any of the characters seem to change before the story ends? How?

Directions

1. ***Brainstorming:*** Spend the first ten minutes just *talking* about your group's question and letting the discussion stimulate everyone's train of thought.
2. ***Note-taking:*** This is the time when someone can begin to write the group's "first draft" of a thesis. The chalkboard is an ideal place to work, because everyone can see what is being written and suggest ways to improve it.

3. ***Revising:*** Now you can read your thesis over together, consider whether it can be supported well, and revise the wording as may be needed. If your group has thought of more than one thesis, work on one at a time.
4. ***Planning:*** Once you have a clearly stated thesis, suggest as a group three or four points that can be used to support it. You may want to cite (refer or allude to) specific passages in the text to back it up.
5. ***Sharing:*** If time permits, share the results of your project with the rest of the class. It will help them to see just how your group used the questioning technique to come up with a thesis and a plan for its development.

Composition

In accordance with your teacher's directions, develop the thesis of your group, or a different one, into a composition.

Angelica Gibbs

Angelica Gibbs is a black author who has written short fiction for The New Yorker *magazine, as well as for other publications. Although intensive searching has not uncovered even the basic facts of her life, most of her published writing apparently was done during the 1930s and 40s.*

One of Angelica Gibbs's stories has appeared in a collection entitled About Women *(H. Reed, editor), and she also has contributed to a volume with the engaging title* A Primer for White Folks *(1945), edited by Bucklin Moon.*

"The Test," originally published in The New Yorker *in 1940, represents a noteworthy example of black literature through its sensitive portrayal of both blatant and subtle forms of the racial prejudice and put-downs so long experienced by black Americans.*

VI

The Test

Story Setting: *A typical suburban town somewhere along the East Coast, probably in one of the Middle Atlantic states such as Maryland or Delaware. The time is around the early 1930s.*

In the Story: *A young black woman, working as a mother's helper for a white woman, encounters white male prejudice when she goes to take her driving test.*

On the afternoon Marian took her second driver's test, Mrs. Ericson went with her. "It's probably better to have someone a little older with you," Mrs. Ericson said as Marian slipped into the driver's seat beside her. "Perhaps the last time your Cousin Bill made you nervous, talking too much on the way."

"Yes, Ma'am," Marian said in her soft unaccented voice. "They probably do like it better if a white person shows up with you."

GLOSSARY

5 **Yes, Ma'am:** a polite form of address toward women, used mostly in the South, where it was always expected from black people and children.
5 **unaccented voice:** with no noticeable accent or dialect.

INFORMAL SPEECH

6 **shows up:** appears, comes along.

STANDARD VOCABULARY

4 **nervous:** anxious, on edge.

"Oh, I don't think it's *that,*" Mrs. Ericson began, and subsided after a glance at the girl's set profile. Marian drove the car slowly through the shady suburban streets. It was one of the first hot days in June, and when they reached the boulevard they found it crowded with cars headed for the beaches.

"Do you want me to drive?" Mrs. Ericson asked. "I'll be glad to if you're feeling jumpy." Marian shook her head. Mrs. Ericson watched her dark, competent hands and wondered for the thousandth time how the house had ever managed to get along without her, or how she had lived through those earlier years when her household had been presided over by a series of slatternly white girls who had considered housework demeaning and the care of children an added insult. "You drive beautifully, Marian," she said. "Now, don't think of the last time. Anybody would slide on a steep hill on a wet day like that."

"It takes four mistakes to flunk you," Marian said. "I don't remember doing all the things the inspector marked down on my blank."

"People say that they only want you to slip them a little something," Mrs. Ericson said doubtfully.

"No," Marian said. "That would only make it worse, Mrs. Ericson, I know."

The car turned right, at a traffic signal, into a side road and slid up to the curb at the rear of a short line of parked cars. The inspectors had not arrived yet.

"You have the papers?" Mrs. Ericson asked. Marian took them out of her bag: her learner's permit, the car registration, and her birth certificate. They settled down to the dreary business of waiting.

"It will be marvelous to have someone dependable to drive the children to school every day," Mrs. Ericson said.

Marian looked up from the list of driving requirements she had been studying. "It'll make things simpler at the house, won't it?" she said.

GLOSSARY

8 **set profile:** a stiff and unmoving facial outline.
9 **boulevard:** a main highway.
15 **slatternly:** careless, sloppy, slovenly, messy.
20 **inspector:** a police officer in charge of testing new drivers for their licenses.
20 **blank:** an application form.
24 **curb:** the concrete border or edge of the street, where the sidewalk begins.
27 **learner's permit:** paper stating that one is learning to drive and does not yet have a license.
27 **car registration:** official papers of ownership that must always be in a car.
27 **birth certificate:** a paper used to prove one's place and date of birth.

INFORMAL SPEECH

10 **headed for:** going in the direction of.
11 **I'll be glad to:** I am very willing to, I don't mind at all.
12 **jumpy:** nervous, jittery, edgy.
13 **for the thousandth time:** (exag) many times.
19 **flunk:** fail to pass a test or a course.
21 **slip . . . something:** given them some money as a small bribe ("grease their palms").
29 **marvelous:** really wonderful (great, super, terrific, fantastic); lit, miraculously wonderful.
32 **at the house:** at home, in the place where you (or we) live.

STANDARD VOCABULARY

7 **subsided:** became quiet.
8 **shady:** with leafy trees overhead.
8 **suburban:** a residential area bordering a city.
12 **competent:** efficient.
14 **been presided over:** been run by, been in charge of.
15 **series:** one after another, several in a row.
15 **demeaning:** humiliating to one's self-image.
16 **insult:** a gross indignity inflicted by another person through words or action; "a nasty crack."
22 ***doubtfully:** with some uncertainty.
24 **at the rear:** at the back, behind.
28 **dreary:** tiresome, depressing.
29 ***dependable:** safe and reliable.

"Oh, Marian," Mrs. Ericson exclaimed, "if I only could pay you half of what you're worth!"

"Now, Mrs. Ericson," Marian said firmly. They looked at each other and smiled with affection.

Two cars with official insignia on their doors stopped across the street. The inspectors leaped out, very brisk and military in their neat uniforms. Marian's hands tightened on the wheel. "There's the one who flunked me last time," she whispered, pointing to a stocky, self-important man who had begun to shout directions at the driver at the head of the line. "Oh, Mrs. Ericson."

"Now, Marian," Mrs. Ericson said. They smiled at each other again, rather weakly.

The inspector who finally reached their car was not the stocky one but a genial, middle-aged man who grinned broadly as he thumbed over their papers. Mrs. Ericson started to get out of the car. "Don't you want to come along?" the inspector asked. "Mandy and I don't mind the company."

Mrs. Ericson was bewildered for a moment. "No," she said, and stepped to the curb. "I might make Marian self-conscious. She's a fine driver, Inspector."

"Sure thing," the inspector said, winking at Mrs. Ericson. He slid into the seat beside Marian. "Turn right at the corner, Mandy-Lou."

From the curb, Mrs. Ericson watched the car move smoothly up the street.

The inspector made notations in a small black book. "Age?" he inquired presently, as they drove along.

"Twenty-seven."

GLOSSARY

33 **half . . . worth:** at least half of your great value. (Domestic help, especially black women, received very low wages until very recently.)
35 **Now, Mrs. Ericson:** a way of protesting politely: "Don't say any more; I understand."
37 **insignia:** special sign or mark (an emblem) representing an organization.
38 **uniforms:** official clothes worn in the line of duty.
42 **rather weakly:** in a way that showed neither one felt very confident.
49 **winking at:** shutting one eye in a gesture that is supposed to mean "You and I understand each other."
50 **Mandy** (and **Mandy-Lou):** a name associated with the stereotype of a black woman long ago in slave times, especially in the deep South.

INFORMAL SPEECH

44 **grinned broadly:** gave a wide smile, from amusement, not from friendliness (in this usage).
44 **thumbed over:** quickly leafed through.
49 **sure thing:** an emphatic "yes," "right!," or "of course!"

STANDARD VOCABULARY

35 **firmly:** definitely.
36 **affection:** warm feeling toward each other.
38 **brisk:** quick and business-like.
38 **military:** associated with the armed services.
38 **neat:** orderly.
39 **stocky:** short and heavy.
40 **self-important:** proud, pompous.
43 **genial:** kindly in appearance.
47 ***bewildered:** confused and puzzled.
48 **self-conscious:** nervous or anxious that one might do something wrong.
52 **notations:** notes.
52 **presently:** in a short time, soon.

He looked at Marian out of the corner of his eye. "Old enough to have quite a flock of pickaninnies, eh?"

Marian did not answer.

"Left at this corner," the inspector said, "and park between that truck and the green Buick."

The two cars were very close together, but Marian squeezed in between them without too much maneuvering. "Driven before, Mandy-Lou?" the inspector asked.

"Yes, sir. I had a license for three years in Pennsylvania."

"Why do you want to drive a car?"

"My employer needs me to take her children to and from school."

"Sure you don't really want to sneak out nights to meet some young blood?" the inspector asked. He laughed as Marian shook her head.

"Let's see you take a left at the corner and then turn around in the middle of the next block," the inspector said. He began to whistle "Swanee River." "Make you homesick?" he asked.

Marian put out her hand, swung around neatly in the street, and headed back in the direction from which they had come. "No," she said. "I was born in Scranton, Pennsylvania."

The inspector feigned astonishment. "You-all ain't Southern?" he said. "Well, dog my cats if I didn't think you-all came from down yondah."

"No, sir," Marian said.

"Turn onto Main Street and let's see how you-all does in heavier traffic."

They followed a line of cars along Main Street for several blocks until they came in sight of a concrete bridge which arched high over the railroad tracks.

GLOSSARY

55 **flock of:** a large group, used for domestic animals, such as chickens or sheep.
56 **pickaninnies:** (Southern dial) informal term for black children, first used during slave times; not in current use.
65 **some young blood:** (OD) a young man looking for a good time with any girl he can pick up.
68 **Swanee River:** an old, once-popular song of the South expressing a longing for "the old plantation."
73 **dog my cats:** a meaningless phrase that's supposed to express great surprise or amazement.
74 **you-all . . . down yondah:** a fake attempt to sound like a black speaker from the deep South.
76 **how you-all does:** an attempt to imitate Black English as spoken in the South.
78 **concrete bridge . . . tracks:** a high overpass made of steel and concrete.

INFORMAL SPEECH

55 **out of the corner of his eye:** a sidelong look, suggesting watchfulness or suspicion of some sort of wrongdoing.
60 **squeezed in:** managed to get into a small place.
65 **sneak out nights:** slip away from the house secretly at night.
66 **shook her head:** indicated "no" without speaking.
67 **let's see you:** an informal way of saying "I'd like to see you. . . ." do a certain thing.

STANDARD VOCABULARY

58 **park:** bring a car to a stop and then wait, usually by backing up into a space between two other cars.
61 **maneuvering:** moving back and forth, using much physical energy.
64 ***employer:** a formal term for the person one works for (the "boss").
68 **homesick:** missing home, wanting to go home (feeling nostalgic).
73 **feigned:** put on an act, faked.
73 ***astonishment:** great surprise.

"Read that sign at the end of the bridge," the inspector said.

" 'Proceed with caution. Dangerous in slippery weather,' " Marian said.

"You-all sho can read fine," the inspector exclaimed. "Where d'you learn to do that, Mandy?"

"I got my college degree last year," Marian said. Her voice was not quite steady.

As the car crept up the slope of the bridge the inspector burst out laughing. He laughed so hard he could scarcely give his next direction. "Stop here," he said, wiping his eyes, "then start 'er up again. Mandy got her degree, did she? Dog my cats!"

GLOSSARY

80 **slippery weather:** rain or ice making roads slippery.
84 **burst out laughing:** suddenly gave an explosive laugh.

INFORMAL SPEECH

STANDARD VOCABULARY

80 ***proceed:** move ahead.
80 ***caution:** care for one's safety.
80 ***dangerous:** unsafe.
83 ***steady:** firm and calm.
84 **crept:** moved very slowly.
84 **slope:** an incline, ramp.
85 **scarcely:** hardly, with the greatest difficulty.

Marian pulled up beside the curb. She put the car in neutral, pulled on the emergency, waited a moment, and then put the car into gear again. Her face was set. As she released the brake her foot slipped off the clutch pedal and the engine stalled.

"Now, Mistress Mandy," the inspector said, "remember your degree."

"*Damn you*!" Marian cried. She started the car with a jerk.

The inspector lost his joviality in an instant. "Return to the starting place, please," he said, and made four very black crosses at random in the squares on Marian's application blank.

Mrs. Ericson was waiting at the curb where they had left her. As Marian stopped the car, the inspector jumped out and brushed past her, his face purple. "What happened?" Mrs. Ericson asked, looking after him with alarm.

Marian stared down at the wheel and her lip trembled.

"Oh, Marian, *again*?" Mrs. Ericson said.

Marian nodded. "In a sort of different way," she said, and slid over to the right-hand side of the car.

GLOSSARY

87 **in neutral:** when the gears are disengaged and the car stands still.
89 **clutch pedal:** the pedal used when shifting gears.
89 **engine stalled:** motor stopped ("went dead").
90 **Mistress Mandy:** mock formality ("Mistress" is OD as a form of address).
90 **your degree:** your college degree; in other words, your college education.
96 **his face purple:** his face flushed with emotion.
98 **her lip trembled:** her mouth was unsteady.

INFORMAL SPEECH

87 **pulled up:** brought the car close to the curb.
91 **Damn you!:** (sw) a mild oath, but still a form of swearing.
96 **brushed past:** hurried by close enough to graze her clothes in passing.

STANDARD VOCABULARY

87 **emergency (brake):** the hand brake. (An *emergency*, literally, is an occasion of crisis.)
91 **jerk:** a sharp motion.
92 **joviality:** jolly, cheerful manner.
93 **at random:** here and there, no particular place.
97 **alarm:** fear of danger.
98 **stared:** fixed her eyes straight ahead.

1. STUDY QUESTIONS

DISCOVERING THE STORY THROUGH OBSERVATION AND INFERENCE

1. ***Observation:*** Where are Marian and Mrs. Ericson going, as the story begins? What do we already know has happened before?
   Inference: Does Marian's "Yes, Ma'am" mean that she agrees with Mrs. Ericson? What *does* it mean? What do you think Mrs. Ericson means by her answer?
2. ***Observation:*** What has been Mrs. Ericson's experience with the girls who have worked for her in the past? What sort of work was involved?
   Inference: In contrast to them, what sort of worker has Marian been? (Suggest examples of the sort of differences that Mrs. Ericson apparently means.)
3. ***Observation:*** Explain the mistake that made Marian fail her first test. What opinion does Mrs. Ericson have of her driving?
   Inference: What do you think Marian is implying when she says that she doesn't remember "doing all the things the inspector marked down" on her application blank? How well do you think Mrs. Ericson really "hears" what Marian is trying to tell her?
4. ***Observation:*** A psychologist, Eric Berne, claims that in our relationships to people we often seem to be acting out the roles of child-to-parent or parent-to-child instead of behaving as equals. Looking back over all of Mrs. Ericson's remarks so far, do you see any signs of her playing such a role with Marian?
   Inference: To what extent do you think that Marian's view of their "roles" corresponds to (agrees with) Mrs. Ericson's?
5. ***Observation:*** How would you describe the sort of feelings that Marian and Mrs. Ericson have toward each other? On what points, if any, do they disagree?
   Inference: Considering Mrs. Ericson's earlier remarks to Marian, what do you think of her reason for wanting Marian to get her driver's license?
6. ***Observation:*** Does Marian get the same inspector who gave her the first test? What sort of inspector does this man seem to be?
   Inference: Why is Mrs. Ericson bewildered at the inspector's comment? What might she be thinking as she stands there on the curb?
7. ***Observation:*** How many times in the story does the inspector call Marian by the wrong name? (Point out each place in the story.)
   Inference: Why doesn't Marian correct him? Why didn't Mrs. Ericson correct him either?
8. ***Observation:*** What are the first two driver's tasks the inspector asks Marian to perform? What driving knowledge does she display in doing them?
   Inference: In your own words, explain what the inspector is saying to Marian in his remarks about pickaninnies and "some young blood." What is he insinuating (implying in a negative way) about her in making these suggestions?

9. ***Observation:*** In what ways does the inspector try to link Marian to the South?
   Inference: To what extent do you think his remarks represent his own attitude or opinion? Could there be any other reasons for him to talk this way to her?
10. ***Observation:*** Marian performs well in her first two driving tasks. What are the last two ways in which the inspector wants her to demonstrate her skill?
   Inference: During slavery times in the United States (ending in 1863), many black people were not taught to read or write. In the light of this fact, how do you interpret the inspector's comments about Marian's ability to read and about her college degree? Do you think that he himself is a college graduate?
11. ***Observation:*** It is following this remark that the story says that "the inspector burst out laughing." At what points in the story has he smiled (or grinned) and laughed?
   Inference: What are some of the reasons why people laugh? Which ones do you think apply to the inspector in this story?
12. ***Observation:*** What do the "four very black crosses at random" represent? What else tells you how the inspector is feeling?
   Inference: Can you explain what Marian means by her last remark? What do you think is Mrs. Ericson's final view of the situation?

2. VOCABULARY STUDY

CONNOTATION IS IMPORTANT, TOO!

In English, as in your own language, many of the words simply *stand for* or represent something, but other words suggest implications or emotional associations. Consider these three sentences about Jim's new suit:

1. His father said it was *inexpensive.*
2. His mother said it was *a bargain.*
3. His girlfriend said it was *cheap.*

Each statement tells you that Jim did not pay much for his suit. The first one is "denotative," because it just gives us the information without any hint of how his father feels. The other two are "connotative," because each one implies something *favorable or unfavorable* about the suit *from the point of view of the speaker.* Is Jim's girlfriend pleased with his new suit? How does his mother feel about his purchase?

Some words are nearly always denotative: many nouns, such as "banana," "automobile," or "building"; verbs like "swim," "travel," or "think"; and certain adjectives such as "social," "molecular," or "silent." You can expect the *nomenclature,* or the special terminology, that is used in any area of knowledge to be denotative: "telescopic lens" (in photography); "pathology" (in medicine); "marketing" (in business); "voltmeter" (in electronics); or "psychoneurosis" (in psychology). It is usually the *denotation* of a word that you are searching for when you look up its meaning in the dictionary.

But you have probably noticed that many of the words you read or hear spoken carry a definite atmosphere or emotional tone. Some words have a clearly *positive,* or *favorable,* connotation: "sunny," "brotherhood," "comforting," "energetic," or "satin." Other words, such as "greedy," "weakness," "sneer," "harsh," or "rotten," carry with them a very unpleasant atmosphere. They are said to have *negative,* or *unfavorable,* connotations.

The most confusing words of all, even for those who are very familiar with the language, are the ones that are sometimes favorable and sometimes unfavorable, according to the way they are used in a particular context: Omer likes *strong* coffee, but he dislikes *strong* language; Americans admire *old* cars, but not *old* women; Mr. Methuselah *manages* his business, while Mrs. Methuselah *manages* her husband. Although you may not immediately recognize all the shades of meaning in the words you read, by increasing your awareness of those delicate variations you can strengthen your language skills.

This exercise will give you an opportunity to see if you can differentiate between connotative and denotative meanings in the context of short passages from the story you have just read. In addition, for the words that seem to you to be connotative, you can try to identify whether they are favorable or unfavorable (positive or negative), as used in that particular context.

Directions

Each of the short passages comes from "The Test," and many of the words can be found among the Vocabulary Aids.

Use an X to indicate whether you would classify the word, as used in that context, as denotative (*Denot.*), connotation favorable (*Connot. favor.*), or connotation unfavorable (*Connot. unfavor.*). The first three are already marked for you: A *soft* voice is attractive in a woman (less so in a man); *beaches* are simply the sandy shores beside the sea; and to feel *jumpy* means to be somewhat nervous and lacking in poise or self-control. (Would you like to be thought of as "jumpy"?)

You will not necessarily be looking for the "right" answers here. The value of this exercise is in your thinking about the way the words are used and discussing them in class together. Since some of the words can be classified in more than one way, there may be some disagreement as to how to interpret them. But you may be surprised at how quickly you can recognize a connotative meaning, identify whether it is positive or negative, and even defend your own point of view.

	PAGE	LINE	DENOT.	CONNOT. FAVOR.	CONNOT. UNFAVOR.
1. *soft,* unaccented voice	85	5		x	
2. headed for the *beaches*	86	10	x		
3. feeling *jumpy*	86	11			x
4. dark, *competent* hands	86	12			
5. *slatternly* white girls	86	15			
6. considered housework *demeaning*	86	15			
7. you drive *beautifully*	86	16			
8. a *steep* hill	86	17			
9. to *flunk* you	86	19			
10. line of *parked* cars	86	25			
11. it will be *marvelous*	86	29			
12. to have someone *dependable*	86	29			
13. it'll make things *simpler*	86	32			
14. smiled with *affection*	87	35			
15. very *brisk* and military	87	38			
16. Marian's hands *tightened*	87	38			
17. *smiled* at each other	87	42			
18. genial, *middle-aged* man	87	43			
19. make Marian *self-conscious*	87	48			
20. watched the car move *smoothly*	87	51			
21. a flock of *pickaninnies*	88	55			
22. to *sneak out* nights	88	65			
23. *middle* of the next block	88	67			
24. swung around *neatly*	88	70			
25. feigned *astonishment*	88	73			

	PAGE	LINE	DENOT.	CONNOT. FAVOR.	CONNOT. UNFAVOR.
26. *slippery* weather	89	80			
27. her face was *set*	90	88			
28. the engine *stalled*	90	89			
29. with a *jerk*	90	91			
30. lost his *joviality*	90	92			
31. four *very black* crosses	90	93			
32. *brushed* past her	90	96			
33. his face *purple*	90	96			
34. *stared* down at the wheel	90	98			
35. her lip *trembled*	90	98			

If you would like some additional practice, you might want to select one of the stories you have already studied and bring in a list of words for your classmates to identify as denotative or connotative.

3. DISCUSSION

THINKING ABOUT WORDS AND IDEAS

A. The word "discrimination" is often used in connection with legal action taken by minority groups. There is a slight difference between the words "discrimination" and "prejudice." Use your dictionary to answer the following questions:

1. What does it mean to "discriminate against?"
2. What does it mean to "discriminate between?"
3. Which expression has a more favorable connotation? Why?
4. What is the basic root meaning of "prejudice?"
5. Give an example of one form of prejudice that you have seen or experienced.
6. Try using each of the following expressions in a sentence:
   prejudiced against
   no discrimination
   discriminate between

B. As a clue to the historical and cultural background to this story (see Study Question 10), look up in an unabridged dictionary (one of the large ones you can find in the library) the term, "grandfather clause." You might also find this phrase in the index of an American history book. Explain what it means, and show how it fits in with the inspector's attitude in "The Test."

C. Americans care very much about what kind of image they project (send out) to others. What do they mean by the word *image?* Look closely at the dialogue between the inspector and Marian, and try reading some of it aloud. Can you explain what kind of image each one is trying to project to the other? How well do they succeed?

D. The title of "The Test" suggests a theme that goes beyond the obvious aspect of the driving test itself. The episode "tested" all three of the characters in a way that had nothing to do with driving a car. How did the whole experience test the moral fiber (the basic character structure) of the inspector, of Mrs. Ericson, and of Marian herself?

E. You may be familiar with an American newspaper, such as *The New York Times, The Washington Post,* and *The Boston Globe,* as well as one of the news magazines like *Newsweek* and *Time.* Check carefully through a current issue of one of these, and find an article that deals with the problem of racial prejudice or discrimination. Cut out the article or photocopy it to bring to class. Be ready to give a brief oral report on your article by:

- Summarizing its content for the class;
- Relating it to other data or observations of your own;
- Comparing it, if appropriate, with "The Test."

4. GRAMMAR REVIEW: FRAGMENTS AND RUN-ON SENTENCES

REVISE FOR SENTENCE ERRORS

Can you recognize when a sentence is incomplete (a *sentence fragment*) or when it is *run-on* (a comma splice or a fused sentence)?

A sentence is the basic unit of written thought; therefore, it must be clear and definite. Each sentence must contain an independent clause with its own subject and its complete verb. However, two or more independent clauses in the same sentence must either be joined by a semicolon (;) or be connected by a conjunction.

If one independent clause follows another without being either clearly separated or properly joined, the reader becomes confused. When a fragment is left standing alone, the reader looks for something more.

It may be necessary to connect or separate groups of words that *look* like sentences in order to make the whole passage read smoothly and correctly. Keep in mind the fact that punctuation and capital letters are signals that should be helpful to the reader, not misleading.

Directions

Use one or more of the following techniques to correct each of the sentence faults in the essay below:

1. Insert periods or semicolons where they are needed.
2. Add words to complete the meaning (such as a pronoun, verb, or connecting word).
3. Circle or cross out punctuation that should be changed or omitted.
4. Change capital letters and verb forms as needed.

When you have finished your revision, read the whole passage again to make sure that:

- Every sentence is complete—not a fragment;
- All sentences make sense and are consistent with the story;
- There are no run-on sentences.

It was a hot day in the month of June, the boulevard was crowded with cars headed for the beach. The first time that Marian took her driving test. It had poured rain, the streets were slippery. The inspector, a stocky, self-important man, who flunked her when the car slid on a steep hill.

This time the inspector seemed friendlier he laughed a lot and invited Mrs. Ericson to ride along. She and Marian both anxious for Marian to pass the test. Mrs. Ericson knew that Marian was actually a competent driver, she had held a license in Pennsylvania for three years.

The inspector was not so friendly as he appeared to be, in fact, he insulted Marian. Continually making demeaning remarks to her. At first, handling the car smoothly and following all his directions. Marian "kept her cool." Most of the time she answered him briefly or not at all. Until his final crack telling her to remember her college degree. Then lost her temper, exploded with a sharp reply. Making him suddenly angry. As though he had been hoping she would make a mistake of some kind. Then, of course, he flunked her, she didn't have a chance.

The first time that she took the test. The rain made the car slip this time it was Marian's tongue that "slipped."

5. COMPOSITION: A. AN IMAGINARY DIALOGUE

A. PROJECT IMAGINATION: WRITE YOUR OWN DIALOGUE

"The Test" is a story that takes place in the afternoon and ends when Marian once again fails her driving test. Although we don't know what happens later, we can imagine that each of the three characters might have described it rather differently. The purpose of this imagination exercise is to allow you to write your own brief dialogue, one that expresses the viewpoint of one of the characters in a conversation with another character whom you invent.

We'll call the inspector "Joe" and have him talk with a friend of his at a bar that evening. Marian will describe what happened for her boyfriend when he calls for her to go on a date. Mrs. Ericson will tell her husband about it at dinner. Of course, none of them can remember all the details. Each will tell just the highlights, or the things that impressed him or her the most.

You may continue the dialogues started below, or you may prefer to invent new ones of your own.

Joe, the inspector (in a bar late that evening)

FRED: Hey, Joe, who was that good-lookin' black girl I saw you riding around with this afternoon? Classy little number, even if she *was* black! I like your taste!

JOE: Cut it, Fred! I *had* to take out that dame. . . .

Marian (getting into her boyfriend's car)

MARIAN: Hi, Greg. What a day it's been! I thought this evening would *never* come!

GREG: Hi, Sugar! Hey, want to drive? I'll change places with you. Just slide over—

MARIAN:

Mrs. Ericson (pouring more coffee for herself and her husband, Martin, as they finish dinner)

MARTIN: Seems to me you've been kind of quiet, Grace. Something bothering you?

MRS. ERICSON: Well, yes, sort of. Today was the day for Marian to take her driver's test again, you know.

MARTIN: She did O.K., didn't she? I can't imagine why a smart girl like Marian would have had any trouble the *first* time.

MRS. ERICSON: Well, something went wrong again. . . .

5. COMPOSITION: B. ALTERNATE TOPIC

A MINORITY GROUP WHERE I COME FROM

Every country seems to have minority groups who do not seem to "belong" in the same way that others do. They may be different from the majority in race, religion, language, culture, or national origin, or a combination of these. (This is called *ethnicity.*) These ethnic groups usually try in various ways to keep their special identity, and often intermarriage between one group and another is discouraged or actually forbidden.

In describing such a minority group that you know about from your own country, you can use a plan or format something like this:

1. ***Introductory paragraph:*** Explain where you come from, and give a few general facts about whether most of the people share a racial or religious background or whether your country has several ethnic groups. You can, if you choose, explain whether you are writing as a member of the group or from the point of view of an outsider. A statement of your *thesis* should also appear in the introductory paragraph—this works best as its last sentence.
2. ***Middle paragraphs:*** In what ways is this group different from the majority of people in your country? Be very specific about these differences: in appearance, dress, customs, language, rules, lifestyle, etc. Choose several of the most important areas or characteristics of this group to describe or explain (about a paragraph for each).
3. ***Concluding paragraph:*** As you conclude your discussion, say something about the relationship of this group to other people in your country or elsewhere. Are they considered to be outsiders there? Is it an advantage or a disadvantage to be one of them?

William E. Barrett (1900–   )

As often happens with a writer, personal experience provided the background for William E. Barrett's story "Señor Payroll." When he was a young man in his twenties, Barrett was appointed Southwestern Advertising Manager of the Westinghouse Company. In this position, where he had to present the "company image" in New Mexico and Arizona, he undoubtedly came into close contact with Mexican workers and their bosses.

While Barrett has written nonfiction in such diverse areas as biography, international affairs, and aviation, his novels reflect his primary interests: race relations and religion. One of his early novels, The Left Hand of God, *is concerned with both themes. It describes the moral dilemma of an American who is taken captive in a remote corner of China and assumes the guise of a priest in order to escape. This popular novel has been translated into ten languages.*

Several other stories that combined religion with race relations were: The Shadows of the Images *(Spanish-American integration and the Roman Catholic faith);* The Glory Tent *(a Negro revival meeting in Missouri); and* The Lilies of the Field *(about a black ex-army sergeant who helped four nuns to build a church). This last novel is best known for its 1963 film version starring the Academy Award-winning actor, Sidney Poitier.*

VII

Señor Payroll

Story Setting: *The Southwest, probably Arizona or New Mexico, a part of the United States where Mexican immigrants often cross the border seeking work in farming or industry.*

Main Idea: *A group of Mexican workers in an American firm cleverly manage to evade the company's policies through some skillful manipulation of the rules.*

Hints About Humor: *It is not always easy to see that something is funny when it is expressed in another language. However, as you become more able to recognize and to enjoy the humor in what you read, you will know that your knowledge of English is becoming more and more sophisticated.*

Humor can arise from a situation itself, from the language used, or from both, as in the story you are about to read, "Señor Payroll." Humor of situation usually involves sudden and unexpected contrasts, or incongruities. We all sometimes make mistakes, and they are not necessarily funny. Why do we laugh, then, when the math teacher does a problem wrong on the board, or the English teacher has trouble spelling a word like "rhythm"? Because teachers are paid to know more *than we do, not* less, *so their mistakes strike us as amusing.*

We expect a dog to go after a cat, but what if the cat turns around and chases the dog? Or what if the robber rushes out of the bank with a bag of money and finds that his getaway car has been stolen? When such things happen, we all can laugh at the joke (and the ironies involved) even when our knowledge of English is limited.

The humor may not be quite so obvious when it involves language itself. For instance, Barrett not only uses a slightly ridiculous situation as the basis for his story, but he deliberately heightens the absurdity by the way he tells it.

As you read "Señor Payroll," watch for some of the devices, or tricks, that a writer employs to produce a comic effect, such as:

Irony: *saying the opposite of what one means.*
Exaggeration: *making something sound much more important than it really is.*
Mixing of language styles: *expressing simple ideas in very formal language, or using both formal and informal styles close together.*

Some of these devices appeared also in "The Loudest Voice." Other approaches to humor and irony will be pointed out as we read later stories.

Larry and I were Junior Engineers in the gas plant, which means that we were clerks. Anything that could be classified as paper work came to the flat double desk across which we faced each other. The Main Office downtown sent us a bewildering array of orders and rules that were to be put into effect.

Junior Engineers were beneath the notice of everyone except the Mexican laborers at the plant. To them we were the visible form of a distant, unknowable paymaster. We were Señor Payroll.

Those Mexicans were great workmen: the aristocrats among them were the stokers, big men who worked Herculean eight-hour shifts in the fierce heat of the retorts. They scooped coal with huge shovels and hurled it with uncanny aim at tiny doors. The coal streamed out from the shovels like black water from a high-pressure nozzle, and never missed the narrow opening. The stokers worked stripped to the waist, and there was pride and dignity in them. Few men could do such work, and they were the few.

GLOSSARY

1 **Junior Engineers:** an important-sounding job title.
2 **paper work:** filling out forms.
3 **bewildering array:** many confusing kinds.
6 **paymaster:** one who pays the employees.
7 **Señor Payroll:** Mr. Payroll—a personification of payroll, the list of workers to be paid.
9 **Herculean:** an adjective referring to a very strong man, Hercules, from ancient Greek mythology.
9 **retorts:** furnaces for burning coal to obtain gas.
10 **shovels:** tools with long, wooden handles attached to large, rounded metal surfaces.
11 **high-pressure nozzle:** small device to force water through a hose very fast.

INFORMAL SPEECH

5 **beneath the notice:** too unimportant even to be seen.
8 **great:** really good, tops, super.
12 **stripped to the waist:** with shirt off, naked from the waist up.

STANDARD VOCABULARY

1 **plant:** a manufacturing company (in this usage).
4 **put into effect:** performed or carried out.
6 ***visible:** seen.
6 **distant:** far off.
8 **aristocrats:** (lit) people of high or noble birth.
9 **fierce:** violent.
10 **huge:** very large, gigantic.
10 **hurled:** threw with force.
10 **uncanny:** amazing.
11 **streamed:** poured.
13 ***dignity:** self-respect.

The Company paid its men only twice a month, on the fifth and on the twentieth. To a Mexican, this was absurd. What man with money will make it last fifteen days? If he hoarded money beyond the spending of three days, he was a miser—and when, Señor, did the blood of Spain flow in the veins of misers? Hence, it was the custom for our stokers to appear every third or fourth day to draw the money due them.

GLOSSARY

17 **the blood of Spain:** (fig) Spanish racial qualities.
18 **draw the money:** collect their pay.

INFORMAL SPEECH

15 **make it last:** not use it up right away but spread it out.

STANDARD VOCABULARY

15 ***absurd:** ridiculous, silly.
16 **hoarded:** kept a hidden supply stored up for personal use.
16 **miser:** one who loves his money more than anything else.
17 **hence:** therefore.
18 **appear:** show (arrive).

There was a certain elasticity in the Company rules, and Larry and I sent the necessary forms to the Main Office and received an "advance" against a man's pay check. Then, one day, Downtown favored us with a memorandum:

"There have been too many abuses of the advance-against-wages privilege. Hereafter, no advance against wages will be made to any employee except in a case of genuine emergency."

We had no sooner posted the notice when in came stoker Juan Garcia. He asked for an advance. I pointed to the notice. He spelled it through slowly, then said, "What does this mean, this 'genuine emergency'?"

I explained to him patiently that the Company was kind and sympathetic, but that it was a great nuisance to have to pay wages every few days. If someone was ill or if money was urgently needed for some other good reason, then the Company would make an exception to the rule.

Juan Garcia turned his hat over and over slowly in his big hands. "I do not get my money?"

"Next payday, Juan. On the twentieth."

He went out silently and I felt a little ashamed of myself. I looked across the desk at Larry. He avoided my eyes.

In the next hour two other stokers came in, looked at the notice, had it explained and walked solemnly out; then no more came. What we did not know was that Juan Garcia, Pete Mendoza, and Francisco Gonzalez had spread the word, and that every Mexican in the plant was explaining the order to every other Mexican. "To get money now, the wife must be sick. There must be medicine for the baby."

The next morning Juan Garcia's wife was practically dying, Pete Mendoza's mother would hardly last the day, there was a veritable epidemic among children, and, just for

GLOSSARY

20 **"advance" against:** earned money given ahead of the regular time.
21 **Downtown:** the Company's main office (an example of personification).
21 **favored us with:** (hum frml) kindly gave us.
23 **genuine emergency:** a really serious need.
31 **exception to the rule:** a time when it's all right to break a rule.
42 **practically dying:** (exag) almost dead.
43 **a veritable epidemic:** could be said to be spreading like a disease.

INFORMAL SPEECH

25 **no sooner . . . when:** just as soon as one thing happened, the next thing happened.
39 **spread the word:** told everyone.
43 **would hardly last the day:** (exag) might not live until nighttime.
43 **just for variety:** to add something different.

STANDARD VOCABULARY

19 **elasticity:** ability to stretch.
21 **memorandum:** a written notice or reminder.
22 ***abuses:** wrong uses.
22 **privilege:** a special favor.
22 **hereafter:** from now on (formal usage).
23 **except:** unless.
25 **posted:** put up in a public place.
28 ***patiently:** in an unhurried way.
28 ***sympathetic:** caring.
29 **nuisance:** a bother or annoyance.
30 ***urgently:** without delay.
35 **silently:** with no sound.
35 **ashamed:** feeling disgraced or embarrassed.
36 **avoided:** took care not to meet.
37 ***explained:** used words to make something plainly understood.
38 **solemnly:** seriously and with great dignity.

variety, there was one sick father. We always suspected that the old man was really sick; no Mexican would otherwise have thought of him. At any rate, nobody paid Larry and me to examine private lives; we made out our forms with an added line describing the "genuine emergency." Our people got paid.

That went on for a week. Then came a new order, curt and to the point: "Hereafter, employees will be paid ONLY on the fifth and the twentieth of the month. No exceptions will be made except in the cases of employees leaving the service of the Company."

The notice went up on the board, and we explained its significance gravely. "No, Juan Garcia, we cannot advance your wages. It is too bad about your wife and your cousins and your aunts, but there is a new rule."

Juan Garcia went out and thought it over. He thought out loud with Mendoza and Gonzalez and Ayala, then, in the morning, he was back, "I am quitting this company for a different job. You pay me now?"

We argued that it was a good company and that it loved its employees like children, but in the end we paid off, because Juan Garcia quit. And so did Gonzalez, Mendoza, Obregon, Ayala and Ortez, the best stokers, men who could not be replaced.

Larry and I looked at each other; we knew what was coming in about three days. One of our duties was to sit on the hiring line early each morning, engaging transient workers for the handy gangs. Any man was accepted who could walk up and ask for a job without falling down. Never before had we been called upon to hire such skilled virtuosos as stokers for handy-gang work, but we were called upon to hire them now.

The day foreman was wringing his hands and asking the Almighty if he was personally supposed to shovel this condemned coal, while there in a stolid, patient line were

GLOSSARY

50 **leaving the service:** giving up their jobs.
51 **board:** a bulletin board, a place where notices are posted.
54 **thought out loud:** (fig) talked it over, discussed the matter.
61 **sit on:** (legal term) to be present and in charge of.
61 **transient workers:** temporary help.
62 **handy gangs:** groups for doing ordinary jobs.
63 **skilled virtuosos:** (iron) artists, usually in musical performance.
65 **day foreman:** boss for the day.
65 **wringing his hands:** (fig) acting very worried, (lit) twisting his hands together in a state of terrible anxiety.
65 **asking the Almighty:** swearing (iron euph).
66 **condemned:** (iron euph) lit. judged and appointed to die; but here, damned.

INFORMAL SPEECH

45 **at any rate:** besides, in any case.
45 **nobody paid . . . to:** it was not part of (our) job to. . . .
48 **to the point:** direct, without wasting words.
52 **too bad:** a casual expression of regret (I'm sorry).
54 **thought it over:** considered what to do.
55 **quitting:** leaving the job.
58 **paid off:** made final payments.
64 **called upon:** expected.

STANDARD VOCABULARY

45 **otherwise:** under other circumstances.
46 ***examine:** inspect closely.
46 ***private:** very personal or intimate business of an individual or a family.
48 **curt:** short and rude.
51 ***significance:** meaning or importance.
51 ***gravely:** soberly, solemnly, very seriously.
57 ***argued:** gave reasons.
59 ***replaced:** found substitutes for.
61 **engaging:** hiring.
66 **stolid:** immovable.

skilled men—Garcia, Mendoza, and others—waiting to be hired. We hired them, of course. There was nothing else to do.

Every day we had a line of resigning stokers and another line of stokers seeking work. Our paper work became very complicated. At the Main Office they were jumping up and down. The procession of forms showing Juan Garcia's resigning and being hired over and over again was too much for them. Sometimes Downtown had Garcia on the payroll twice at the same time when someone down there was slow in entering a resignation. Our phone rang early and often.

Tolerantly and patiently we explained: "There's nothing we can do if a man wants to quit, and if there are stokers available when the plant needs stokers, we hire them."

Out of chaos, Downtown issued another order. I read it and whistled. Larry looked at it and said, "It is going to be very quiet around here."

The order read: "Hereafter, no employee who resigns may be rehired within a period of 30 days."

Juan Garcia was due for another resignation, and when he came in we showed him the order and explained that standing in line the next day would do him no good if he resigned today. "Thirty days is a long time, Juan."

It was a grave matter and he took time to reflect on it. So did Gonzalez, Mendoza, Ayala and Ortez. Ultimately, however, they were all back—and all resigned.

We did our best to dissuade them and we were sad about the parting. This time it was for keeps and they shook hands with us solemnly. It was very nice knowing us. Larry and I looked at each other when they were gone and we both knew that neither of us had been pulling for Downtown to win this duel. It was a blue day.

In the morning, however, they were all back in line. With the utmost gravity, Juan Garcia informed me that he was a stoker looking for a job.

"No dice, Juan," I said. "Come back in thirty days. I warned you."

His eyes looked straight into mine without a flicker. "There is some mistake, Señor," he said. "I am Manuel Hernandez. I work as the stoker in Pueblo, in Santa Fe, in many places."

GLOSSARY

77 **out of chaos:** in all the confusion.
77 **whistled:** made the sound of "Whew!" to show surprise.
81 **due for:** about ready for.
85 **ultimately:** at last, finally.
89 **duel:** (hist) a fight between two individuals to defend their honor (usually with swords or pistols).
93 **without a flicker:** without blinking one's eyes, thus, a steady gaze, as though telling the solemn truth.

INFORMAL SPEECH

70 **jumping up and down:** (fig) excited, and usually happy, (can be iron).
72 **was too much for them:** upset them very much, "got them down."
82 **do him no good:** be of no use.
86 **did our best:** tried very hard.
87 **for keeps:** to last permanently.
89 **pulling for:** wanting.
89 **a blue day:** sad or dismal day.
92 **no dice:** it can't be done ("nothin' doing").

STANDARD VOCABULARY

69 **resigning:** leaving a job.
70 ***complicated:** very difficult, complex.
71 **procession:** long marching line, parade.
75 **tolerantly:** in an accepting manner.
76 **available:** there to be used.
77 **issued:** put forth.
84 **reflect on:** think.
86 **dissuade:** persuade them to change their minds.
90 **utmost:** most extreme, greatest.
92 **warned:** told in advance of danger.

I stared at him, remembering the sick wife and the babies without medicine, the mother-in-law in the hospital, the many resignations and the rehirings. I knew that there was a gas plant in Pueblo, and that there wasn't any in Santa Fe; but who was I to argue with a man about his own name? A stoker is a stoker.

So I hired him. I hired Gonzalez, too, who swore that his name was Carrera, and Ayala, who had shamelessly become Smith.

Three days later the resigning started.

Within a week our payroll read like a history of Latin America. Everyone was on it: Lopez and Obregon, Villa, Diaz, Batista, Gomez, and even San Martin and Bolivar. Finally Larry and I, growing weary of staring at familiar faces and writing unfamiliar names, went to the Superintendent and told him the whole story. He tried not to grin, and said, "Damned nonsense!"

The next day the orders were taken down. We called our most prominent stokers into the office and pointed to the board. No rules any more.

"The next time we hire you hombres," Larry said grimly, "come in under the names you like best, because that's the way you are going to stay on the books."

They looked at us and they looked at the board; then for the first time in the long duel, their teeth flashed white. "Si, Señores," they said.

And so it was.

GLOSSARY

106 **Superintendent:** the person in charge, the boss.
110 **hombres:** Spanish for "men" (usually inf).
113 **Si, Señores:** Yes, sirs.

INFORMAL SPEECH

106 **the whole story:** everything that had happened.
106 **grin:** wide smile, usually open, friendly, and unrestrained.
107 **damned nonsense:** (inf sw) just plain stupid, senseless, a waste of time and effort, a big fuss over nothing.

STANDARD VOCABULARY

96 **stared:** gazed steadily and curiously.
100 **swore:** vowed solemnly.
105 **weary:** tired.
105 ***familiar:** well-known.
108 **prominent:** important and well-known.
110 **grimly:** firmly, severely, with determination.
113 **flashed:** appeared suddenly and brightly.

1. STUDY QUESTIONS

DISCOVERING THE STORY THROUGH OBSERVATION AND INFERENCE

1. ***Observation:*** The narrator says that he and Larry are "Junior Engineers," but what kind of work do they actually *do?*
   Inference: How do they feel about their jobs? Why were they given such a title?
2. ***Observation:*** What is the basis for the title of the story?
   Inference: What attitude is implied by the workers' use of this term? In what ways might it influence the sympathies of Larry and the narrator toward either the workers or the Company?
3. ***Observation:*** What kind of work do the stokers do?
   Inference: Why does the narrator call them "the aristocrats" among the workers?
4. ***Observation:*** Can you explain the problem about paydays?
   Inference: The language in the fourth paragraph (beginning "The Company paid. . . .") is intentionally formal, almost poetic. How does this produce a mildly comic affect? How does it indirectly elevate (raise) the stokers' status?
5. ***Observation:*** What is the rule about "genuine emergencies"? How are the stokers going to deal with it?
   Inference: What do you think of the *method* they use? Can you explain why their lies seem amusing rather than shocking?
6. ***Observation:*** On page 105 the narrator says that "nobody paid Larry and me to examine private lives." What does that mean?
   Inference: Why is this statement important to the story?
7. ***Observation:*** Can you explain the content and meaning of the second Company order?
   Inference: Do you think the Company is being reasonable and fair to the workers? What do Juan Garcia and the other stokers intend to accomplish by quitting?
8. ***Observation:*** On page 105, the paragraph beginning with "The day foreman . . ." and the next two paragraphs achieve their comic effects through the use of both irony and exaggeration. Can you point out places where this "tongue-in-cheek" language is used?
   Inference: What other factors contribute to the humor in this passage?
9. ***Observation:*** What is the reaction of Larry and the narrator to the Company's 30-day rule?
   Inference: What do you think the Company expects to accomplish by making this new rule? What do you think the narrator and Larry expect to happen?
10. ***Observation:*** By looking at the language, can you explain why each of these passages is comical? What happens when you simply restate the meaning?

"His eyes looked straight into mine without a flicker."
". . . who was I to argue with a man about his own name?"
". . . and Ayala, who had shamelessly become Smith."

Inference: Can you tell where the writer's sympathies might be in this story? Do you think the author is in favor of telling lies?

2. DISCUSSION

THINKING ABOUT WORDS AND IDEAS

A. Look up the word "bureaucracy" and explain it in your own words. Then answer the questions below:
   1. Can you tell, by the definition you found, whether the word has a favorable or an unfavorable connotation? Explain.
   2. In what sense was the Company a form of bureaucracy? Why?
   3. What other examples of bureaucracies can you think of from your own observation or experience?
   4. Check the meaning and the connotation of the word "bureaucrat." Do you think that Larry and the narrator were bureaucrats? Why?
   5. Use each of the words in original sentences of your own:
      bureaucracy   bureaucrat   bureaucratic

B. Although "Señor Payroll" is not an especially "deep" or "heavy" story, it does have some of the features of the standard short story. Glance back at the list of Literary Terms in Chapter I so that you can identify the functions of some of those terms in this story:
   1. The *characters* and their *motivation* in each case.
   2. The *protagonist,* the *antagonist,* and the conflict that constitutes the *plot.*
   3. The point of *climax* and what is resolved. Is anyone changed as a result?
   4. The role of the *narrator,* as compared with the narrator in one of the stories read earlier.
   5. What *tone* is established in the first sentence and two or three later sentences that express the same attitude?

C. Each of the colloquial or slang expressions below could be related in some way to the story. Give the meaning for each one, and explain what connection each has with "Señor Payroll":
   1. Have the upper hand; come from behind; gain the upper hand.
   2. The game of one-upmanship. Can you give any examples from your own experience or observation?
   3. An old American saying: "We'd better hang together or we'll all hang separately."

4. Why do Americans favor the underdog but have little sympathy for a loser? What is the difference between "a loser" and "the loser"?
5. Keep a straight face; tongue-in-cheek remarks. Give some examples from the story.

3. GRAMMAR REVIEW: SUBJECT-VERB AGREEMENT

MAKE THE VERB AGREE WITH ITS SUBJECT

Adding the letter "s" to a noun or a verb often seems like a very unimportant thing to worry about when one is studying much more complicated grammar, learning many new vocabulary words every day, and struggling to master college-level courses in a foreign language. Even advanced ESL students sometimes consider the final "s" on a plural noun or on a third person singular, present-tense verb to be a rather trivial matter. After all, isn't one's meaning obvious anyway? Why make a fuss about such a small mistake?

There are several reasons why it is worth your while to pay attention to the rule of making the verb agree with its subject:

- Management of this grammatical detail is one indicator of your control of the language, since you must recognize the subject and must allow it to govern the verb.
- Subject-verb agreement errors are readily noticed by Americans and are generally associated with ignorance. Frequent mistakes of this kind present a poor impression, as if they were coming from a rather casual or careless writer.
- Conversely, you are showing both regard for your reader and meticulous care in expressing what you mean when you make precise distinctions between singular and plural nouns and verbs.
- Finally, taking a little extra time and trouble to write correctly will help you to develop the habit of writing English accurately and well.

The following exercises will give you an opportunity to review and to practice subject-verb agreement. If you have to pause and think whether or not you should add "s" to a verb, perhaps you need to review the rules. If you can write these exercises easily and get them correct, *be sure that you are doing equally well when you write your compositions.*

Although this small, unnecessary error is one of the most common mistakes to be found in ordinary ESL writing, you can be among those exceptional ESL students who *never* make it!

Most stories are written in the past tense; however, as we have noted earlier, when we discuss them we often use the historical present tense (see Chapter I, Language Conversion). For instance:

"Tony walked down the street and entered a cafe"

becomes, when we discuss it,

"Tony walks down the street and enters a cafe."

In this exercise, you will be changing past-tense verbs from the story into the historical present, or the regular present tense. Since the verb in the present tense must agree with its subject, you will need to identify that first.

To complete the exercise:

1. Locate the past-tense verb in the text (page and line numbers are given).
2. Write down the subject for that verb in the left-hand column. (It may not necessarily be the subject for the whole sentence.)
3. If the subject is a pronoun, write in parentheses the noun to which it refers, or its antecedent.
4. Write the present-tense form of the verb in the right-hand column.

The first three have been filled in as examples:

	PAGE	LINE	SUBJECT	PAST TENSE	PRESENT TENSE
1.	102	3	we (Larry and I)	faced	face
2.	102	3	main office	sent	sends
3.	102	9	men	worked	work
4.	102	10	They (the stokers)	hurled	hurl
5.	102	11	The coal	streamed	streams
6.	103	14	The Company	paid	pays
7.	103	3–4	the blood of Spain	did flow	does flow
8.	104	21	Downtown	favored	favores
9.	104	25	stoker Juan Garcia	came	comes
10.	104	35	He	went	goes
11.	104	35	I	felt	feel
12.	104	38	two other stokers	walked	walk
13.	104	40	the plant	was explaining	is explaining
14.	105	46	nobody	paid	pays
15.	105	47	Our people	got paid	get paid
16.	105	54	Juan Garcia	thought	thinks
17.	105	55	he (Juan Garcia)	was	is
18.	106	67	We	hired	hire

	PAGE	LINE	SUBJECT	PAST TENSE	PRESENT TENSE
19.	106	70		became	
20.	106	72		was	
21.	106	74		rang	
22.	106	83		resigned	
23.	106	84		took	
24.	106	85		resigned	
25.	106	87		shook	
26.	106	88		had been pulling	
27.	106	91		informed	
28.	107	100		swore	
29.	107	101		had become	
30.	107	102		started	
31.	107	106		tried	
32.	107	109		pointed	
33.	107	110		said	
34.	107	113		flashed	
35.	107	113		said	

For More Practice

The following paragraphs are taken from earlier stories in this book. Rewrite each of the paragraphs, changing the verbs from the past tense to the *historical present* or regular present.

1. Silence crept into the coach again and presently the businessman turned away. But the boy continued to look at him, . . . without once blinking his eyes or shifting his stare. The businessman was conscious of the boy's scrutiny, for he looked up again, fixed the boy with his eyes, and said, "Your dad's been gone some time. . . ." ("On the Outside")
2. In the morning it snowed. On the street corner a tree had been decorated for us by a kind city administration. In order to miss its chilly shadow our neighbors walked three blocks east to buy a loaf of bread. The butcher pulled down black window shades to keep the colored lights from shining on his chickens. Oh, not me. . . . I tossed it a kiss of tolerance. Poor thing, it was a stranger in Egypt. ("The Loudest Voice")
3. Marian pulled up beside the curb. She put the car in neutral, pulled on the emergency, waited a moment, and then put the car into gear again. Her face was set. As she released the brake her foot slipped off the clutch pedal and the engine stalled. . . . Mrs. Ericson was waiting at the curb where they had left her. As Marian stopped the car, the inspector jumped out and brushed past her, his face purple. ("The Test")

4. VOCABULARY PRACTICE: WORD FORMS

FIND THE RIGHT WORD FORMS

Each of the words in the exercise comes from the group of starred words in the Standard Vocabulary. It is given in the same form as it appeared in the text, so the word will need to be changed into other forms in order to complete the sentence.

Fill in each of the blanks with the word form that most accurately expresses the meaning called for. Decide first what part of speech, or word form, is needed; then consult your own chart or the dictionary to find the right form. The first blank has already been completed for you with the noun form of the word "visible."

1. visible (adjective)
   In their position as payroll clerks, Larry and the narrator had greater *visibility* for the Mexican workers than did the Company managers, who were much harder for them to visualize.
2. absurd (adjective)
   To the Company the payroll issue was absurdly simple, until the series of new rules brought matters to the point of absurdity.
3. abuses (noun)
   Downtown believed that the workers were abusing the freedom to get advances on their pay and when privileges were abused, the Company would have to withdraw them.
4. sympathetic (adjective)
   Although we might have expected Larry and the narrator to sympathize with the Company that employed them, we can see that their sympathies were actually with the Mexican workers.
5. urgently (adverb)
   As the urgency of the workers' need for money increased, their wives were probably urging them to try some other way to get an advance.
6. explained (verb, past)
   Thinking that the rule about emergencies was easily explained, Larry and the narrator made little explanatory speeches telling the Mexican workers that they must come up with an explanation every time they wanted their pay in advance.
7. private (adjective)
   While the narrator and Larry privately suspected what was really

going on, they refused to invade the workers' __________ by checking up on them.

8. significance (noun)
The workers felt that each new rule __________ a change in Company policies that would involve a __________ alteration in their own customs and habits.

9. argued (verb, past)
Whether telling lies was the right way to deal with the Company is an __________ question, but to the workers it was quicker and more efficient than __________.

10. gravely (adverb)
When Larry and the narrator saw the third rule they really looked __________, for they felt that the Mexican workers did not realize or appreciate the __________ of the situation.

11. complicated (past participle)
After the Company finally decided to stop __________ the issue and abolish the new rules, everyone was relieved that all the __________ were now eliminated.

12. familiar (adjective)
Thanks to the narrator and Larry's friendly __________ with the Mexican workers, and to the Company's belated attempt to __________ itself with their ways, both the labor dispute and the story ended happily.

5. COMPOSITION: A. "CONTROLLED" COMPOSITION

"WHO IS REALLY ON THE OUTSIDE"—AGAIN!

The theme of the model composition in Chapter II can also be applied to "Señor Payroll" simply by showing how each group of characters in this story, too, could be considered outsiders.

Reread the model essay, and then follow the same structure, style, and topic, this time for Barrett's story. You will have:

- An introduction that includes the title, author, and main idea,
- Several paragraphs discussing how each group of characters in "Señor Payroll" could be called outsiders,
- A conclusion that follows up and completes what you have said.

5. COMPOSITION: B. ORIGINAL, YET RELATED, TOPICS

WORK, WORK, WORK!

"Señor Payroll" is all about work and the problems of the workplace. Does it make you think of any similar or related experience you have had? Perhaps one of the question-topics below will start you thinking, or your instructor may suggest a different one to you:

Can you remember how you felt as you began your first job? Explain some of the things you learned on that job.

What was the hardest work you have ever done?

Did you ever get involved in a labor dispute, or in a conflict with your boss or with another worker?

Is there a day on a particular job that you would most like to forget? Why?

If one of these questions fits your experience, try to answer it by writing a good, strong thesis statement—and then go on from there.

William Saroyan (1908–1981)

The author's own home town of Fresno, California, may have been the basis for the town in "Going Home," which first appeared in his short story collection Inhale and Exhale *in 1936. Born in 1908 of Armenian immigrant parents, William Saroyan had to overcome the handicaps of poverty and a limited education in order to accomplish his dream of being a writer.*

His style is often called impressionistic. It reflects his own outlook, which was emotionally oriented and a bit impulsive rather than logically organized. Much of Saroyan's writing expresses his always hopeful belief in the American dream of inexhaustible opportunity in this country. His warm interest in all kinds of people is reflected in many of his works, including his Pulitzer prize-winning play The Time of Your Life, *about a very ordinary but lovable group of people in a waterfront saloon.*

Saroyan wrote a great number of books and plays, many of them having a California setting and featuring child characters as important figures. One of these, My Name is Aram, *became a best-seller in the early 1940s, and it was followed two years later by his very popular novel* The Human Comedy. *At that time the United States was deeply involved in World War II, and Americans enthusiastically welcomed the stories of this amiable, upbeat author.*

More information about William Saroyan can be found in his autobiographical work Here Comes, There Goes You Know Who.

VIII

Going Home

Story Setting: *The San Joaquin Valley, in central California, around the early 1930s. The climate here is delightfully warm and sunny, and the rich soil produces an abundance of vegetables all year round. However, it seldom rains except during the winter (from November to January), so that irrigation, or frequent watering, is usually necessary.*

In the Story: *A young man returns to his home town, and we share his impressions, his memories, and his mixed feelings about being there, although we are never told his name.*

I

This valley, he thought, all this country between the mountains, is mine, home to me, the place I dream about, and everything is the same, not a thing is changed, water sprinklers still splash in circles over lawns of Bermuda grass, good old home town, simplicity, reality.

Walking along Alvin Street he felt glad to be home again. Everything was fine, common and good, the smell of earth, cooking suppers, smoke, the rich summer air of the

GLOSSARY

2 **water sprinklers:** attachments to a hose to turn a stream of water into a spray.
3 **lawns of Bermuda grass:** same as English term, "gardens"; front yards.

INFORMAL SPEECH

2 **not a thing:** (emph) nothing.

STANDARD VOCABULARY

3 **splash:** (onomat) fall and scatter about.
3 ***simplicity:** plainness, uncomplicated state, innocence.
3 ***reality:** the quality of being true to the facts of life.
5 **common:** ordinary.

valley full of plant growth, grapes growing, peaches ripening, and the oleander bush swooning with sweetness, the same as ever. He breathed deeply, drawing the smell of home deep into his lungs, smiling inwardly. It was hot. He hadn't felt his senses reacting to the earth so cleanly and clearly for years; now it was a pleasure even to breathe. The cleanliness of the air sharpened the moment so that, walking, he felt the magnificence of being, glory of possessing substance, of having form and motion and intellect, the piety of merely being alive on the earth.

Water, he thought, hearing the soft splash of a lawn sprinkler; to taste the water of home, the full cool water of the valley, to have that simple thirst and that solid water with which to quench it, fulfillment, the clarity of life. He saw an old man holding a hose over some geranium plants, and his thirst sent him to the man.

Good evening, he said quietly; may I have a drink?

The old man turned slowly, his shadow large against the house, to look into the young man's face, amazed and pleased. You bet, he said; here, and he placed the hose into the young man's hands. Mighty fine water, said the old man, this water of the San Joaquin valley; best yet, I guess. That water up in Frisco makes me sick, ain't got no taste. And down in Los Angeles, why, the water tastes like castor oil; I can't understand how so many people go on living there year after year.

While the old man talked he listened to the water falling from the hose to the earth, leaping thickly. Cleanly, sinking swiftly into the earth. You said it, our water is the finest on earth.

He curved his head over the spouting water and began to drink. The sweet rich taste

GLOSSARY

6 **grapes . . . peaches:** fruits that ripen in the late summer.
6 **oleander bush:** an evergreen bush with clusters of sweet-smelling flowers.
7 **swooning:** (OD) fainting.
16 **geranium plants:** brightly colored (red, pink, or white) flowered plants, often in window boxes.
20 **San Joaquin Valley:** a long stretch of very fertile but dry land in California.
21 **Frisco:** a colloquialism for San Francisco.
22 **Los Angeles:** the largest city in Southern California.
22 **castor oil:** unpleasant-tasting medicine.

INFORMAL SPEECH

7 **the same as ever:** just the way it always was.
19 **you bet:** a term of emphatic agreement.
20 **mighty fine:** very good.
21 **makes me sick:** makes me disgusted; a very informal way of saying "It's just terrible!"
21 **ain't got no:** (vulgar) hasn't any.
25 **you said it:** emphatic agreement.

STANDARD VOCABULARY

8 **reacting to:** acting in response to.
10 **cleanliness:** purity.
10 **magnificence:** a grandly impressive quality.
11 **glory:** heavenly splendor.
11 ***possessing:** owning, having.
11 ***substance:** something physical or material.
11 ***intellect:** mind or intelligence.
11 **piety:** devotion to God, worshipfulness.
14 **thirst:** need for water.
15 **quench:** satisfy one's thirst.
15 ***fulfillment:** complete satisfaction.
15 ***clarity:** clearness, sometimes transparency.
15 **hose:** a flexible tube, usually attached to a faucet or tap, for watering plants.
19 **amazed** (at): very much surprised (at).
27 **spouting:** coming up or out with great force, used regarding liquids.

of the water amazed him, and as he drank he thought, God, this is splendid. He could feel the cool water splashing into his being, refreshing and cooling him. Losing his breath, he lifted his head, saying to the old man, We're mighty lucky, us folks in the valley.

He bent his head over the water again and began again to swallow the splashing liquid, laughing to himself with delight, It seemed as if he couldn't get enough of it into his system; the more he drank, the finer the water tasted to him and the more he wanted to drink.

The old man was amazed. You drunk about two quarts, he said.

GLOSSARY

INFORMAL SPEECH

30 **mighty lucky:** very fortunate.
30 **us folks:** (used as subj) we.

STANDARD VOCABULARY

28 **splendid:** wonderful, magnificent, fantastic.
29 **his being:** his body and more; throughout his whole consciousness.
33 ***system:** the inner workings of something, such as a body or a machine; also, a plan.

Still swallowing the water, he could hear the old man talking, and he lifted his head again, replying, I guess so. It sure tastes fine. He wiped his mouth with a handkerchief, still holding the hose, still wanting to drink more. The whole valley was in that water, all the clarity, all the genuineness, all the goodness and simplicity and reality.

II

Man alive, said the old man. You sure was thirsty. How long since you had a drink, anyway?

Two years, he replied, I mean two years since I had a drink of *this* water. I been away, traveling around. I just got back. I was born here, over on G Street in Russian town; you know, across the Southern Pacific tracks; been away two years and I just got back. Mighty fine too, let me tell you, to be back. I like this place. I'm going to get a job and settle down.

He hung his head over the water again and took several more swallows; then he handed the hose to the old man.

You sure was thirsty, said the old man. I ain't never seen anybody anywhere drink so much water at one time. It sure looked good seeing you swallow all that water.

He went on walking down Alvin Street, humming to himself, the old man staring at him.

Nice to be back, the young man thought; greatest mistake I ever made, coming back this way.

Everything he had ever done had been a mistake, and this was one of the good mistakes. He had come south from San Francisco without even thinking of going home; he had thought of going as far south as Merced, stopping there awhile, and then going back, but once he had got into the country, it had been too much. It had been great fun standing on the highway in his city clothes, hitchhiking.

One little city after another, and here he was walking through the streets of his home town, at seven in the evening. It was great, very amusing; and the water; splendid.

GLOSSARY

37 **handkerchief:** a square of cloth, usually white, for wiping or blowing one's nose.
43 **Russian town:** a section of town inhabited by Russian immigrants.
44 **Southern Pacific:** the name of an important railroad.
50 **humming:** singing with the mouth closed (an onomatopoetic word).
56 **Merced:** town southeast of San Francisco, in the San Joaquin Valley.

INFORMAL SPEECH

40 **man alive!:** exclamation of wonder.
40 **you sure was:** (inf) you certainly were.
42 **I been:** (inf) I have been.
44 **across the . . . tracks:** on the poor people's side of town.
45 **settle down:** set up a permanent home and way of life.
57 **it had been too much:** the emotional tug or pull of being so close to his home had become too hard to resist.
58 **hitchhiking:** the practice of walking along a road and signaling (by raising the right thumb) that a person wants a ride.

STANDARD VOCABULARY

39 **genuineness:** true reality of something.
52 **mistake:** error, wrong move or action.
60 **amusing:** funny or entertaining.

He wasn't far from town, the city itself, and he could see one or two of the taller buildings, the Pacific Gas and Electric Building, all lit up with colored lights, and another, a taller one, that he hadn't seen before. That's a new one, he thought; they put up that one while I was away; things must be booming.

He turned down Fulton Street and began walking into town. It looked great from where he was, far away and nice and small, very genuine, a real quiet little town, the kind of place to live in, settle down in, marry in, have a home, kids, a job, and all the rest of it. It was all he wanted. The air of the valley and the water and the reality of the whole place, the cleanliness of life in the valley, the simplicity of the people.

In the city, everything was the same: the names of the stores, the people walking in the streets, and the slow passing of automobiles; boys in cars trying to pick up girls; same as ever; not a thing changed. He saw faces he had known as a boy, people he did not know by name, and then he saw Tony Rocca, his old pal, walking up the street toward him, and he saw that Tony recognized him. He stopped walking, waiting for Tony to come into his presence. It was like a meeting in a dream, strange, almost incredible. He had dreamed of the two of them playing hookey from school to go swimming, to go out to the county fair, to sneak into a moving-picture theatre; and now here he was again, a big fellow with a lazy, easy-going walk, and a genial Italian grin. It was good, and he was glad he had made the mistake and come back.

He stopped walking, waiting for Tony to come into his presence, smiling at him, unable to speak. The two boys shook hands and then began to strike one another with affection, laughing loudly, swearing at one another. You old bastard, Tony said; where the hell have you been? and he punched his friend in the stomach, laughing loudly.

Old Tony, he said; good old punchdrunk Tony, God, it's good to see you. I thought maybe you'd be dead by this time. What the hell have you been doing? He dodged another

GLOSSARY

76 **county fair:** an annual event where prizes are awarded for farm produce, and there is family entertainment.
77 **moving-picture theatre:** cinema or movie house.
81 **shook hands:** shaking hands in the accepted and customary American form of either greeting or saying good-bye.
83 **in the stomach:** just above the belt.
84 **punchdrunk:** term used for fighters who get beaten up a lot, thus one who does a great deal of fighting (One who is punchdrunk usually can't speak clearly.)

INFORMAL SPEECH

62 **all lit up:** with all the lights on; bright.
64 **booming:** (used for a town, city, or business) prospering and growing.
71 **pick up girls:** fig, give them a ride, hoping to get better acquainted.
73 **old pal:** a good friend known for a long time, one that a person likes to spend time with.
76 **playing hookey:** staying out of school without a proper excuse (sl).
77 **sneak:** go somewhere covertly, not wanting to be seen.
78 **easy-going:** relaxed.
79 **grin:** broad smile.
82 **you old bastard:** term of friendly insult.
82 **where the hell:** "hell" considered to be swearing, used for emphasis.
83 **punched:** hit with the fist.

STANDARD VOCABULARY

74 **recognized:** found to be familiar, knew.
74 **(into his) presence:** (to) his vicinity, or the space in front of him, nearby.
75 **incredible:** unbelievable.
77 **lazy:** avoiding as much effort as possible.
79 **genial:** pleasant, friendly.
81 ***strike:** hit or slap (either in a friendly or in an unfriendly way).
82 **affection:** warm feeling toward someone.
82 **swearing:** cursing, using "bad" language, usually involving religious terms, thus can be considered blasphemous. (Note other meanings when combined with *by, in, off,* and *to.*)
85 **dodged:** avoided quickly.

punch, and struck his friend in the chest. He swore in Italian at Tony, using words Tony taught him years ago, and Tony swore back at him in Russian.

I've got to go out to the house, he said at last. The folks don't know I'm here. I've got to go out and see them. I'm dying to see my brother Paul.

He went on down the street, smiling about Tony. They would be having a lot of good times together again; they might even go swimming again the way they did as kids. It was great to be back.

Walking by stores, he thought of buying his mother a small gift, A little gift would please the old lady. But he had little money, and all the decent things were expensive. I'll get her something later, he thought.

He turned west on Tulare Street, crossing the Southern Pacific tracks, reached G Street, then turned south. In a few minutes he would be home again, at the door of the little old house; the same as ever; the old woman, the old man, his three sisters, and his kid brother, all of them in the house, living simple lives.

III

He saw the house from a distance of about a block. and his heart began to jump. He felt suddenly ill and afraid, something he had forgotten about the place, about the life which he had always hated, something ugly and mean. But he walked on, moving slower as he came closer to the house. The fence had fallen and no one had fixed it. The house suddenly appeared to be very ugly, and he wondered why in hell the old man didn't move to a better house in a better neighborhood. Seeing the house again, feeling all its old reality, all his hatred for it returned, and he began to feel again the longing to be away from it, where he could not see it. He began to feel, as he had felt as a boy, the deep inarticulate hatred he had for the whole city, its falseness, its meanness, the stupidity of its people, the

GLOSSARY

100 **about a block:** as far as the length of a city block (approximately 325 meters).

INFORMAL SPEECH

88 **to the house:** go home.
89 **I'm dying to:** I very much want to; I'm crazy to, I can't wait to.
92 **great to be back:** wonderful to be home again.
94 **the old lady; the old woman:** a somewhat rude but friendly term for one's mother.
94 **decent:** all right, satisfactory. Can mean proper or modest.
98 **the old man:** rude but friendly term for one's father.
98 **kid brother:** younger brother (friendly term).
100 **(heart) began to jump:** began to pound, or beat fast and hard.
104 **why in hell:** questioning in a complaining, angry mood.

STANDARD VOCABULARY

94 **expensive:** costly.
102 **ugly:** very offensive to see, hideously unattractive.
102 **mean:** (see *meanness*).
102 **neighborhood:** people living near one another, a community.
106 **longing:** deep desire.
107 **inarticulate:** unable to say what one is thinking.
108 **falseness:** dishonesty, phoniness.
108 **meanness:** here a quality of being very ordinary. (Sometimes also *unkindness.*) Note: neither definition has any connection with the verb *mean*, or the gerund *meaning.* Can you find other definitions for words using the root word, *mean?*
108 **stupidity:** lack of intelligence; deliberate carelessness or ignorance.

emptiness of their minds, and it seemed to him that he would never be able to return to such a place. The water; yes, it was good, it was splendid; but there were other things.

He walked slowly before the house, looking at it as if he might be a stranger, feeling alien and unrelated to it, yet feeling that it was home, the place he dreamed about, the place that tormented him wherever he went. He was afraid someone might come out of the house and see him, because he knew that if he was seen, he might find himself running away. Still, he wanted to see them, all of them, have them before his eyes, feel the full presence of their bodies, even smell them, that old strong Russian smell. But it was too much. He began to feel hatred for everything in the city, and he walked on, going to the corner. There he stood beneath the street lamp, bewildered and disgusted, wanting to see his brother Paul, to talk to the boy, find out what was going on in his mind, how he was taking it, being in such a place, living such a life. He knew how it had been with him when he had been his brother's age, and he hoped he might be able to give his brother a little advice, how to keep from feeling the monotony and the ugliness by reading.

He forgot that he hadn't eaten since breakfast, and that he had been dreaming for months of eating another of his mother's meals, sitting at the old table in the kitchen, seeing her, large and red-faced and serious and angry toward him, loving him, but he had lost his appetite. He thought he might wait at the corner; perhaps his brother would leave the house to take a walk and he would see the boy and talk to him. Paul, he would say, and he would talk to the boy in Russian.

The stillness of the valley began to oppress him, losing its piety, becoming merely a form of the valley's monotony.

IV

Still, he couldn't go away from the house. From the corner he could see it, and he knew that he wanted to go in and be among his people, a part of their lives; he knew this was what he had wanted to do for months, to knock at the door, embrace his mother and

GLOSSARY

117 **going to the corner:** walking on to the next intersection beyond his house.
120 **such a place . . . such a life:** a derogatory (negative) way of suggesting it was a very poor place to be.
132 **be among his people:** be back with his own family and relatives, feeling that he belonged there.

INFORMAL SPEECH

119 **how he was taking it:** how he was adjusting himself to such a life.
120 **how it had been with him:** what his own experience and feelings had been like.
127 **take a walk:** go for a stroll, go walking with no aim to go anywhere.

STANDARD VOCABULARY

112 ***alien:** strange, foreign.
112 **unrelated to:** having no connection with.
113 **tormented:** caused him continuous, agonizing pain.
118 **bewildered:** confused, unable to think what to do.
118 **disgusted:** feeling great distaste or annoyance, "put off by."
122 ***advice:** words of wisdom. ("Advice" is never used in the plural form.)
122 ***monotony:** boring sameness of things.
125 **serious:** sober, thoughtful.
126 **appetite:** a desire to eat.
129 **stillness:** quietness.
129 ***oppress:** to crush or burden one, spiritually or physically.
133 **embrace:** put his arms around.

his sisters, walk across the floors of the house, sit in the old chairs, sleep in his bed, talk with his old man, eat at the table.

And now something he had forgotten while he had been away, something real but ugly in that life, had come swiftly, changing everything, changing the appearance and meaning of the house, the city, the whole valley, making it all ugly and unreal, making him wish to go away and never return. He could never come back. He could never enter the house again and go on with his life where he had left off.

Suddenly he was in the alley, climbing over the fence, walking through the yard. His mother had planted tomatoes, and peppers, and the smell of the growing plants was thick and acrid and very melancholy to him. There was a light in the kitchen, and he moved quietly toward it, hoping to see some of them without being seen. He walked close to the house, to the kitchen window, and looking in saw his youngest sister Martha washing dishes. He saw the old table, the old stove, and Martha, with her back turned to him; and all these things seemed so sad and so pathetic that tears came to his eyes, and he began to need a cigarette. He struck a match quietly on the bottom of his shoe and inhaled the smoke, looking at his little sister in the old house, a part of the monotony, Everything seemed very still, very clear, terribly sad; but he hoped his mother would enter the kitchen; he wanted to have another look at her. He wanted to see if his being away had changed her much. How would she look? Would she have that old angry look? He felt angry with himself for not being a good son, for not trying to make his mother happy, and he knew it was impossible.

He saw his brother Paul enter the kitchen for a drink of water, and for a moment he wanted to cry out the boy's name, everything that was good in him, all his love, rushing to the face and form of the boy; but he restrained himself, inhaling deeply, tightening his lips. In the kitchen, the boy seemed lost, bewildered, imprisoned. Looking at his brother, he began to cry softly, saying, Jesus, O Jesus, Jesus.

He no longer wished to see his mother. He would become so angry that he would do something crazy. He walked quietly through the yard, hoisted himself over the fence, and jumped to the alley. He began to walk away, his grief mounting in him. When he was far

GLOSSARY

141 **alley:** a small, narrow lane or roadway bordering the back part of a yard or piece of property.
141 **yard:** an enclosed land around a house or a building.
143 **acrid:** unpleasantly sharp-smelling or bitter-tasting.
143 **kitchen:** the room where families prepare the meals and often eat informally.
159 **Jesus, O Jesus:** one name of the Christians' God, used here to express anguish and misery.
161 **hoisted himself:** lifted himself, climbed.

INFORMAL SPEECH

140 **go on:** continue.
140 **left off:** stopped.
148 **struck a match:** lit a match to light his cigarette.
151 **have . . . (a) . . . look at:** try to look quickly, but also carefully. (Note the word *look* in each of the next two lines.)
160 **do something crazy:** lose his self-control and behave in a strange or wild manner.

STANDARD VOCABULARY

137 **swiftly:** rapidly, fast.
138 **meaning:** profound significance.
143 **melancholy:** depressingly sad.
147 **pathetic:** arousing pity, tenderness, or both.
148 **inhaled:** drew into the lungs.
154 **impossible:** not able to be done.
157 ***restrained:** kept under tight control.
158 **imprisoned:** kept in jail, fig or lit; locked in.
162 ***grief:** deep sadness, usually because of a great loss.
162 **mounting:** rising.

enough away not to be heard, he began to sob, loving them passionately and hating the ugliness and monotony of their lives. He felt himself hurrying away from home, from his people, crying bitterly in the darkness of the clear night, weeping because there was nothing he could do, not one confounded thing.

GLOSSARY

165 **bitterly:** very unhappily and hopelessly.

INFORMAL SPEECH

166 **confounded:** mild swearing, a polite substitute for "damned." (Standard meaning: confused.)

STANDARD VOCABULARY

163 **passionately:** with strong, unchecked feelings.

1. COMPOSITION: IMAGINING YOUR OWN ENDING

WHO WILL OPEN THE DOOR?

Since "Going Home" is a story to stir one's feelings and fantasies, you may not be ready right away to analyze and discuss all the meanings that can be found there. That can come later.

Instead, let your imagination carry the story on a bit farther, perhaps even to what might have happened if the young man had *not* walked away from his home. . . .

Suppose, in fact, he went up and knocked on the door. Would it be opened by his sister Martha, his brother Paul, his mother, or his father? Would he go away again, or would he decide to stay there? Would the greeting he received make any difference? Never mind about using proper punctuation at first. What is important is your own interpretation and the way you use your imagination:

1. Make up a name for the young man, and decide who will answer when he knocks.
2. You may add details, such as his feelings as he stands waiting for someone to come, or a description of the one who opens the door.
3. Try to write your dialogue the way you imagine their conversation would sound.
4. Keep the whole scene fairly short—no more than a page or two.
5. Be prepared to share your ending by reading it aloud to your classmates.

Remember, there is no "right" or "wrong" point of view when one is using one's imagination. Different ways of seeing or interpreting the story will simply make it more interesting to everyone else.

2. SPECIAL PROJECT: READ . . . AND READ AGAIN

SEARCHING FOR THE DEEPER MEANINGS

A Special Project to Work On Together in Four Small Groups

Occasionally we read a story that is not quite like any other. Saroyan's "Going Home" is just such a story.

On the surface it looks very simple, as the one-sentence preview ("In the Story") seems to suggest. But there are little things about it—mysterious things—that make you wonder. For instance:

Why isn't the man ever named?

How does he happen to arrive so unexpectedly here in his hometown?

What is really behind those surprising swings of his moods from one extreme to the other?

What sort of conversation is this supposed to be, with no quotation marks to set it off from the rest of the text?

Since these questions may not even *have* any definite answers, let's try some others that might point the way to a deeper understanding and a greater appreciation of Saroyan's story as the work of art that it is.

For the sake of convenience, the story has been divided into four parts labeled I, II, III, and IV. Although the sections are not equal in length, each one represents an important "stage" or psychological process that the young man seems to reach and has to go through in his experience of going home. Each of the four groups will work together on *one* section.

Directions

1. Even though everyone in the class has read the story, now is the time to take another look by giving it what we call a "close reading." Each member of the group can take turns with the others in reading your group's section aloud. Take your time, and check the vocabulary whenever you need to.
2. After reading aloud your part of the story together, silently read through all the study questions for your section. Your teacher will give you some directions or guidelines as to how he or she would like you to handle and report on them.
3. The last group of questions is for the class to consider and talk about together after each group has reported on its own section.

Section I

In this beginning part, the author makes us feel that *we are there.* Watch closely to see how he does it.

1. ***Observation:*** The young man's experience in arriving in his home town is described in a very physical way, through his senses. What does he see, hear, and smell?
   Inference: How are the senses of taste and touch also suggested?
2. ***Observation:*** In the first three paragraphs, list all the words that are about living and growing.
   Inference: What do you think that the writer is trying to communicate to us about the young man's feelings and state of mind through those words, as well as through those strange philosophical expressions at the end of paragraph 3?
3. ***Observation:*** What makes the young man notice the water? What words would you use to describe the old man's behavior?
   Inference: Why do you think that the young man drinks so much water?

4. ***Observation:*** Check or make a list of all the words having a pleasant or favorable connotation:

    In the first three paragraphs;
    In the rest of your section, the part about *water.*

    Inference: What effect (or tone) do these connotative words produce? What kind of title do you think would fit this section?

Section II

In this part, we continue to go with the young man as he strolls along the streets of his home town, but now we are also sharing his memories:

1. ***Observation:*** How long has the young man been away? What additional facts do we learn about him here?
   Inference: The old man says, "You sure was thirsty." What do you think the young man's thirst might represent? What does his drinking so much water mean?
2. ***Observation:*** The young man calls it a "mistake" that he is here in his home town. How did he get here (and why?), and what plans does he have?
   Inference: A "memory trip" is an experience of reliving one's memories. What memories does he recall *before* he meets Tony, and how do they make him feel?
3. ***Observation:*** What memories does he associate with Tony Rocca? In what ways are his memories mixed up with his dreams?
   Inference: Dreams are often rather idealistic; that is, one sees life as one would *like* it to be. In what sense are some of his memories (and his dreams) about Tony idealistic?
4. ***Observation:*** Check or make a list of all the words in this section that have a pleasant or a favorable connotation:

    Before he meets Tony;
    After he sees Tony.

    Inference: Why does the young man continually use expressions like "the same as ever" and "again"? Can you point to one or two passages that show a relationship between his memories and his idealism? As a group, what title would you give to this section?

Section III

This important section, although shorter than the first two, marks the beginning of a *transition process.* (*Transition* means "passage from one position to another.")

1. ***Observation:*** What is the cause of the sudden change in the young man's mood? What was his former position or viewpoint, and what has it become now?

Inference: We are not told specifically what he is remembering about his early life, but from the hints provided in this part, what are some of those other things that you imagine he might have experienced?

2. ***Observation:*** List in a column (on separate lines) all the words having negative connotations in the long paragraph beginning, "He saw the house. . . ."
Inference: Negative types of words usually express negative feelings. Beside each of the words in your list, write what emotion it seems to indicate.
3. ***Observation:*** Check back to the paragraph (in Section II) that begins: "He turned down Fulton Street. . . ." Both that paragraph and the one beginning "He saw the house. . . ." are about his home town. What differences do you see in these two descriptions? What does the sentence mean that begins: "The stillness of the valley. . . ."?
Inference: Ambivalence is a feeling of being attracted to something, while at the same time wanting to get away from it. It is like loving and hating someone, both at once. What kind of ambivalent feelings, or conflicts, is this young man having about:

    His relationship to his home?
    The sight of his family?
    The thought of a "home-cooked meal"?
    The memory of his relations with his mother?

4. ***Observation:*** What sort of thoughts does he have regarding his younger brother Paul? Do you see any conflicts in this relationship?
Inference: Is he being idealistic or realistic about his role as an older brother? Why do you think he is taking that role so seriously? What title would your group consider to be appropriate for this section?

Section IV

The real nature of the young man's emotional conflict becomes clearer in the last part of the story. His relations with his family certainly are involved, but something else very important is there also.

1. ***Observation:*** What are the young man's feelings about his family as this section begins? Do these feelings seem to be in line or agree with the attitude he expressed toward them:

    When he talked to Tony?
    When he "walked slowly before the house"?

   Inference: Do you think that his "something real but ugly" refers to anything definite that actually happened, or not? What do you think he might be talking about?
2. ***Observation:*** The author returns to some very physical description in the last scene, beginning with "Suddenly he was in the alley. . . ." What senses are involved in this description?
Inference: Describe the effects of these sensory impressions as compared with those of the first three paragraphs of the story.

3. ***Observation:*** Family relationships are often ambivalent: that is, people can feel opposite ways about each other at the same time. Where does this sort of ambivalence appear in this family's relations?
   Inference: What is meant by the sentence that begins: "He felt angry with himself for. . . ."? (What does he mean by being "a good son"?) In addition to anger, what else is the young man feeling?
4. ***Observation:*** What is the nature of the conflict that is going on inside this young man? How does he "resolve" his struggle?
   Inference: In what way or ways do you think the young man will be changed as a result of his decision?

For the Whole Class to Consider Together

1. Water is a favorite natural symbol with writers because, like fire, it can suggest so many things. Consider:
   a. *Its practical usefulness.* In addition to satisfying a very thirsty young man, what are some of the *other* uses that might be found for water? Which can you associate with this story?
   b. *Its emotional symbolism.* In this statement, "The water; yes, it was good. . . ." (p. 123, line 110), what does the water seem to be symbolizing? Why is the young man now rejecting it? When Paul finally does appear, what does he do? Could there be any symbolic meaning here?
   c. *Its religious or moral symbolism.* Water is employed in several important religious rituals. Mention several that you know about, and explain its symbolic significance in each one. What connection can you make between this moral significance of water and the young man's comments about feeling "angry with himself" and earlier, his "mistakes"?
2. Psychologists have given much study and attention to the stage in a person's life that they call "the identity crisis," which usually comes in late adolescence. At this time the young person realizes that he or she can no longer depend upon the parents to supply all of one's needs and to make the important decisions in one's life. It is time for him or her to become an adult:
   a. From ancient times to the present, many societies have recognized and celebrated this vital process by means of initiation rites. Look up these words and explain the meaning. The term "rite of passage" is also used for the same process. What is the literal meaning of this expression?
   b. Many great writers have used the symbolism of "going on a journey" to describe this experience. How does the story "Going Home" become a symbolic "journey":

      From the young man's outward experience to his inner feelings?
      From idealism to realism?
      From childhood to adulthood?

   c. Some literary artists have portrayed this type of journey as a "descent into hell," while others have emphasized the universal human yearning (desire) to "return to paradise." Which interpretation would you apply to the story "Going Home"?

3. The sad aspects of such a story and its implications are obvious, but it has *positive* (beneficial) elements also. What positive or constructive factors can there be:

    About getting acquainted with (in touch with) our own inner feelings?
    About becoming more realistic?
    About learning to depend more on ourselves?

    In the long run, how might this process have constructive or beneficial effects on our relationships with our families?

3. GRAMMAR: PUNCTUATING DIRECT QUOTATIONS

YOUR READERS LOOK FOR SIGNALS, TOO!

Motorists who are driving along city streets depend on traffic lights to let them know when to cross a busy intersection and when to wait for their turn. Without signals, drivers could get mixed up in a real traffic jam.

Readers, too, could become pretty mixed up if the passage they were reading had no "signals" and the words and sentences simply went right on without stopping. The cues or signals that are used in English to help guide the reader are capital letters, spacing, and punctuation. Occasionally, a writer such as Saroyan, for reasons of his own, omits the usual or conventional punctuation in written conversation. It is easier for the reader, however, if the conversation or dialogue is punctuated to look like what it is: the exact words spoken by two (or more) people to each other.

Whether or not you ever have occasion to write a story yourself, by learning to use conventional punctuation, capitalization, and spacing you will gain greater control over the language and more awareness of what the reader expects. In order to show how this works and also to practice managing direct quotations in your own writing, try the following exercise.

Each of the following numbered passages comes from one of the stories in this book. All the selections contain direct quotations, some of which involve more than one speaker.

A. First, read the entire passage.
B. Underline the *exact words only* of each speaker so that you will know what to enclose in quotation marks.
C. Then rewrite the passage, using conventional spacing (indentation when needed), capitalization, and punctuation. Add the kind of end punctuation you think is required.
D. If time permits, check back on the composition-dialogue you wrote, and make any necessary revisions in the punctuation, capitalization, and spacing.

1. Business is bad one undertaker told me. people don't die like they used to.
2. Capitalism said the student patiently is bound to collapse within a few decades.
3. Yes I shouted. more like it he said. now Shirley can you put a ribbon in your hair or a bobby pin. it's too messy. yes I bawled.
4. They are all at work he said my wife, my daughter, and her husband.
5. I made a little church of my hands and said hear O Israel . . . then I called out in Yiddish please, good night good night. Ssh.
6. He tried not to grin, and said damned nonsense.
7. Bosh said the businessman. that's an extreme view. hunger said the second student is always extreme.
8. Ach, Clara my father asked what does she do there till six o'clock she can't even put the plates on the table. Christmas said my mother coldly. ho! ho! my father said. Christmas. what's the harm.

When you have finished writing out this exercise, you may check your rewritten passages with the original versions. In a few instances there may be a difference of opinion regarding commas or end punctuation; your instructor can be the final authority. For the rest of the corrections, however, ask yourself:

Are my quotation marks in the same places as the author's?
Did I indent and capitalize in all the right places?
The author did not place any commas or periods under or outside of the quotation marks. Did I?

4. LANGUAGE USAGE: TWO-WORD VERBS

CONNECTIONS: A CROSS-CLUE PUZZLE COMPOSED OF TWO-WORD VERBS

You can do this puzzle in pairs, in groups, or on your own.

When prepositions or adverbs follow a verb in such a way that the verb takes on a new, idiomatic meaning, we call such a combination a "two-word verb."

The adverbs or prepositions needed to solve this cross-clue puzzle are all connected with either one of the two verbs: *look* or *swear*. The definition given below matches the two-word verb combination of the corresponding number.* The two-word verbs in the puzzle may go either across or down.

Each answer connects with a previous solution by way of one or more common letters. Study the two examples beginning with 1:

*The definitions are adapted from those found in *The Oxford Advanced Learner's Dictionary* (London, 1974).

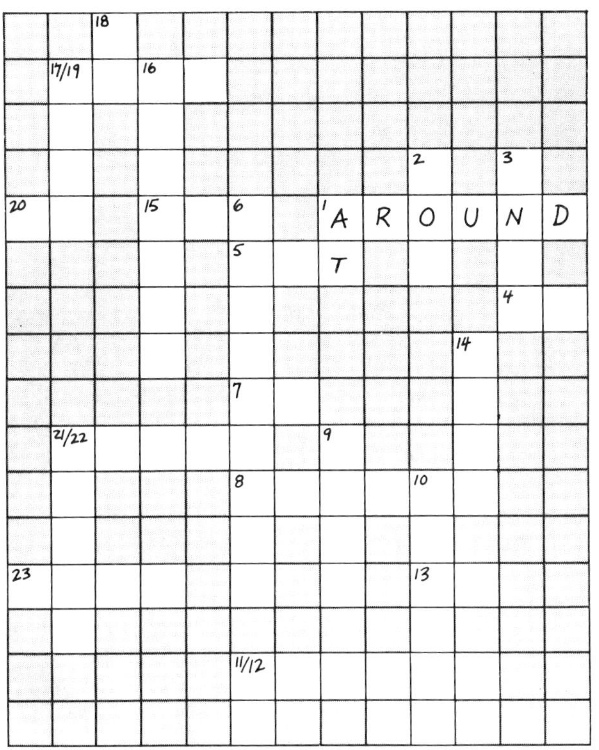

1. Casually inspect, or shop in various places:
   look a r o u n d.
   Turn the eyes toward:
   look a t.
2. Try to find:
   look __ __ __.
3. Investigate something:
   look __ __ __ __.
4. Watch, as a spectator:
   look __ __.
5. Gaze through a window:
   look __ __ __.
6. Anticipate with pleasure:
   look __ __ __ __ __ __ __ __ __.
7. Denounce by cursing:
   swear __ __.
8. Consider oneself better, despise:
   look __ __ __ __ __ __.
9. Turn one's eyes to another direction:
   look __ __ __ __.
10. Take care of, or beware of:
    look __ __ __ __ __ __.
11. Remember or recall:
    look __ __ __ __ __ __.
12. Have great confidence in:
    swear __ __.
13. Declare or say emphatically:
    swear __ __.
14. Pay a short visit to:
    look __ __ __ __.
15. Declare that one will stop doing something:
    swear __ __ __.
16. Check carefully, or skim (as a book):
    look __ __ __ __ __ __ __ __.
17. Admire:
    look __ __ __ __.
18. Appear better, or search for information:
    look __ __.
19. View or consider:
    look __ __ __ __.
20. Cause to take the oath of office:
    swear __ __.
21. Take care of:
    look __ __ __ __ __.
22. Move or work fast (colloq):
    look __ __ __ __ __.
23. Scan or inspect:
    look __ __ __ __.

Leonard Q. Ross (1908–)

It was the writer's own experience of teaching English to adult immigrants that inspired the Hyman Kaplan stories of Leo C. Rosten, who wrote them under the pseudonym (pen name) of Leonard Q. Ross. In a sense, the author is an immigrant, having been born in Poland in 1908 and been brought to the United States in his infancy.

Rosten was educated at the University of Chicago, where he earned his Ph.D. degree in 1937. As a political scientist and teacher, he made some thoroughgoing studies of Washington newsmen and their operations in his book, The Washington Correspondents *(1937), while another work of his,* Hollywood: The Movie Colony, the Movie Makers *(1941), presents an objective, sociological study of the film capital during the most active years of moving picture production.*

For many years, Rosten's humorous writings have been published in books and periodicals (such as The Wall Street Journal*). He has also written the screenplays for eight movies and has published over thirty books, including a witty, yet serious, novel about an Army psychiatrist entitled* Captain Newman, M.D. *(1961). A more recent work is his readable nonfiction book* The Joys of Yiddish *(1968).*

In addition to The Education of H*Y*M*A*N K*A*P*L*A*N *(1937), from which our story is taken, he brought out another collection of favorites,* The Return of H*Y*M*A*N K*A*P*L*A*N *(1959), twenty-two years after the popular original work.*

IX

*Mr. K*A*P*L*A*N and Vocabulary*

Story Setting: *An ESL classroom for adult immigrants in New York City is the setting for* The Education of H*Y*M*A*N K*A*P*L*A*N, *a collection of short stories first published separately in national magazines. Since the same familiar characters appeared in them all, these humorous and popular stories soon were among the best sellers of the 1930s.*

In the Story: *Mr. Parkhill, the ESL teacher, spends another evening session trying very hard to help his students to improve their mastery of the English language. The vocabulary lesson begins enthusiastically, but, as usual, the teacher's efforts are somewhat hampered by the amazing mistakes of our favorite pupil, Mr. Hyman Kaplan.*

More on Humor: *As you may already suspect, "Mr. K*A*P*L*A*N and Vocabulary" is a humorous, friendly story. As though sharing an "inside" joke with the author, we chuckle at each character's mistakes, while we recall our own equally ridiculous blunders from the past.*

The same comic devices discussed earlier ("Hints About Humor," p. 101) can be found in the story we are about to read. One aspect of humor that was suggested in both "The Loudest Voice" and in "Señor Payroll" but is more prominent in this story is satire, *a form of mockery of people or institutions that take themselves too seriously. For instance, Mr. Abramovitch understands very well that his Jewish neighbors have reason to feel "uptight" about the Christmas program, so he jokes lightly about both Christians and Jews in order to keep the peace. In "Señor Payroll" it is "the Company"—and perhaps bureaucracy in general—that is the target of Barrett's satire.*

The humor that appears in Ross's story, as in all the other Hyman Kaplan tales, is poking gentle fun at all his characters for their weaknesses and failings. (In a more exaggerated, unsympathetic form, this kind of satire could become caricature, *in which a person is seen only by way of his or her particular faults.) In fact, it is that very human quality that charms us, so that we identify with each character in turn, even while we smile at the absurdity of their behavior. In the end, we recognize that we are really laughing at ourselves and at our own sense of superiority, which seems to persist in spite of all our mistakes.*

*Since "Mr. K*A*P*L*A*N and Vocabulary" involves the subject of language and learning, the author appropriately relies especially on the familiar device of contrasting highly formal, correct speech with outrageous examples of broken English. In addition, we can expect to find some less obvious, but equally comic, types of wordplay such as puns and words with double meanings (double entendres).*

A final note: In order to indicate Hyman Kaplan's unique way of pronouncing (or mispronouncing) English words, the author spells them phonetically—as they sound—*according to English pronunciation rules. The best way to figure them out is to read them aloud, trying to pronounce the words just as they are written.*

"VOCABULARY!" said Mr. Parkhill. "Above all, we must work on vocabulary."

He was probably right. For the students in the beginners' grade, vocabulary was a dire and pressing need. Spelling, after all, was not of such immediate importance to people who did little writing during their daily lives. Grammar? They needed the substance—words, phrases, idioms—to which grammar might be applied. Pronunciation? Mr. Parkhill had come to the reluctant conclusion that for some of them accurate pronunciation was a near impossibility. Take Mr. Kaplan, for example. Mr. Kaplan was a willing, an earnest, aye! an enthusiastic pupil. And yet, despite Mr. Parkhill's tireless tutelage, Mr. Kaplan referred to the most celebrated of movie lovers as "Clock Gebble," who, it appeared, showed a fine set of teeth "venever he greens." Mr. Kaplan, when asked to use "heaven" in a sentence, had replied promptly, "In sommer, ve all heaven a fine time."

Yes, vocabulary—that, Mr. Parkhill thought, was the greatest need.

". . . And so tonight I shall write a list of new, useful words on the blackboard. To each student I shall assign three words. Write a sentence in your notebooks using each

GLOSSARY

8 **aye:** (OD) yes, indeed! Also an affirmative vote, as opposed to the negative, "nay."
8 **tireless tutelage:** (hum frml) patient instruction.
9 **"Clock Gebble":** Clark Gable, the best-known and one of the most popular of the Hollywood film lovers during the 1930s.
10 **venever he greens:** whenever he grins, or smiles broadly.

INFORMAL SPEECH

1 **above all:** the most important thing.
3 **after all:** in spite of everything else.

STANDARD VOCABULARY

3 **dire:** terrible, dreadful.
3 **immediate:** direct, not to be put off.
4 ***substance:** matter, real meaning.
5 ***applied:** given practical use.
6 ***reluctant:** unwilling.
6 **accurate:** exact, correct.
7 **earnest:** serious.
8 **despite:** in spite of.
9 **celebrated:** famous.
10 **heaven:** home of God, place of supreme happiness.

word. Make sure you have no mistakes. You may use your dictionaries, if you wish. Then go to the blackboard and copy your three sentences for class analysis."

The class was impressed and pleased. Miss Mitnick's ordinarily shy expression changed to one of eager expectancy. Mrs. Moskowitz, simple soul that she was, prepared her notebook with stolid solemnity. And Mr. Kaplan, in the middle of the front row, took out his box of crayons, smiled more broadly than ever (a chance to use his crayons always intensified Mr. Kaplan's natural euphoria), turned to a fresh page in his notebook, and printed, slowly and with great love:

VOCAPULERY

(Prectice in Book. Then Going to Blackb. and putting on.)

by

H*Y*M*A*N K*A*P*L*A*N

For the title he chose purple crayon; for the methodological observation in parentheses, orange; for the "by," yellow. His name he printed, fondly, as always: in red and blue and flamboyant green. As he handled the crayons Mr. Kaplan smiled with the sweet serenity of one in direct communication with his Muse.

Mr. Parkhill assigned three words to each student and the beginners' grade went into action. Lips pursed, brows wrinkled, distant looks appeared in thoughtful eyes; heads were scratched, chins stroked, dictionaries fluttered. Mr. Kaplan tackled his three words

GLOSSARY

17 **Miss Mitnick's . . . Mrs. Moskowitz:** two of the characters who regularly appeared in the Hyman Kaplan stories. Use of the formal titles "Miss" and "Mrs." was a common practice at this time, especially when students were of college age or older.
20 **crayons:** wax pencils in different colors, usually used by children.
21 **natural euphoria:** (hum exag) a usual state of feeling extremely happy; "high."
23 **methodological observation:** (hum frml) notation or comment on what was supposed to be done.
23 **in parentheses:** within the punctuation marks, as: (. . .).
26 **his Muse:** (spec) In ancient mythology, one of the goddesses who inspired poets and artists (hum frml).
28 **lips pursed:** lips drawn together in tiny wrinkles; puckered.
29 **fluttered:** (onomat) made the sound of turning pages.

INFORMAL SPEECH

27 **went into action:** began to work hard and fast.

STANDARD VOCABULARY

16 **analysis:** critical judgment.
17 ***impressed:** affected seriously and deeply.
17 **ordinarily:** usually.
17 **shy:** timid with other people, self-conscious.
18 ***expectancy:** the state of happily awaiting something; anticipation.
19 **stolid:** not easily excited.
19 **solemnity:** sober dignity.
20 ***broadly:** widely.
21 **intensified:** made stronger.
24 **fondly:** lovingly.
25 **flamboyant:** very vivid and noticeable; loud.
26 **serenity:** peacefulness.
26 **communication:** contact, usually by words.
29 **stroked:** rubbed gently.
29 **tackled:** (fig) began to work on them very energetically.

with gusto: *pitcher, fascinate, university*. Mr. Parkhill noticed that Mr. Kaplan's cerebration was accompanied by strange sounds: he pronounced each word, and tried fitting it into a sentence, in a whisper which could be heard halfway across the room. He muttered the entire process of his reasoning. Mr. Kaplan, it seemed, thought only in dialogue with his other self. There was something uncanny about it.

"Pitcher . . . pitcher," Mr. Kaplan whispered. "Is maybe a pitcher for milk? Is maybe a pitcher on de vall—art! Two minninks! 'Plizz take milk from de pitcher.' Fine! 'De pitcher hengs cockeye.' Also fine! Pitcher . . . pitcher."

This private colloquy was not indulged in without a subtle design, for Mr. Kaplan watched Mr. Parkhill's facial expressions carefully out of the corner of his eye as he whispered to himself. Mr. Kaplan hoped to discover which interpretation of "pitcher" was acceptable. But Mr. Parkhill had long ago learned to beware of Mr. Kaplan's strategies; he preserved a stern facial immobility as Mr. Kaplan's stage whispers floated through the classroom.

When Mr. Kaplan had finished his three sentences he reread them proudly, nodded happily to Mr. Parkhill (who, though pretending to be watching Miss Schneiderman at the blackboard, was watching Mr. Kaplan out of the corner of *his* eye), and went to the board. He whispered the sentences aloud as he copied them. Ecstasy illuminated his face.

"Well," said Mr. Parkhill after all the students had transcribed their work, "let's start at this end. Mr. Bloom, I think?"

Mr. Bloom read his sentences quickly:

GLOSSARY

30 **pitcher:** a container from which a liquid is poured.
30 **cerebration:** (hum frml) brainwork, thought processes.
34 **uncanny:** weird, strange.
38 **colloquy:** (hum frml) conversation.
38 **subtle design:** secret, underlying purpose.
41 **strategies:** carefully calculated plans.
42 **immobility:** lack of motion, rigidity.
47 **ecstasy:** delight, blissful happiness.
48 **transcribed:** copied (in this case, on the board).

INFORMAL SPEECH

37 **cockeye:** cockeyed, or crooked.
39 **watched . . . out of the corner of his eye:** looked in a stealthy, surreptitious way, not wanting to be seen.
42 **stage whispers:** (lit) whispers loud enough to be heard from the stage to the audience.

STANDARD VOCABULARY

30 **fascinate:** enchant, charm.
31 ***was accompanied by:** occurred at the same time as, went with.
32 **whisper:** (onomat) softly spoken sound.
32 **muttered:** (onomat) spoke under his breath, too low to be understood.
38 **private:** secret and personal.
38 ***indulged in:** (hum frml) carried on, enjoyed.
40 ***interpretation:** meaning or explanation.
41 **beware of:** be careful about.
42 **preserved:** kept unchanged (maintained).
42 **stern:** displeased, hard.
42 **floated:** drifted through the air.
44 **proudly:** feeling pleased with himself.
44 **nodded:** moved the head up and down in agreement.
45 ***pretending:** putting on an act, making believe.
47 **illuminated:** lit up.

She *declined* the money.
In her red hat she falt *conspicuous.*
Last Saturday, I saw a *remarkable* show.

"Excellent!" said Mr. Parkhill. "Are there any questions?" There were no questions. Mr. Parkhill corrected "falt" and the exercise continued. On the whole, all went surprisingly well. Except for those of Mrs. Moskowitz, who worked havoc with "niggardly" ("It was a niggardly night."), the sentences were quite good. Mr. Parkhill was delighted. The experiment in vocabulary-building was proving a decided success. At last Mr. Kaplan's three sentences came up.

"Mr. Kaplan is next, I believe." There was a note of caution in Mr. Parkhill's voice.

Mr. Kaplan went to the board. "Mine foist void, ladies an' gantleman," he announced smiling (Mr. Kaplan always did things with a certain bravado), "is 'pitcher.' So de santence is: 'Oh, how beauriful is dis pitcher.'"

Mr. Parkhill saw that Mr. Kaplan had neatly straddled two words by deliberately noncommittal usage. "Er—Mr. Kaplan. The word is 'p-i-t-c-h-e-r,' not 'p-i-c-t-u-r-e.'"

Too late did Mr. Parkhill realize that he had given Mr. Kaplan the clue he had been seeking.

"Mr. Pockheel," Mr. Kaplan replied with consummate simplicity, "dis void *is* 'p-i-t-c-h-e-r.'"

"But when you say, 'Oh, how *beautiful* this pitcher is,'" said Mr. Parkhill, determined to force Mr. Kaplan to the wall, "you suggest—"

"Ah!" Mr. Kaplan murmured, with a tolerant smile. "In som houses is even de *pitchers* beauriful."

"Read your next sentence, Mr. Kaplan."

GLOSSARY

56 **worked havoc:** (hum exag) caused chaos and destruction.
56 **niggardly:** cheap, stingy, miserly.
60 **a note of caution:** a slightly questioning tone of voice, since Mr. Parkhill's experience with Hyman Kaplan had led him to expect surprising answers.
64 **straddled:** (fig) seemed to favor two sides; lit, to sit or stand with legs spread on each side of something.
68 **consummate simplicity:** the utmost innocence (hum frml and exag).

INFORMAL SPEECH

55 **on the whole:** in general, for the most part.
59 **came up:** came next by turn.
64 **neatly:** cleverly.
71 **force . . . to the wall:** make someone admit he is wrong; corner a person or crowd one into a corner.

STANDARD VOCABULARY

51 **declined:** refused.
52 **conspicuous:** very noticeable, in an embarrassing way.
53 ***remarkable:** outstanding.
58 **experiment:** new effort or undertaking in the process of learning.
58 **decided:** (adj.) definite.
62 **bravado:** a brave appearance, a good front.
64 **deliberately:** intentionally.
65 **noncommittal:** indefinite.
66 **clue:** idea or information that suggests a possible answer (key to a solution).
67 **seeking:** looking for.
70 **determined:** unshakeable in his purpose.
72 **tolerant:** kindly, indulgent.

Mr. Kaplan went on, smiling. "De sacond void, ladies an' gantleman, is 'fescinate'— an' believe me is a planty hod void! So is mine santence: 'In India is all kinds snake-fescinators.'"

"You are thinking of snake-*charmers*." (Mr. Kaplan seemed to have taken the dictionary's description of "fascinate" too literally.) "Try 'fascinate' in another sentence, please."

Mr. Kaplan gazed ceilingward with a masterful insouciance, one eye half-closed. Then he ventured: "You *fescinate* me."

GLOSSARY

78 **snake-charmers:** Indian entertainers or holy men (fakirs) who tame poisonous snakes with their music.
80 **ceilingward:** toward the ceiling (top) of the room.
80 **with a masterful insouciance:** (hum frml) with an air (attitude) of complete control and indifference or nonchalance.

INFORMAL SPEECH

STANDARD VOCABULARY

81 **ventured:** cautiously tried out or attempted.

Mr. Parkhill hurried Mr. Kaplan on to his last word.

"Toid void, faller-students, is 'univoisity.' De santence usink dis void: 'Elaven yiss is married mine vife an' minesalf, so is time commink for our tvalft *univoisity*.' "

It was the opportunity for which Miss Mitnick had been waiting. "Mr. Kaplan mixes up two words," she said. "He means 'anniversary.' 'University' is a high college—the *highest* college."

Mr. Kaplan listened to this unwelcome correction with a fine sufferance. Then he arched his eyebrows and said, "You got right, Mitnick. Hau Kay! So I'll givink anodder santence: 'Som pipple didn't have aducation in a *univoisity*' "—he glanced meaningfully at Miss Mitnick—" 'but just de same, dey havink efter elaven yiss de tvalft *annivoisery*.' "

With this retort courteous Mr. Kaplan took his seat. Through the next few recitations he was strangely silent. He did not bother to offer a correction of Miss Kowalski's spectacular misuse of "guess." ("Turn out the guess.") He did not as much as volunteer an opinion on Miss Hirschfield's "The cat omits a cry." For all his proud smile it was clear that Mr. Kaplan had suffered a deep hurt: like a smoldering cinder in his soul lay the thought of his humiliation at the mundane hands of one Rose Mitnick. He smiled as bravely as ever, but his silence was ominous. He seemed to be waiting, waiting. . . .

"Miss Mitnick, please," said Mr. Parkhill. A flame leaped into Mr. Kaplan's eyes.

Miss Mitnick's first sentence was "*Enamel* is used for painting chairs." Before she could read it Mr. Kaplan's voice rang out in triumph.

"Mistake by Mitnick! Ha! Mit *enimals* she is painting chairs? Ha!"

GLOSSARY

85 **Miss Mitnick:** In the Hyman Kaplan stories, Miss Mitnick is the star pupil and Mr. Kaplan's arch rival.
88 **fine sufferance:** (hum frml) extreme patience.
89 **arched his eyebrows:** raised his eyebrows, showing dignified displeasure.
92 **retort courteous:** (OD, hum frml) polite put-down.
95 **omits a cry:** she meant "emits," or lets out.
96 **had suffered a deep hurt:** to "suffer" means to be forced to experience great pain. An older (OD) meaning also is: to allow, or put up with.
96 **smoldering cinder:** (lit) a slow-burning piece of coal; (fig) a sore spot that rankles, a "slow burn."
97 **mundane:** worldly, profane (hum exag).
97 **one Rose Mitnick:** (hum form) a certain person named, used to show contempt and a sense of superiority.

INFORMAL SPEECH

82 **hurried . . . on to:** encouraged (or fig "pushed") him to go on without any delay or discussion.
93 **did not bother to:** didn't take the trouble or make any effort to.
94 **did not as much as:** didn't even try to.
95 **for all his . . . :** in spite of his. . . .
97 **at the . . . hands of:** by means of, suggesting that someone is responsible for.
101 **rang out:** sounded out very loudly.

STANDARD VOCABULARY

85 ***opportunity:** chance to accomplish something.
86 **anniversary:** yearly date marking an important event, such as one's marriage (a *wedding* anniversary).
88 **unwelcome:** not wanted.
92 **recitations:** students' oral replies to the teacher's questions.
93 ***spectacular:** (hum exag) sensational, striking.
94 **volunteer:** offer.
94 ***opinion:** a personal viewpoint.
96 **soul:** spirit, or conscious awareness.
97 ***humiliation:** deep embarrassment.
98 **ominous:** threatening.
99 **flame:** a spark of fire.
101 ***triumph:** joy in victory.

"The word is *'enamel,'* " said Mr. Parkhill coldly. "Not 'animal.' "

Rebuffed, Mr. Kaplan let Miss Mitnick's reading of that sentence, and her next, go unchallenged. But the flame burned in his eyes again when she read her final effort: "The prisoner stood in the *dock.*"

"Well," suggested Mr. Parkhill, before Mr. Kaplan, squirming with excitement in his chair, could offer a rash correction, "that's one way to use the word. The English use it that way. But there is a—er—more common usage. Can you use 'dock' in a more familiar meaning, Miss Mitnick?"

Miss Mitnick was silent.

"Anyone?"

"I like roast *duck!*" cried Mr. Kaplan promptly.

"*Dock!*" Mr. Parkhill said severely. "Not *duck!*" Once again Mr. Kaplan bowed to a cruel fate.

" 'Dock' isn't hard," said Mr. Parkhill encouragingly. "I'll give you a hint, class. Each of you, in coming to America, has had *direct experience with a dock.*" He smiled almost gaily, and waited.

The class went into that coma which signified thought, searching its collective memory of "coming to America." Mrs. Moskowitz closed her eyes as the recollection of her seasickness surged over her like a wave, and searched her memory no more. Mr. Kaplan, desperate to make the kill, whispered his associations tensely: " 'Dock' . . . Commink to America . . . boat . . . feesh . . . big vaves . . . cremps."

It was clear they were getting nowhere. (Mr. Norman Bloom, indeed, had forgotten all about "dock" in his sweet recollection of the pinochle game on the boat when he had won four and a half dollars.)

"Well, I'll make it even easier," said Mr. Parkhill lightly. "Where did your boats *land?*"

GLOSSARY

103 **enamel:** a kind of paint with a high gloss.
106 **prisoner:** someone accused of and held for law-breaking.
106 **in the dock:** British term for "before the court." The usual meaning of "dock" is a pier or a wharf where a ship (or boat) is tied up.
114 **bowed to a cruel fate:** (hum exag) accepted his miserable destiny in life.
119 **coma:** state of prolonged unconsciousness (hum exag).
121 **surged:** flowed or poured.
122 **make the kill:** (lit) said of a hunter who moves close to kill the animal he has been hunting.
123 **cremps:** cramps, stomach pains.
125 **pinochle game:** card game used for gambling.

INFORMAL SPEECH

107 **squirming:** moving his body in his chair, wiggling. (The British word is "wriggling.")
116 **give . . . a hint:** offer a clue to the meaning, give a helpful suggestion.
124 **getting nowhere:** not making any progress.

STANDARD VOCABULARY

104 **rebuffed:** rejected, put down.
105 **unchallenged:** without being questioned.
108 **rash:** impulsive, usually unwise.
109 **common:** ordinary or frequent, everyday.
114 **severely:** in a tone of sharp reproof.
116 **encouragingly:** offering support and hope.
117 **gaily:** cheerfully.
119 **signified:** meant, indicated.
119 ***collective:** combined recollection, memory of an event.
120 **recollection:** memory.
122 **desperate:** frantically anxious.
122 ***associations:** mental connections.
122 ***tensely:** nervously.
127 **lightly:** casually.

"New York!" cried Mr. Kaplan eagerly.

Mr. Parkhill cleared his throat. "Yes—of course. But I mean—"

A cry of joy came from the lips of Hyman Kaplan. "I got him! Ufcawss! *'Dock!'* Plain an tsimple! Ha!" He shot a look of triumph toward Miss Mitnick. "I'm soprize so high-cless a student like Mitnick, she knows all abot fency voids like 'univoisities' and 'annivoiseries,' she shouldn't know a leetle void like 'dock'!"

Something in Mr. Parkhill warned him. Not for a moment could he believe that Mr. Kaplan's confidence and enthusiasm were authentic indications of a correct answer. Mr. Parkhill would have preferred that some other student try a sentence with "dock." But no one volunteered.

"Very well, Mr. Kaplan," he said staring at his fingers, as if to break the impact of Mr. Kaplan's contribution.

Mr. Kaplan rose, inspiration in his eyes. His smile was so wide that his face seemed to be one ecstatic cavern. He cast majestic glances to both sides, as if reading the tribute in the faces of his fellow-students. Then he said, in one triumphant breath, "Hollo, Doc!"

Peace fell upon the room. Through the windows, from far away, there came the muted rumble of the Third Avenue elevated. The features of Abraham Lincoln on the wall took on, somehow, a softer understanding. But Mr. Parkhill was aware only of a strange and unaccountable ringing in his ears ("Hello, Doc!" . . . "Hello, Doc!") and, while shaking his head sadly to show Mr. Kaplan that he was wrong, he thought to himself with feverish persistence, "Vocabulary. Above all, vocabulary."

GLOSSARY

130 **cleared his throat:** consciously half-coughed, a sign of nervousness.
139 **break the impact:** soften by force.
143 **"Hollo, Doc":** When immigrants arrived at Ellis Island, New York harbor, they were immediately given immunization shots. The "doc" (doctor) was thus one of the first Americans to greet newcomers.
144 **fell upon:** settled over.
145 **rumble:** (onomat) noisy sound of a large vehicle.
145 **Third Avenue elevated:** N.Y. subway train on elevated tracks.
145 **Abraham Lincoln:** one of the most admired of all U.S. Presidents (1860–1865).
147 **ringing in his ears:** a sound in the head that usually means the blood pressure has risen, thus indicating higher inner tension.

INFORMAL SPEECH

135 **not for a moment could he believe that:** he did not believe it was at all likely or possible that. . . .
141 **inspiration:** a clever thought; a bright idea.
146 **took on:** assumed, seemed to have.
147 **shaking his head:** moving his head back and forth to indicate "No."
149 **above all:** more than anything else.

STANDARD VOCABULARY

132 **shot:** aimed, fired, as a gun.
136 **confidence:** sureness of oneself, self-certainty.
136 ***authentic:** true, reliable.
136 ***indications:** signs.
140 ***contribution:** offering.
141 ***inspiration:** (hum exag) divine influence (see also IS).
142 **ecstatic:** the adjective form of "ecstasy" (see Gloss).
142 **majestic:** kingly.
142 **tribute:** profound respect and appreciation (hum exag).
145 **muted:** somewhat softened in sound.
145 **features:** facial parts such as the nose or eyes.
147 **unaccountable:** mysterious, inexplainable, inexplicable.
149 **feverish:** agitated, intense, irrational.
149 ***persistence:** determination to continue.

1. STUDY QUESTIONS

DISCOVERING THE STORY THROUGH OBSERVATION AND INFERENCE

1. ***Observation:*** As an ESL teacher, why does Mr. Parkhill consider the teaching of vocabulary to be so important—more so than spelling and grammar, for instance?
   Inference: Would you call Mr. Parkhill the "persona" in this story? (For a definition, see "Point of View" under the Literary Terms.) Explain how you can tell.
2. ***Observation:*** We are first introduced to Hyman Kaplan through examples of his use (and misuse) of English. What are the kinds of mistakes that he makes? Give some examples.
   Inference: What can we infer about him both from his method and from his manner of writing his name?
3. ***Observation:*** What is each of the following expressions saying about the person referred to:

   "Mr. Parkhill's tireless tutelage"?
   "Miss Mitnick's . . . eager expectancy"?
   the "stolid solemnity" of Mrs. Moskowitz?

   Inference: Can you recognize this somewhat exaggerated formality as irony? (See Literary Terms and More on Humor, p. 135.) What quality in each of the characters is the author satirizing, and why?
4. ***Observation:*** What is Mr. Kaplan's problem with his vocabulary word, "pitcher"?
   Inference: Why has Mr. Parkhill "preserved a stern facial immobility"? What does this tell us about the teacher-student relationship of Mr. Parkhill and Hyman Kaplan?
5. ***Observation:*** How does Mr. Kaplan solve his little problem? Are your sympathies with him or with his teacher? Why?
   Inference: What are the implications of Mr. Kaplan's answering Mr. Parkhill "with consummate simplicity" (p. 139, line 68) at one point and "masterful insouciance" (p. 140, line 80) a moment later?
6. ***Observation:*** What goes wrong when Hyman Kaplan first tries to use his word, "fascinate"?
   Inference: Why has Mr. Parkhill "hurried Mr. Kaplan on to his last word" after Mr. Kaplan's second attempt at using the word? Do you think Mr. Kaplan meant anything improper by it?
7. ***Observation:*** What does the conversation about the word "university" tell us about the attitudes of Miss Mitnick and Mr. Kaplan toward each other?
   Inference: What is Hyman Kaplan "waiting" for, in line 98 (p. 141).

8. ***Observation:*** When the word "duck" comes up, how does Mr. Kaplan respond? How does his behavior here compare with his earlier actions?
   Inference: So far, what seems to be Mr. Kaplan's motivation as a student? What could you recommend for him to do to improve his English?
9. ***Observation:*** What is Mr. Parkhill's method for trying to help his class get the right meaning of "dock"?
   Inference: What effect does this have on each of the members of the class? Is it a good method for teaching, do you think?
10. ***Observation:*** The final scene is humorous because it is such a letdown after a suspenseful build-up. What are the ways (and words) the author uses to build up the reader's expectations to this point?
    Inference: What final impression is created by the last paragraph?

2. VOCABULARY STUDY: A. WORD FORMS

USE THE RIGHT WORD FORMS

"VOCABULARY!" said Mr. Parkhill. "Above all, we must work on vocabulary."

A story like this provides us with an especially good opportunity for vocabulary enrichment, and so more words than usual have been starred in the Standard Vocabulary columns.

In keeping up your word forms chart, or in completing the word forms exercises, you have probably found that you sometimes have to hunt a bit to identify all the possible forms for a word. You have also discovered that some forms may *appear* to belong to that word, but in fact they are related to another (perhaps similar) word.

The same can be true of the meanings. Although a simple, appropriate meaning has been provided in the Vocabulary Aids, you can often find a long list of varied meanings in the dictionary. But, like the forms of words, the meanings, too, depend largely on the context, or the way a word is used in the sentence.

Both of these exercises require you to refer to an English dictionary for further information about the words. Exercise A asks you to supply the correct forms of the words, while Exercise B asks you to identify the accurate meaning of each word when it is in a different form from the one you were given.

All the words included in these exercises are among those starred in the Standard Vocabulary of "Mr. K*A*P*L*A*N and Vocabulary."

Each of the words in this exercise is given in the same form as it appears in the text. Change the word to the correct form that is required to fill the blank in the sentence.

Example: interpretation (*noun*)
When Gloria's parents arrived from Hong Kong, she met them at the airport and acted as their *interpreter* with Customs and Immigration.

1. impressed (*verb, past participle*)
   Chantalle had accumulated an ______________ grade point average by the time she applied to graduate school.
2. tensely (*adverb*)
   Although the three had been good friends for a year, they found that there were too many ______________ when they became roommates.
3. inspiration (*noun*)
   ______________ by his father's hard-working example, Josef studied long hours to prepare for medical school.
4. remarkable (*adjective*)
   Sociologists note that people whose marriages have failed are often ______________ eager to try again.
5. collective (*adjective*)
   Although he needed money desperately, he was very reluctant to sell his valuable stamp ______________.
6. broadly (*adverb*)
   Extensive travel can be ______________ as well as educational.
7. applied (*verb, past participle*)
   Some people feel that if young men are required to register for the draft, the same law should be ______________ to young women also.
8. persistence (*noun*)
   "No matter how much we complain," said Al-Noor and Khaled, "the guy upstairs ______________ in turning up his stereo to full volume."
9. contribute (*verb*)
   Annette's nearsightedness was not the only reason for her difficulties in school, but it was a ______________ cause.
10. expectancy (*noun*)
    Americans are generally more pleased to see their friends when they are ______________ than when they just drop by without an invitation.
11. triumph (*noun*)
    After winning the Boston Marathon, Bill Rodgers made his ______________ appearance before the huge crowds and the TV cameras in order to be crowned with the laurel wreath.
12. authentic (*adjective*)
    When Nyurka found what appeared to be an emerald ring and took it to a jeweler, he said there was no question about its ______________.

13. humiliation (*noun*)
Boys who had not learned their lessons used to be subjected to the ______________ experience of being caned (beaten) by the schoolmaster.

14. indulged in (*verb, past participle*)
Some religions forbid any ______________ in alcoholic beverages or tobacco, as well as in harder drugs.

15. substance (*noun*)
"He's lied to me before," said my uncle, "and I'll never believe that story until he ______________ every word of it."

2. VOCABULARY STUDY
B. MEANINGS IN CONTEXT

CHOOSE THE MEANING THAT FITS

The *italicized* portion of each sentence contains one of the vocabulary words, but in a form other than the one in the Standard Vocabulary list. Paraphrase or rewrite the *italicized* part so that the same thing is expressed in different words. Note that sometimes the meaning of a word changes slightly in its various forms, so you would be wise to check with your dictionary often.

For instance, you are probably familiar with "remark" (about) as the verb meaning "to comment." However, it has another meaning: "to take notice of and then to comment about." It is this meaning that is associated with "remarkable," the word in the Standard Vocabulary list.

Sentence example: *Having remarked Sonia's special genius for computer science,* Mr. Venuti gave her an excellent recommendation.

Paraphrase: Since he had particularly noticed and spoken about Sonia's special ability in computer science, Mr. Venuti. . . .

1. Children whose parents *are too indulgent* become very self-centered and unhappy.
Children whose parents ____
____

2. In order to buy refreshments for the office party, the committee decided *to collect money by passing around an envelope.*
. . . the committee decided ____
____

3. American children are not supposed to miss school *unless they have a substantial reason to do so.*

   . . . not supposed to miss school unless ____________________________________

   ____

4. Sam had been dating Cindy for a year and a half, and *he was waiting for an opportune moment to ask her to marry him.*

   . . . and he was waiting ____

   ____

5. Most of us *prefer to associate with people* whose economic level is somewhat close to our own.

   Most of us ____

   ____

6. Juanita was having fun dancing with all the guys until her brother told her angrily, *"You are making a spectacle of yourself!"*

   . . . her brother told her angrily," ______________________________________

   ____

7. Little Jennifer cried when the school bus came for her in the morning, but *she didn't have any reluctance about boarding it later to go home.*

   . . . but she ____

   ____

8. "I'm the champion!" *Sasha told his father triumphantly,* after having won their third chess game.

   "I'm the champion!" Sasha ____

   ____

9. Parents need to be careful what TV shows are watched at home, *because young children are so very impressionable.*

   . . . what TV shows are watched at home, because young children _______

   ____

10. Although Sondra didn't understand much about football, *she made a pretense of liking the game* because her boyfriend played fullback on the team.

    . . . didn't understand much about football, she __________________________

    ____

11. You may have noticed that *a person's unfriendly behavior is sometimes indicative of shyness.*

    You may have noticed that ____

    ____

12. Peter did not enjoy having discussions with his friend George, because *he thought George was too opinionated.*
    . . . because he ____
    ____

13. Louise performed a violin solo at the concert, *with her friend Margie playing the piano accompaniment.*
    Louise performed a violin solo . . . ______________________________
    ____

14. The murder suspect was detained by the police *until his alibi (story) of having been in Baltimore that night could be authenticated.*
    . . . detained by the police until __________________________________
    ____

15. Classroom discussions always go better *when everyone contributes something to them.*
    . . . go better when ____
    ____

3. SPECIAL COMPOSITION PROJECT: ORGANIZING AN OUTLINE

YOU CAN LEARN TO WORK WITH AN OUTLINE

Although most writers seldom compose from a formal outline, many do some sort of drafting or planning on paper in the form of notes or a list of points. Even though you may not want or need to rely on an outline as the basis for most of your writing, there are a few occasions when it can be very useful.

An outline is a clear and convenient way to show the structure for more complicated types of writing such as a report, an analysis, a proposal, or a case study. Outlines are usually expected to be done with term papers also. In fact, you may occasionally be asked to submit *just an outline,* in order to provide a brief but organized picture of how you would plan to treat the whole subject.

Here is what an outline can and should do:

1. It includes the basic contents or information.
2. It clearly indicates which are the writer's main (major) points.
3. It shows what minor points will be used to support the major points.
4. It offers an organized plan for arranging the writer's major and minor points.
5. It follows a conventional format, using Roman numerals, capital letters, Arabic numbers, and small letters in descending order, indenting farther to the right as the items of the outline become more detailed.

In this composition exercise, you will not actually be composing an outline, but you will *complete* two outlines that have been started for you, taking your major and minor points from the list of items provided for each one. Both outlines use material from the story you have just read, but each one takes a different analytical approach.

Directions for Completing Outline A

1. This outline has been divided into two sections, part I and parts II and III combined, to make it easier for you to fill it in.
2. Below Roman numeral I is a list containing two levels of items, all of which you are to arrange in the fill-in spaces under the heading, "I. Pronunciation."
3. Study the thesis to see what the outline is about.
4. Select the larger headings for A and B; then decide how to arrange all the other items.
5. Complete part I first; then go on to parts II and III. Note that there are three main points under "II. Grammar," but *no supporting* details under them.
6. Since the items for parts II and III are mixed together, you will have to decide how to separate the points that belong under each heading.

A. AN ANALYSIS OF ESL ERRORS IN "MR. K*A*P*L*A*N AND VOCABULARY"

Thesis: The story, "Mr. K*A*P*L*A*N and Vocabulary," offers a broad sampling of the errors commonly made by students of English as a second language.

I. Pronunciation
   A. ______________________
      1. ______________________
      2. Saying *ar* like *ä* or *ah* (hod).
      3. ______________________
      4. ______________________
   B. ______________________
      1. ______________________
      2. ______________________
      3. ______________________
      4. ______________________

Pronouncing *ē* to sound like *ĭ* (pipple)
Instead of *w*, saying *v* (void)
For a final *g* substituting *k* (havink)
Difficulties with vowel sounds
Making *er* or *ur* sound like *oi* (foist)
In past-tense verbs, omitting the *d* (I'm soprize)
In place of *th*, making it *d* or *t* (de, tvalft)

Difficulties with consonant sounds

Pronouncing *ā* and *ă* like *ĕ* (Gebble, hengs)

II. Grammar

A. ______

B. ______

C. ______

III. Vocabulary

A. ______

1. ______
2. ______

B. ______

1. ______
2. ______
3. ______

Failure to distinguish aurally (to *hear* the differences) between English words

Substituting German *mit* (with) for *with*

Mixing up *pitcher* with *picture* and *guess* with *gas*

Errors in -ing verb combinations (I'll givink)

Misreading *university* as *anniversary*

Omission of pronouns (Is maybe pitcher . . . ?)

Substitution of native language for English words

Confusing *omits* with *emits* and *enamel* with *animal*

Confusing *mein* (my) with *mine*

Reversals in word order (. . . so is time commink for . . .)

Directions for Completing Outline B

This time only two of the supporting points have been given in the outline. Decide which are the main points and whether each belongs to I, II, or III. Then complete the remainder of the outline, being careful to keep your supporting points under the right headings.

B. SITUATIONAL HUMOR IN "MR. K*A*P*L*A*N AND VOCABULARY"

Thesis: One of the features of the story that especially adds to the humor is the typical classroom psychology that dominates the whole scene.

I. ______

A. ______

B. ______

C. His childish rivalry with Miss Mitnick.

D. ______________________________

II. ______________________________

A. ______________________________

B. ______________________________

C. ______________________________

D. ______________________________

III. ______________________________

A. Assigns tasks that are uninteresting and impractical.

B. ______________________________

C. ______________________________

D. ______________________________

His certainty that his answer will be the right one.

Wasting time by means of elaborate preparations before getting to work.

Even Mr. Parkhill becomes a comic figure because he relies on such typical teaching techniques.

His eagerness to be the first to answer all the questions.

Expects students to make no mistakes.

We smile when we see the students pulling the same tricks that much younger students try in the classroom.

Trying to make an impression on the teacher by looking studious and acting busy.

Tries to drop hints to make them guess the "right" answer.

It's amusing to see a grown-up man like Hyman Kaplan behaving like a child.

Giving vague answers with more than one possible interpretation.

Gives students very little explanation or help.

His loving care in using his crayons.

Trying to get clues from other people to help find the answers.

When You Have Finished:

1. Check them over again to be sure that:
   What you have filled in under the main points (I or II) are, in fact, major points.
   You have identified where the supporting points should go.
   You have listed the points in the best possible order.
2. Look for examples of *parallelism*, or the use of similar grammatical structures such as participial phrases, prepositional phrases, and complete sentences. What do you notice about parallelism in an outline?
3. If your instructor would like you to develop parts of either outline into paragraphs, you might try one or more of the following:

a. Compose an introductory paragraph for one of the outlines, incorporating the thesis in the paragraph.
b. Select one main section as the basis for writing a paragraph. In the first outline you might write on: I. Pronunciation, A or B; part II; or part III. In the second outline you might develop any one of the main parts. Be sure to write a topic sentence for your paragraph.
c. Write a concluding paragraph to wind up one of the two discussions. This should refer back in some way to what has been said (without repeating it), and it would also include comments and conclusions of your own, such as something similar from your own experience, or your opinion about the difficulties ESL students often have with these or other language problems.

4. LANGUAGE CONVERSION: A. FORMAL TO INFORMAL SPEECH

REWRITE IT THE SIMPLE WAY

One of this author's most successful comic devices is his exaggerated use of formal expressions. Although Mr. Parkhill doesn't actually *talk* in these elegant phrases, we suspect that he likes to think of himself as an educator and a scholar—perhaps making that sort of impression on his ESL students also.

On the other hand, Hyman Kaplan's fractured English makes a startling contrast to the highly formal language. Ross has intentionally combined two extremes in style time and time again for the incongruous (and humorous) effect of mixing them.

Most of the time, however, a good writer tries to avoid either extreme. The best or most effective use of English is to make it simple, clear, and unpretentious: that is, to avoid fancy or flowery language and just try to be easily understood. A careful writer uses correct grammar for exactly the same reason: to make it easier for the reader to understand his meaning.

Keep these points in mind as you write the first of these two practice exercises.

Each of these sentences is based on formal language used in the story, but they can be said in a much simpler way. Refer to the Vocabulary Aids for help with the meanings. Then complete the unfinished sentence so that it paraphrases (means the same as) the first one. Use any idioms or colloquial expressions that express the meaning well. (You may need more words than are used in the original.)

1. Mr. Kaplan continued to mispronounce many words, despite Mr. Parkhill's tireless tutelage.

   Mr. Kaplan kept on mispronouncing words, even though________________

   ____

2. A chance to use his crayons always intensified Mr. Kaplan's natural euphoria.
   Whenever Mr. Kaplan could use his crayons, he ______________________
   ____

3. He chose an orange crayon for the methodological observation.
   He used an orange crayon to ______________________
   ____

4. Mr. Parkhill noticed that Mr. Kaplan's cerebration was accompanied by some strange sounds.
   Mr. Parkhill noticed that Mr. Kaplan was ______________________
   while ____

5. This private colloquy was not indulged in without a subtle design.
   Mr. Kaplan had an underlying reason for ______________________
   ____

6. Mr. Parkhill had learned to beware of Mr. Kaplan's strategies, so he preserved a stern facial immobility.
   Mr. Parkhill had learned to watch out for ______________________
   so ____

7. Mr. Parkhill saw that Mr. Kaplan had neatly straddled two words by deliberately noncommittal usage.
   Mr. Parkhill saw that Mr. Kaplan had managed to ______________________
   ____

8. Mr. Kaplan listened to this unwelcome correction with a fine sufferance.
   Mr. Kaplan did not like it when ______________________
   but ____

9. Like a smoldering cinder in his soul lay the thought of his humiliation by Miss Mitnick.
   Hyman Kaplan felt very ______________________
   because Miss Mitnick ______________________

10. When Mr. Parkhill tried to give the students a hint, the class went into that coma which signified thought.
    When Mr. Parkhill tried to give the students a hint, the class looked as though ______________________
    while ____

4. LANGUAGE CONVERSION: B. NONSTANDARD TO STANDARD USAGE

REWRITE IT THE CORRECT WAY

You will recognize the passages below as typical speech of Mr. Kaplan. The punctuation is correct, but the grammar and the spelling should be revised, and words sometimes need to be added.

You may make corrections right on the paper here in the same way that you would proofread and revise your own paper:

Cross out the word that has a mistake and write the correct word above it;
Use a caret (‸) to indicate where a word is missing; then add that word above the caret.

It is better not just to cross out letters or try to squeeze extra ones in. Instead, rewrite the whole word in its correct form.

1. In sommer, ve all heaven a fine time.
2. Is maybe a pitcher for milk? Is maybe a pitcher on de vall—art! Two minninks!
3. "Plizz take milk from de pitcher." Fine! "De pitcher hengs cockeye."
4. In som houses is even de *pitchers* beauriful.
5. So is mine santence: "In India is all kinds snake-fescinators."
6. Elaven yiss is married mine vife an'minesalf, so is time commink for our tvalft univoisity.
7. You got right, Mitnick . . . So I'll givink anodder santence.
8. Mistake by Mitnick! Ha! Mit *enimals* she is painting chairs?
9. I got him! Ufcawss! . . . Plain an tsimple!
10. I'm soprize so high-class a student like Mitnick, . . . she shouldn't know a leetle void like "dock"!

Peter L. Sandberg (1934–   )

Born in Winchester, Massachusetts, Peter L. Sandberg went down South for his college education, graduating from Florida Southern College in 1958. He traveled to the West and Midwest for graduate study (at the University of Colorado and the University of Iowa), then on to the Southwest to teach at Phoenix College, Arizona, in the early 1960s. From there he moved "back East," spending some years in writing and editorial work in Pennsylvania before returning to his roots in Massachusetts in 1968.

For the next few years Sandberg settled down to teach English at Northeastern University in Boston, where he is still remembered by some of his former colleagues in the English Department as "a great teacher of creative writing," "a conscientious, thoroughly nice person," and someone who "wrote an outdoorsy sort of fiction that was published in Playboy Magazine.*"*

Since the early 1970s Sandberg has been living and working in New Hampshire as a full-time writer. In addition to his numerous short stories, which have appeared in Best Little Magazine Fiction *(1970),* Best American Short Stories *(1974), and* Playboy's Laughing Lovers *(1975), Sandberg has published several novels of adventure and suspense, including* Wolf Mountain, Stubb's Run, *and* King's Run. *He also collaborated with another writer, Berent Sandberg, to produce* Brass Diamonds, *a thriller about a CIA agent and ex-Vietnam fighter on a drug investigation in Cambodia.*

An enthusiastic mountain climber himself, the author of "Hawsmoot" once was seriously hurt in a fall during a mountain-climbing expedition in Arizona. "I have always been intrigued with the ways in which a man can define his courage and/or cowardice in a confrontation with nature," he comments in his biographical notes for Contemporary Authors *(1976), and continues: "The first story I wrote had to do with a young man climbing a mountain, and I suspect the last one will have to do with an old man climbing a mountain—though I hasten to add I do write about other things."*

X

Hawsmoot

Story Setting: *A steep cliff that happens to be a favorite site for mountain climbers, its fictitious location being in Wisconsin, possibly beside one of the Great Lakes. In this north-central part of the country, the fall season becomes wintry rather early.*

In the Story: *A middle-aged man finds his mountain climbing skills, experience, and stamina challenged by a daring young climber, who has come from across the sea to scale the cliff.*

One day at the base of the cliffs high above the Wisconsin lake came a young German climber who carried no rope and said that no one could follow him unroped on a climb of the Grand Giraffe.

"Climbers who are good climb with ropes," he said. "But climbers who are great climb alone."

GLOSSARY

1 **base of the cliffs:** a level place beneath the high, steep face of a rocky mass.
2 **unroped:** without using a rope as a safety precaution.
3 **the Grand Giraffe:** the name of a steep, rocky cliff.

INFORMAL SPEECH

4 **who are good:** those who are really highly skilled.
4 **who are great:** those who stand out as so remarkable that few will ever match them.

STANDARD VOCABULARY

2 **rope:** a thick, strong cord made of fibers twisted together and used by mountain climbers to prevent falls.

The German was eighteen and wore lederhosen and an orange climbing parka. While he talked his gray eyes sparkled and his lips parted in a smile over his square white teeth, but the smile was as distant as the lake below him and his eyes were as cold as the autumn sun which hung in the sky above him like a frozen amulet.

"I will be great," he said. "So I climb unroped where other climbers will not follow."

Gathered at the base of the cliff hearing the German speak was a group of young men and women with coiled ropes on their shoulders and belts hung with climbing iron. Most of them wore blue parkas or windbreakers with the insignias of climbing clubs sewn to the sleeves. In back of them was one older man who carried no rope or gear or insignia, and who rested on a walking cane. He looked like a trail walker of the Audubon variety.

When the German had finished speaking the young men and women did not answer him, but the older man did.

"I'll follow you," he said.

The young German's eyes softened. The Prussian lines of his jaw relaxed and a shock of blond hair fell over his forehead.

"Do you climb?" he asked.

The man, who was fifty-four, stepped out from the group of younger people. He was an ordinary looking man with gentle and undistinguished features like those of a regular army corporal or a custodian at a school for small children. He wore an army surplus shirt and pants and soft leather climbing shoes, and he used the cane when he walked because the pain in his back was terrible without it.

"I'll follow you," he said.

The German was watching him carefully. "You climb?" he repeated.

"Sure," the man said.

GLOSSARY

6 **lederhosen:** leather leggings (leg coverings).
9 **like a frozen amulet:** small, carved good-luck charm. (In the northern United States, the sun does not seem warm in the fall.)
12 **climbing iron:** spikes for digging into rock to hold on when climbing.
15 **Audubon:** a national society of nature lovers.
19 **Prussian:** a north German racial group known for stern military discipline.
19 **shock of blond hair:** an untidy mass of light-colored hair.
24 **army corporal:** the second lowest rank in the army (just above a private).
24 **army surplus:** bought in a store that sells outdated army clothing cheaply.

INFORMAL SPEECH

15 **of the —— variety:** of a certain type.
26 **terrible:** very bad.

STANDARD VOCABULARY

6 **parka:** a waterproof jacket with an attached hood.
8 ***distant:** (fig) faraway, not inviting friendliness.
8 **autumn:** a synonym for the season of fall (September 21 through December 21 in the United States).
12 **coiled:** loosely wound or rolled together.
13 **windbreakers:** lightweight, tightly woven jackets that keep out wind.
13 **insignias:** cloth patches symbolizing organizations.
13 **sewn:** stitched, attached with thread.
14 **gear:** equipment or apparatus needed for a special purpose.
15 **cane:** a strong stick with a curved handle, to aid in walking.
19 ***relaxed:** loosened up.
23 ***ordinary:** rather common.
23 **undistinguished:** plain, not noticeable.
24 **custodian:** a person who cleans and takes care of a building.

The German gestured at the cliff behind him. The sleeves of his parka were rolled back to the elbow and the muscles of his forearms bulged under the skin like rocks in a silk sock.

"The Giraffe?" he said.

"Sure," the man said.

The German kept smiling as he looked at the man, but his eyes were like gimlets. The man looked back calmly, wishing that the German would begin to climb for his back hurt and really he had climbed enough for one day. It was time to drive back to North Fork and make a meal of corn muffins and franks and then get under the heat lamp. But the German was arrogant and the young climbers, who were quite good, would not answer the challenge to climb alone because they were used to the safety of a rope. As for himself, he had climbed on these cliffs for thirty years; he had done the most difficult climbs, and never in all that time had he used a rope.

"If you climb the Giraffe," the German said smiling, "even as far as the overhang, even with a rope for safety, I'll buy you a supper tonight."

"Sure," the man said. The German was insulting and cocksure and for a moment the man became angry, until his own pain and weariness came over him. Then all he wanted to do was sit down.

"*Ja,*" said the German. "Good. It's a good joke."

He walked to the start of the climb and looked up. The cliff rose nearly vertical a hundred and twenty feet and was split by a long crack which looked like a lightning bolt. Aside from the crack the gray rock was quite smooth, broken now and then by small nubbins and ledges where it was possible to place usually no more than one half inch of the sole of a boot. The crack itself was big enough in some places to take a man's hand and in others to take his fist or toe. Twenty feet from the top a small overhanging roof jutted out

GLOSSARY

31 **forearm(s):** the part of the arm between the hand and elbow.
31 **silk sock:** short stocking made of very thin material.
35 **gimlets:** small tools used for boring holes in wood.
38 **corn muffins and franks:** individual, cup-sized bread made of corn meal, and hot dogs.
38 **heat lamp:** infrared lamp directing heat to any part of the body.
43 **overhang:** a part of a cliff that extends out overhead.
48 **Ja:** German for "yes," pronounced "yah."
50 **a lightning bolt:** a sharp, jagged flash of lightning.
52 **nubbins:** very small, projecting parts.
52 **ledges:** somewhat larger projections than nubbins, big enough to stand or sit on.

INFORMAL SPEECH

34 **sure:** yes, of course ("okay" or "O.K.").
39 **quite:** noticeably or somewhat.
40 **as for himself:** referring to himself, expressing his own preferences.
45 **cocksure:** overconfident, very certain that he could not fail.
46 **came over him:** seemed to hit him with a great rush or surge of feeling.
48 **It's a good joke:** You're just trying to be funny, or you can't be serious.

STANDARD VOCABULARY

30 **gestured:** made a sign or motion with the hand.
31 **bulged:** swelled outward noticeably.
39 ***arrogant:** proud and insolent in behavior.
39 ***challenge:** an invitation to compete.
40 **safety:** freedom from danger.
45 **insulting:** deliberately intending to hurt another's dignity or feelings.
49 **vertical:** straight up and down.
51 **aside from:** except for.
53 **sole:** bottom of a shoe.
54 **jutted out:** stuck out, protruded.

from the cliff about four feet. To the people who had first made the climb the long crack resembled the neck of a giraffe and the overhang resembled its head.

"*Ja,*" the German said again. "*Es ist alles nur Spass.*"

He studied the beginning of the climb, then raised his hands above his head fitting them carefully into the crack. In that attitude he paused for a moment, looking like a brightly colored still from a ballet. "A good one," he said glancing over his shoulder. Then he raised his right foot lightly to a small hold and began to climb.

The man, who was Will Hawsmoot, found a rock and sat down resting his chin on his hands which he folded over his cane. You're right, he thought as he watched the German climb. A man can get to be known by climbing without a rope. But maybe I'm too old to climb that way anymore. I don't know. Maybe I am. The decision was one he would have to make soon. He knew that. Perhaps he should have made it before now.

The wind blew up from the lake in gusts, up the cliff where it ballooned the orange parka until the German looked huge and then the wind suddenly died and the air went out of the parka and the German looked small again, high on the cliff, sixty feet up, resting on small holds.

"He'll eat crow," one of the young climbers said.

The German yodelled, tilting his head up, a sharp Bavarian yodel that echoed down the cliffs.

"He's an egotistical so and so isn't he, Mr. Hawsmoot," a young girl said.

Hawsmoot smiled. They were nice people these young climbers, and certainly meant well. But there were some things they didn't understand. There were some things that a man decided for himself; about the rope for instance. They had wanted him to use a rope when he climbed. They offered to climb with him every weekend so he would always be sure to have a partner, and when he kept refusing, or tried politely to change the subject, they had thought he was too poor to buy a rope and offered to buy one for him.

GLOSSARY

57 **Es . . . Spass:** German for "It is all nothing but a joke."
59 **attitude:** (here) his physical position.
60 **ballet:** a graceful, formal dance.
67 **ballooned:** filled with air and bulged out.
72 **Bavarian yodel:** a musical call, changing back and forth from normal to high falsetto tones.

INFORMAL SPEECH

60 **a good one:** comment meaning "a clever joke."
64 **get to be known:** become famous.
71 **eat crow:** admit that he was wrong.
74 **so and so:** a polite way of avoiding calling someone an insulting name.
75 **meant well:** had good intentions and a kindly attitude.
79 **kept refusing:** continued to say no.
79 **change the subject:** talk about something else.

STANDARD VOCABULARY

56 ***resembled:** looked like.
56 **giraffe:** an African spotted animal with a very long neck.
60 **still (noun):** a photograph showing arrested motion.
60 **glancing:** looking very briefly.
61 **hold (noun):** a place to grasp firmly with one's hand.
67 **gusts:** sudden strong rushes of wind.
68 ***huge:** very, very large, like a monster.
72 **yodelled:** see "Bavarian yodel" in the Glossary.
72 **echoed:** sounded and then resounded.
74 ***egotistical:** extremely self-centered.
77 **for instance:** for example.
79 **partner:** someone who shares equally in responsibility, effort, and rewards.

The German had begun to climb again moving slowly, high enough up now that a fall would kill him, moving slowly but easily the way a squirrel can climb the trunk of a big barked tree. You are good, Hawsmoot thought watching the young German climb. And they won't offer you a rope because you're young. And I'm old. I guess that's the real difference between you and me.

The young climbers came to the lake every spring as soon as the ice was off the cliffs. They climbed for a week or two weeks. Some of them climbed all summer until the leaves turned yellow and the air got so cold their hands turned numb on the rock. Not just young climbers either, but young and middle-aged and old. Some came back for a second season. Some came back year after year for four or five years. Then they would disappear and he would never see or hear of them again. In thirty years he had seen so many climbers come and go from the lake that all their faces seemed the same to him, and while he remembered certain climbs he had taught them to do—or had done while they watched gazing up at him like a half circle of interested possums—he could not remember anything particular about them except that most of them climbed well and that all of them used ropes; that each year there would be a few new ones among them, and a few of the old ones would have gone.

He would remember the German. Not the orange parka, or the blond hair that the wind was whipping up there, or the powerful arms and legs that lifted his weight like jacks, but the fact that the German was making a difficult climb without the protection of a rope. He was already to the overhang, standing on small holds a hundred feet above the ground, so close under the overhang that his head was bent sideways, his cheek pressed flat against the cold stone of the roof.

"He'll see what it's all about now," one of the young climbers said. "The cheese will get more binding."

Some of the others laughed dryly but the sounds were meaningless to Hawsmoot who at this moment was bound body and soul to the climber who clung to the rock so high up that when he dislodged a small pebble it took a long time to hit the ground, and when it did it broke. The orange parka luffed in the breeze which blew up suddenly and then

GLOSSARY

82 **squirrel:** a small, bushy-tailed animal (a rodent) skilled at climbing trees.
82 **big barked tree:** the rough, hard surface on the trunk of a large tree.
89 **a second season:** again at the same time next year.
94 **like . . . possums:** looking like an attentive group of small animals.
98 **jacks:** devices for raising heavy objects off the ground.
103 **The cheese . . . more binding:** an expression used among dairy farmers and meaning the situation is going to get tougher (or tighter) yet.
105 **laughed dryly:** laughed without enthusiasm or real humor.
108 **luffed:** a nautical term used when a sail shakes from a strong wind.

INFORMAL SPEECH

83 **you are good:** see Informal Speech, p. 157.
98 **whipping:** sharply blowing and flapping.
103 **what it's all about:** what the real difficulties are.
106 **body and soul:** in a total sense.

STANDARD VOCABULARY

88 **numb:** lacking any feeling.
90 **disappear:** go away and not return.
94 ***particular:** special or specific.
99 ***protection:** a guard or shield against injury.
101 **pressed:** pushed or squeezed tightly against something.
106 ***bound:** (past tense of *to bind*) fastened together. (Look up its related meanings.)
106 **clung:** (past tense of *to cling*) held on very tightly.
107 **dislodged:** forced out of a secure or settled position.
107 **pebble:** a very small piece of rock, its sharp edges worn down and somewhat rounded from its exposure to the weather.

stopped. The dry leaf rustle on the slope died. A silence came over the cliff. The German moved his left hand out to the edge of the overhang in such silence that Hawsmoot heard his ring scrape. Then he let his feet come away from the wall and hung by his hands four feet out from the cliff like a man on a high trapeze. The group at the base of the cliff watched. The German raised himself up slowly as if to gain the overhang, then lowered himself to arm's length again. The people watching caught their breath. Hawsmoot felt his heart begin to hammer. He had hung like that many times and knew exactly how it felt, like hanging onto life by the fingertips. The German raised himself, paused, then lowered himself again.

"Look at him show off," one of the young men said, "Crazy bastard."

The German hung motionless above them for a moment longer, then raised himself up again, but not stopping this time, following through by kicking a foot high up, moving with great precision, levering himself up quickly until he stood on top of the roof. Then he finished the last twenty feet and sat at the cliff edge smiling down at them.

When Hawsmoot got up and walked to the start of the climb, one of the girl climbers followed him. There were club insignias sewn to the sleeves of her parka.

"Don't climb without a rope, Mr. Hawsmoot," she said. "You shouldn't."

She was a pretty girl, long dark braids like panther tails almost reached her waist. There were usually a few like her each summer, prettier than most. He tried to remember the one last summer, the one he had taught to climb the overhang on the Leaning Tower. But he couldn't remember. Maybe it had been the summer before, or any one of thirty summers.

"I guess I'll be all right," he said laying his cane carefully against the cliff as a man who would come back for it. "It's a good climb. I know it pretty well."

The massive cliff was in shadow now for it faced east and the sun had passed behind it. Know it well? Yes, he knew it well. He knew how it looked in all seasons; how it was in sun and shade, in snow and ice. He knew where it was easy to climb and where it was hard, and where, so far at least, it had been impossible. He knew intimately the long crack

GLOSSARY

112 **high trapeze:** swinging bar from which circus acrobats perform their feats of daring and skill.
116 **by the fingertips:** by the ends of one's fingers.
126 **braids:** long strands of hair woven together in three sections.
126 **panther:** a catlike animal with a long, slim tail.
126 **waist:** the middle part of the body, where a belt is worn.
128 **the Leaning Tower:** the name of another favorite mountain of climbers, named after the Tower of Pisa in Italy.

INFORMAL SPEECH

114 **caught their breath:** gasped in sudden fear.
115 **heart began to hammer:** his heart began to beat very fast and hard.
118 **show off:** try to attract attention by his abilities.
118 **crazy bastard:** (pejor) a silly fool.
131 **guess:** suppose, in a hopeful, although not certain, tone.
131 **be all right:** a vague expression, meaning (here), "probably nothing will happen to me."
132 **pretty well:** a modest, understated way of saying "very well."

STANDARD VOCABULARY

109 **rustle:** (onomat) a soft, gentle sound.
109 ***silence:** a noticeable state of quietness.
111 **scrape:** (onomat) make a rough, hard sound.
113 ***gain:** reach.
119 ***motionless:** without moving.
120 **following through:** performing an act all the way to its conclusion.
121 **precision:** exactness.
121 **levering:** raising or prying oneself up by means of something.
121 **roof:** the top outside part, usually of a building.
133 **massive:** impressively large or huge.
136 **intimately:** in a close, personal way.

that looked like the neck of a giraffe, knew the size of each nubbin of rock on either side, how long he could stand on it comfortably, which way it sloped and which foot must be placed on it to make the climb smoothly.

It did not seem surprising to him that he knew the rock so well. The cliffs from end to end measured less than a mile, and he had spent half a lifetime studying them.

The wind blew up in gusts and died and blew again. His back began to throb, the torn muscles drawing up in spasm against the cold. For a minute it seemed to him that he had been standing in front of the cliff since spring and that whole seasons had gone by until suddenly it was winter. Foolish, because it had only been a minute or so. He reached his hands over his head and placed them in the crack, a little lower down than the German had, and as soon as a little of his weight was on his hands, his back stopped hurting.

"You shouldn't do it," the girl said. He was startled by her voice so close to him. "We can run up the trail to the top and lower a rope. It wouldn't take long."

"Don't worry about me," he said. "I want to do the climb."

He started. The rock felt good, a little cold which he liked because his hands stuck hard to the holds and did not perspire as they did sometimes in summer. The young climbers were talking below him. He heard them say that Hawsmoot was still one of the best climbers in the country and that the German would eat crow, but soon the words and the sounds of their voices became meaningless and he was alone with his climb as he had been for so many years.

He tried to think just when it was he had begun. It was after the old man had been killed in the brutal accident with the mower. It was after the farm went under which he remembered so vividly as the day when the auctioneer came out and sold all the furniture and took down the big sign on the barn that said *Hawsmoot.* It was either just before or just after his mother's death, right about the time he took the job in the cannery. He still worked at the cannery, worked on a belt culling the cans that got fouled up in the labelling machine and came out with tattered labels or no labels at all. It was not what he had

GLOSSARY

142 **torn muscles:** injured body tissues (in his back).
143 **spasm:** a sudden quick tightening, a twinge (here, of pain).
145 **foolish:** absurd or silly (to feel that way).
158 **mower:** a large farm machine with heavy, sharp blades for cutting grain.
159 **auctioneer:** An auction (here) is a sale of nearly all one's personal property in order to pay one's debts. The auctioneer handles the sale.
161 **cannery:** a canning factory.
162 **belt:** a continuously moving, flat surface (carrying cans to be filled).
162 **culling:** removing for a special reason.
162 **labelling machine:** the machine that placed paper covers on the cans to indicate their contents.

INFORMAL SPEECH

137 **on either side:** on each side.
140 **from end to end:** from one end to the other.
145 **a minute or so:** a minute, more or less.
157 **the old man:** a familiar reference to his father.
158 **went under:** lost money until it went bankrupt and had to be sold.
161 **right about the time:** very near the same time.
162 **worked on:** had a job at or with.
162 **got fouled up:** did not go through the process correctly (got "screwed up").

STANDARD VOCABULARY

138 ***comfortably:** restfully, without physical distress.
138 **sloped:** slanted.
142 **throb:** seem to vibrate or pulsate, sometimes with pain.
148 **startled** (by): given a mild shock, as by a sudden noise or appearance.
149 **lower:** let down.
152 **perspire:** to sweat, give off body moisture.
158 ***brutal:** violent.
159 **vividly:** in very clear detail.
163 **tattered:** badly torn.

wanted to do with his life, not at all. But the farm had failed and no better job was open to him. There was no money, and he had to eat.

He reached down to brush some grit from a foothold and watched the pieces fall like drops of water far below him to the ground where the younger climbers gazed up at him. From the corner of his eye the forested slope of yellow-leafed trees fell steeply away to the mud shore of the lake. That was right. He remembered now. It was early spring of the year his mother had died when he had come out to the lake to swim and had seen the climbers working the cliffs. He had put on his boots and levis and climbed the steep slope to the cliffs and watched all that afternoon, and he had come back the next day to watch again. This was the sport, better than football or baseball which he had never cared much for. He watched long enough to see how the climbers moved on the rock, then he went off to a cloistered section of the cliffs and began practicing on his own. He had always been shy. Too shy to ask if he could climb with the others.

For the next three years the careful study of the rock, the discovery of force and counterforce and the delicacy of balance, all the myriad techniques of moving up and down steep rock let him forget the loss of his family and home, and made it easier to work on the belt where he performed his job as a faceless, nameless man, lost like a pebble in the rock pile of the cannery.

The wind blew so hard for a moment that his eyes watered. The overhang was not far above him now. The climb was going nicely and he felt good except that his hands ached a little, probably from the cold. He paused to rest, taking one hand from the rock and putting it in his pocket, letting the stiff tips of his fingers rest in the warm crease of his groin.

GLOSSARY

166 **foothold:** a small place where he could safely put his foot.
168 **forested slope:** the wooded side of the mountain.
171 **levis:** blue jeans, or denim trousers for casual wear. (Actually a trademark for "Levi's," this brand name has been used so frequently that it is often thought to be a synonym for *jeans.*)
177 **force and counterforce:** laws of physics relating to the balancing of one weight or strength against another.
178 **delicacy of balance:** a condition where the weight or force could very easily be shifted to one side or the other.
180 **faceless, nameless:** (fig) without a face or a name.
180 **rock pile:** (lit, a heap of stones) here, a metaphor for the factory where Hawsmoot works.
182 **eyes watered:** tears came to his eyes.
185 **crease of his groin:** the warm place between his legs.

INFORMAL SPEECH

164 **to do with his life:** what sort of career or life work he had wanted.
168 **from the corner of his eye:** from what he could see sideways.
168 **fell . . . away:** rapidly extended downward and outward.
171 **working the ———:** keeping up constant activity on or about.
173 **This was the sport:** the one for him, the sport of his choice.
175 **on his own:** without help from anyone.
183 **going nicely:** proceeding well, without any trouble.

STANDARD VOCABULARY

164 ***failed:** not succeeded; gone bankrupt and had to be sold.
166 **grit:** grains of dirt or sand.
175 **cloistered:** hidden away and undiscovered, as though in a convent or a monastery.
176 **shy:** self-conscious around other people.
178 **myriad:** very many, innumerable.
178 ***techniques:** exact methods.
183 **ached:** felt tired and sore.
185 ***stiff:** straight and hard to bend.

Five years went by. Sometime, he couldn't remember exactly when or how it happened, he had begun climbing on the big cliffs and gradually the other climbers began to recognize him and they gathered to watch as he climbed the most difficult climbs alone and unroped. Sure. It was a little after that that a short blond haired man with a stiff brown beard asked to climb with him.

"I'm Joe Meyers," he said. "You're Hawsmoot, aren't you?"

Hawsmoot said yes that was his name, and wondered how this stranger knew it.

"You know all the best climbs I guess," Meyers said.

"Sure."

"I'd like to climb some of them with you."

"Sure," Hawsmoot said.

They climbed. Without a rope Hawsmoot led climb after climb and Meyers followed. No matter how severe the pitch, Meyers followed with such grace that Hawsmoot knew this man was the best that had ever come to the lake.

At the end of the day when they stood at the base of the highest climb, Hawsmoot pointed up the rock and said, "The overhang is hard."

Meyers nodded. He stood on the ground watching Hawsmoot climb up the crack that looked like a lightning bolt, and when he saw Hawsmoot swing out from the cliff hanging by his hands from the edge of the overhang, feet swinging free, Meyers smiled and shook his head slowly and said, "I'd want a rope for that one." And he did not follow.

It was as clear in Hawsmoot's mind as if it had happened yesterday, or today, as though it were happening again. Joe Meyers. The other climbers told Hawsmoot who he was. He was one of the five best climbers in the country, and he had hitchiked from California to see Hawsmoot climb.

"How'd he know my name?" Hawsmoot had asked.

A girl had replied a little disdainfully, "Everybody knows you."

Others came. Peters came from Utah, Turner from Colorado, Mrs. Ann Brisket from Anchorage, Dietrich from Austria, Steffano from Italy; famous climbers on their way to make first ascents in all the mountain ranges of the hemisphere stopped at the lake to see Hawsmoot climb, the man they had heard of who did extreme climbs unroped.

Himself, he had never been thirty miles beyond his own town. But these climbers brought the world to him and took him to the world.

GLOSSARY

198 **how severe the pitch:** how difficult the upward climb.
200 **at the base:** at the very bottom.
208 **hitchhiked:** traveled by walking along a road in the hope of being given a ride ("thumbing a ride").
212 **Utah, Colorado:** states in the western United States.
213 **Anchorage:** the largest city in Alaska.
214 **mountain ranges of the hemisphere:** the most well-known mountains in North or South America.

INFORMAL SPEECH

194 **sure:** a casual expression meaning "of course" or "naturally."
198 **no matter how:** however steep it might be.
202 **nodded:** moved his head up and down to indicate agreement.
216 **himself, he:** an informal emphasis.

STANDARD VOCABULARY

188 ***recognize:** know by sight.
192 ***stranger:** someone new and unknown in an area.
198 ***grace:** agility and ease.
211 ***disdainfully:** in a superior, unpleasant manner.
215 **extreme:** most advanced and most difficult.

He was about to smile thinking this when suddenly he saw something above him, blocking his way. He was startled and for the first time he grew tense on his holds. The hell. It was the overhang, that's all it was. But it seemed to loom over his head, dark and

GLOSSARY

219 **blocking his way:** stopping him from passing.

INFORMAL SPEECH

219 **the hell:** mild swearing expression indicating a sudden disturbance or annoyance.
220 **that's all it was:** a way of downplaying something difficult or dan-

STANDARD VOCABULARY

219 **tense:** tight in one's muscles.
220 **loom:** extend above one's head in a sinister or threatening way.

fatal looking. Until now he had hardly been conscious of the climb, his hands and feet working automatically. Now he must keep his mind on the rock. He inched up until his head was bent under the overhang and his cheek rested against the cold stone roof. No need to hurry here, there's time. Far down there he could see the young climbers gazing up like possums, and behind them the slope of trees dropped into the lake. It gave him the impression of being a thousand feet up, so high up in the heavens he wanted to let go, fall back into the soft oblivion of a cloud. He was very still, hugging the stone closely, his cheek pressed against it as if he were embracing a close friend he was leaving and knew he might not see again.

Then the left hand moved out to the edge of the roof and caught in the familiar hold, the rock gritty against his nails. Then the right hand went slowly out to meet the left; and instantly after that his feet pulled from the wall. *Hawsmoot! Hawsmoot!* Something was wrong. He kept hearing his name, someone was shouting his name, and his arms weren't working. The wind was blowing from the lake so cold it numbed his hands and his arms weren't pulling him up. He dangled above the ground, confused, alarmed. He felt a great desire to drop off, to let go; he was weary, tired out. It had just been too much for one day, too damn much. He was exhausted. But he forced the arms to work until slowly by inches his head was level with his hands. He forced the arms again, forced them so hard he thought the muscles would burst through the skin, forced them until his wrists were level with his hands. Wobbling he kicked his shoe up, and missed the hold. He hung out over the emptiness, hung out over the abyss with every fibre of his body screaming to let go. But he kicked again and this time made it. He pressed his weight up on that leg and reached for higher hand holds. He was over.

GLOSSARY

241 **abyss:** a hole so deep as to seem bottomless.
241 **every fibre:** every small living part.

gerous to make it sound less important.
222 **keep his mind on:** concentrate, think hard.
226 **let go:** stop holding on.
233 **weren't working:** were not functioning as well as usual.
237 **too damn much:** the swear word adds feeling and emphasis.

STANDARD VOCABULARY

221 **fatal:** causing death.
221 **conscious:** aware, thinking about.
222 ***automatically:** in a precise, machinelike way, without thinking.
222 **inched:** went very slowly.
226 **impression:** a feeling.
227 ***oblivion:** a place of unconsciousness and forgetting.
230 **familiar:** comfortable because well-known.
235 **dangled:** hung loosely.
235 ***confused:** mixed up, uncertain.
235 **alarmed:** suddenly fearful.
236 **weary:** tired.
237 ***exhausted:** completely tired out.
238 **level with:** on the same plane as.
238 **forced:** struggled to make an effort regardless of difficulties and resistance.
240 **wobbling:** moving in a shaky way.
241 **screaming:** (fig) shouting loudly from pain.

On top of the overhang, he rested. It had not been close, only a little clumsy missing the foothold the first time. Plenty of good young climbers had missed that hold and fallen from the overhang, caught by their rope. *You should climb with a rope, Mr. Hawsmoot.* He had climbed it many times, a hundred times, at least that. He had first climbed it when he was thirty and the only difference now was that he climbed it more slowly and had missed the foothold the first time. Had they been calling his name? He guessed not. They were standing down there, so far now that they were hard to make out, dim white faces all the same. *Mr. Hawsmoot, use a rope.*

It was getting to be twilight and he felt saddened at the thought of having to walk the hiking trail back to the base of the cliff without a cane, the back sore in the damp evening air. He did not think about making the German eat crow, the German was all right. He was young and cocksure and good, and probably he had little money and was trying to make a name for himself in the States. The German was all right. What he thought about as he stood on the steep cliff high above the ground was that this year he would be fifty-five and sixty in five years; and that one day his hands would not hold. *You should wear a rope, Mr. Hawsmoot.* Yes, that would save him all right.

He looked at his hands on the knobby rock and thought of the lifetime he had spent building their power. He thought of Meyers coming from California to climb with him. He thought of Dietrich, Steffano, Peters, and all the others who had come to see him climb. He thought of the faceless, nameless hundreds who had come to the lake to climb roped and had left forgotten. *You should wear a rope.* Maybe so. Maybe I'm too old to climb without one. Maybe it was close just now, I don't know. He began climbing again, the last twenty feet.

The German was waiting at the top of the cliff. When he came forward his face seemed softer in the shadows. They stood facing each other in the stiff wind that blew up the cliffs causing the leaves to make sounds like pebbles down tin chutes.

"You are a great climber," the German said. "If I had known . . ."

"I guess we better get down the trail before dark," the man said. He did not want the German to feel humble.

"Yes," the German said. "Surely. My name is Fuchs, and yours . . ."

"Hawsmoot."

GLOSSARY

252 **twilight:** early evening, between sunset and darkness.
260 **knobby:** rough and uneven.
269 **tin chutes:** small, hollow passageways made of thin metal.

INFORMAL SPEECH

250 **hard to make out:** difficult to see clearly.
254 **The German was all right:** . . . was a "good guy." (Compare with the earlier IS definition of "all right" on page 162, line 131).
255 **trying to make a name for himself:** trying to do something that would make him famous.
264 **maybe so:** an expression of partial, but doubtful, agreement.

STANDARD VOCABULARY

244 ***clumsy:** awkward, not skillful.
252 **saddened:** somewhat sorrowful.
261 ***power:** dynamic strength.
268 **softer:** kinder and gentler.
268 ***stiff:** strong and steady (compare with the Standard Vocabulary definition on p. 164, line 185).
272 ***humble:** submissive, not proud or arrogant.

The sound of that name as it fell from his lips carried from the cliffs out over the land to the shores of seas and beyond. It beaconed his soul. It carried his decision. Go on climbing without the rope. Go on climbing as always. Hope I am high up when the hands don't hold.

GLOSSARY

276 **beaconed:** functioned as a guiding light or a lighthouse at sea.
276 **carried his decision:** "carried" in this sense means to cast the final or deciding vote.

INFORMAL SPEECH

277 **go on:** continue, do not stop.

STANDARD VOCABULARY

275 **carried:** sounded for a long distance.

1. READING: A REVIEW OF THE LITERARY TERMS

SURVEY THE STRUCTURE AND COMPARE

Instead of the usual study questions, we will take a different approach to the story "Hawsmoot." First, we'll use the literary terms as convenient labels, or "handles," for briefly studying the structure and content. Then we'll do a more careful reading of the story as we follow the discussion questions in the next activity section: "Close Reading: Special Group Reports."

By now you are probably familiar with most of the terminology, but you may want to refresh your memory by reviewing it once again (see "Literary Terms," Chapter I), either before completing the statements below or while you are working on them. You will notice that some of the sentences contain references to other stories we have been reading. As you try to recall those stories and make a few comparisons with "Hawsmoot," you may be surprised at how much you can remember and how readily you can use terminology well known to more advanced students of literature.

1. *Setting*
   a. The place where "Hawsmoot" is located is ______________________________ ______________.
   b. The time of year is ______________, when the weather in this part of the country is ______________.
   c. The setting for "Hawsmoot" is important because ______________________ ____.
   d. Two of the earlier stories with very different settings are: "______________ ______________," which takes place ______________________________; and "______________________," whose setting is ______________________.
   e. Of these three stories, I think that the setting of "______________" is the most important to the story because ______________________________ ____.

2. *Characters*
   a. The major characters in "Hawsmoot" are ______________________________, and the minor characters are ______________________________________.
   b. Although there is no narrator in this story, it is told from the point of view of ______________.
   c. Three of the stories we read that *were* told by narrators are: "______________ ______________________________," told by ______________________________; "______________________________," told by ______________________________; and "______________________________," told by ______________________________.

d. Although few short stories have time to develop "round" characters, we could call Hawsmoot a round character because ____________________
____.

e. Another "round" character from a different story might be ______________, from "______________," because ____________________
____.

f. ______________ and ______________, from the stories, "______________" and "______________," are really no more than "flat" characters because ____
____
____.

3. ***Plot***

a. In "Hawsmoot" the central conflict that involves the action takes place between the protagonist, ______________, and the antagonist, ______________.

b. The strongest motivation behind the protagonist is to ____________________
____,
while the aim of the antagonist, on the other hand, is ____________________
____.

c. Another story's plot that clearly involves two people is "______________
______________," in which ______________ tries to prevent ______________
______________ from ______________.

d. "Hawsmoot" is told partly by means of flashbacks, which give us information about ______________ by way of ______________.

e. In another story, "______________," flashbacks are also used, in this case to give information about ______________.

f. An important *subplot* in "Hawsmoot" involves the inner conflict of ____
______________, who must ____.

4. ***Theme***

a. The most obvious theme of the story, "Hawsmoot," concerns the struggle between ______________ and ______________, because it represents ___
____.

b. Although the subplot is related to a specific decision, there is an underlying theme here also of ____
____.

c. Two other stories whose themes I can remember are:
"______________," with the theme, ______________________________
____; and
"______________," whose theme is ______________________________
____.

2. CLOSE READING: A. SPECIAL GROUP REPORTS

RESEARCH, REFLECT, REPORT YOUR FINDINGS

Both "Hawsmoot" and "Going Home" give us close-up portrayals of the loner, an individual who is obviously an outsider. Both stories also have a poetic quality in their authors' imaginative use of language, as well as in the psychological implications of an individual's "inner landscape"—his unspoken feelings and the more or less unconscious workings of his mind.

Searching out these subtle implications and hidden motives can be very rewarding for the reader, because they can lead to exciting new territory for discovery—unexpected insights about the meaning of life itself, along with one's own values and priorities.

Each of the first four parts of the following project is designed for several people to work on together and then to share their observations, as a group, with the rest of the class. The concluding section, "Character and Symbol in 'Hawsmoot,'" is for the whole class to think about and discuss together in open forum.

A. Development of the Plot.

The main plot of this story begins with the first sentence and involves what happens on that one day only.

1. How does the first sentence suggest the dual nature of the plot of Hawsmoot's struggle: with a man? with a mountain? How does this sentence set the tone of the story?
2. List as many contrasting factors as you can find between the protagonist and the antagonist (appearance, personality, etc.).
3. Trace (follow step by step) the series of small episodes that happen that day and that constitute the plot. In each case, note whether Hawsmoot is contending here with a man or a mountain, or both.
4. In this dual plot, explain where each climax comes, or at what point Hawsmoot's conflict is actually resolved with the mountain and with the man.

B. The Flashback Technique.

Authors often make use of flashbacks, but Sandberg has made them add another whole dimension, or a subplot, to his story. Begin with the first flashback, which occurs in the paragraph beginning, "Hawsmoot smiled" (p. 160, line 75). Your instructor will help you to divide up the rest of the story into manageable portions, so that your group can report on the flashbacks in your section, as follows.

1. Give the page and lines where each flashback appears;
2. Tell what information it provides;
3. Explain how the author leads into it, then returns to the story.

C. **Poetic Language.**
The effectiveness of Sandberg's style is greatly increased by his poetically descriptive language, particularly the frequent use of figures of speech. (For definitions, see abbreviations from the Vocabulary Aids, under *fig sp, met, person,* and *sim.*)

1. It is easy to recognize similes because they are always introduced by either "like" or "as." Find and be ready to point out three examples of similes that refer to the young German.
2. Find and be ready to point out three other similes that appear in the story. For each one:
   a. Mention what is being described;
   b. Explain what sort of feeling the simile suggests.
3. Metaphor appears in several places in the story also. In each of the following examples, what sort of image or picture does the metaphor lead you to imagine?
   a. ". . . where it ballooned the orange parka . . ." (p. 160, lines 67–68).
   b. ". . . who at this moment was bound body and soul to the climber" (p. 161, line 106.)
   c. ". . . in the rock pile of the cannery" (p. 164, lines 180–81.)
   d. ". . . fall back into the soft oblivion of a cloud" (p. 167, lines 226–27.)
   e. "It beaconed his soul" (p. 169, line 276.)

D. **The Significance of the Title.**
The title "Hawsmoot" is itself an important clue to the plot, and it also links the plot to the underlying theme.

1. Where in the story do we first see its importance to him? Locate and point out each place where there is a reference to his name, or even to the idea of a name.
2. What effects has his feeling about his name had on his choices in life thus far? (Mention some specific choices.)
3. In some cultures people are very reluctant to give their names to strangers. Do any of these associations with a name enter into Hawsmoot's confrontation with the German?
4. What double meaning do you see in the repeated word, "carried," in the last paragraph?

2. CLOSE READING:
B. GENERAL DISCUSSION

CHARACTER AND SYMBOL IN "HAWSMOOT"

1. Decide which of the following qualities and expressions would apply to Hawsmoot, to Fuchs, or to neither or both of them:

adventuresome	foolhardy	courage	mettle
intrepid	invincible	"true grit"	heroism
energetic	plucky	stubborn	"guts"
ambitious	rash	fearless	vanity

2. The word "pebble" appears as both a metaphor and a symbol for Hawsmoot himself in the following passages:

   ". . . Hawsmoot who at this moment . . . when it did it broke" (p. 161, 105–108).

   "They stood . . . down tin chutes" (p. 168, lines 268–269).

   In what sense does the pebble seem to be symbolizing:

   a. His American type of rugged individualism?
   b. His sense of alienation from society?
   c. The possibility that a younger man could easily outdo him?
   d. His famous reputation as a climber?

3. (*Optional*) A psychological interpretation: If you enjoy searching out deep, psychological themes, you might like to look for one in this story. For instance, Freudian psychology uses the ancient Greek myth about Oedipus to explain a young boy's conflicting feelings about his parents. Oedipus, who did not know who his parents were, killed his father in a battle and then married his father's wife, not realizing she was his mother.

   According to Freud, this represents the antagonism or hostility that fathers and sons often have toward each other, a feeling partly caused by the special love the boy has for his mother. With this background in mind:

   a. Can you explain how the rivalry between the young German and Hawsmoot could represent the Oedipal conflict described by Freud? If so, who or what would symbolize the "mother"?
   b. Can you explain how each of the following passages would support this interpretation?

      "The young German's eyes softened." (p. 158, line 19).

      "The German kept smiling as he looked at the man, but his eyes were like gimlets." (p. 159, line 35).

      "He was very still, hugging the stone closely, his cheek pressed against it. . . ." (p. 167, lines 227–228).

4. Two final questions to consider:

   a. If you were Hawsmoot, would you make the same decision as he did?
   b. Would you object if your father had made a similar type of decision regarding his life?

3. VOCABULARY: SYNONYMS AND ANTONYMS

A. SYNONYMS

Below is a list of twenty synonyms, which you are to match with the Standard Vocabulary words. Each synonym is to be used *only once.*

All the words in the left-hand column are taken from the Standard Vocabulary list for "Hawsmoot." However, some of them are in a different form from the one in which they appeared on the list. Each word is in the same form as the corresponding synonym that goes with it.

List of Synonyms

alien	fasten	increase	self-centered
awkwardness	forgetfulness	mechanical	similarity
common	gigantic	methods	still
dare	haughty	rigidity	strong
ease	identification	safeguard	violence

	SYNONYM		SYNONYM
1. bind	__________	11. resemblance	__________
2. stiffness	__________	12. clumsiness	__________
3. huge	__________	13. arrogant	__________
4. brutality	__________	14. recognition	__________
5. strange	__________	15. egotistical	__________
6. oblivion	__________	16. techniques	__________
7. ordinary	__________	17. protect	__________
8. motionless	__________	18. powerful	__________
9. comfort	__________	19. gain	__________
10. automatic	__________	20. challenge	__________

B. ANTONYMS

An *antonym* is a word that means the opposite of another word. Below is a list of twenty antonyms, which you are to match with the words in the Standard Vocabulary list. Each antonym is to be used only once.

Again, all the words in the column are from the Standard Vocabulary list of "Hawsmoot," some of them in different forms from the way they appeared in the original list. The antonym is in the same form as its corresponding (opposite) word.

List of Antonyms

admiring	friends	loose	rarely
aware	general	lose	success
awkward	gentle	nearby	tension
clearness	gracefully	noisy	threat
differed	humbly	pride	weaken

		ANTONYM			ANTONYM
1.	ordinarily	______	11.	disdainful	______
2.	graceful	______	12.	clumsily	______
3.	gain	______	13.	silent	______
4.	distant	______	14.	relaxation	______
5.	resembled	______	15.	oblivious	______
6.	brutal	______	16.	confusion	______
7.	failure	______	17.	bound	______
8.	arrogantly	______	18.	humility	______
9.	protection	______	19.	strangers	______
10.	particular	______	20.	empower	______

4. STYLE: USING PARTICIPLES FOR SMOOTHER WRITING

STREAMLINE YOUR SENTENCES!

Children's writing is easily recognizable, not only by the näiveté of the ideas expressed, but even more by its immaturity of style. In a child's composition we can expect to find a very limited vocabulary, as well as short sentences with little variety in the sentence structure.

When older students are learning to write in another language, they sometimes unconsciously slip into an immature style such as they would not think of using in their native language. Although their ideas are on an adult level and they practice grammatical forms and add more words to their vocabulary, their writing continues to sound childish.

One reason is that *they are writing one sentence at a time,* without thinking about its relation to the one that came before it and the one that will follow. You can connect your own choppy sentences and also reduce their wordiness by making use of dependent clauses and participles, as Sandberg does in "Hawsmoot." Read one of his paragraphs aloud and see how smoothly it flows along by means of carefully built-in connecting links.

In this exercise, some of the longer sentences from the story have been broken up into shorter units. You can try your hand at rewriting them in a more coherent, easy-reading style with the help of the same present and past participles that Sandberg used. (For a review of the correct use of participles, see Chapter V.)

Follow the method used in the example and combine each of the sets of sentences to make one smooth sentence. For this practice exercise, do not use relative clauses or adverbial connectors such as "when" or "although." Change the underlined verb to its correct participial form. You may need to add a comma to indicate a brief pause before the participial phrase.

Example: The man found a rock and sat down. He *rested* his chin on his hands.

The man found a rock and sat down, resting his chin on his hands.

1. He stood on the ground. He *watched* Hawsmoot climb up the crack. ______

2. The people *were watching*. They caught their breath. ______

3. He raised his hands above his head. He *fitted* them carefully into the crack.

4. Far down there he could see the young climbers. They *gazed* up like possums. ______

5. He paused to rest. He *took* one hand from the rock. He *put* it in his pocket.

6. "I guess I'll be all right," he said. He *laid* his cane carefully against the cliff.

7. His head was bent sideways. His cheek *was pressed* flat against the cold stone. ______

8. The stiff wind blew up the cliffs. It *caused* the leaves to make sounds like pebbles. ______

9. The German yodelled. He *tilted* his head up. ______

10. He *wobbled*. He kicked his shoe up. ______

11. He paused for a moment. He *looked* like a brightly colored still from a ballet.

12. He saw something above him. It *blocked* his way. ______

13. He had seen the climbers. They *were working* the cliffs. ______

14. He finished the last twenty feet and sat at the cliff edge. He *smiled* down at them. ____

____

15. The gray rock was quite smooth. It *was broken* now and then by small ledges.

____

____

16. His back began to throb. The torn muscles *drew* up in spasm against the cold. ____

____

17. He saw Hawsmoot swing out from the cliff. He *hung* by his hands from the overhang. His feet *swung* free. ____

____

18. Nameless hundreds had come to the lake to climb. They *were roped.* They left and *were forgotten.* ____

____

19. The man looked back calmly. He *wished* the German would begin to climb.

____

20. The German hung motionless for a moment, then raised himself up. He *did not stop* this time. He followed through by kicking a foot high up. He *moved* with great precision. ____

____

____

5. COMPOSITION: DESCRIPTIVE WRITING

DESCRIPTION IN 3–D

A. Describe Imaginatively

As we noted in "Close Reading: Poetic Language," Sandberg describes things both sensitively and imaginatively, with the help of similes and metaphors. You are already familiar with this technique in the literature of your native language, but you may wonder if you would ever have occasion to try it in English, or whether you could manage it if you tried.

The answer to both questions is "Yes!" When you want to describe creatively but do not know the right vocabulary words, experiment with using "like" or "as." You may find that the result is even more effective than if you had composed literally or technically correct definitions.

In this exercise you will have a chance to try your hand at writing similes. Let your imagination take over as you think up some interesting and vivid clauses or phrases to complete the sentences below:

1. That music is awful. It sounds like ______________________________

   ______________________________.

2. My mother makes the best soufflé you ever tasted. It's as light as ________

   ______________________________.

3. When the bus driver shut the door and we all were packed in tightly, I felt like ______________________________

   ______________________________.

4. My girlfriend has such lovely hair. It looks like ______________________

   ______________________________.

5. I've been so busy moving that I haven't eaten all day. I'm as hungry as ___

   ______________________________.

6. So you've been playing mud football all afternoon, have you! You look like

   ______________________________.

7. As evening approached, all the lights began to come on, and those tall buildings looked like ______________________________

   ______________________________.

8. We didn't have any heat in our apartment for a whole week last winter, and I got as cold as ______________________________

   ______________________________.

B. Describe Accurately

How well do you "see" what you are looking at? Can you describe something accurately enough so that another person can "see" it too?

Sharpen your skill at observation and your writing, as well, by doing the following exercise:

1. Look in your pocket, purse, or backpack and take out a small object (something other than a book or a notebook), and put it on the writing surface in front of you.
2. Without naming the object, make a detailed list of notes describing it. Include its size, shape, material(s), surface texture (smoothness, hardness, etc.), its color(s), and any other features you can see. Recheck your list to make sure you have mentioned everything you can say to describe it.

3. When you have finished, exchange objects and descriptions with someone near you. Each of you then look closely to find out if either of you can see something that the other one missed. If so, add more details to the other person's description.

C. Describe Meaningfully

Like any other form of writing, a description should be purposeful. When you are describing lab results or reporting a car accident, your details must be *objective,* that is, not influenced or colored by your imagination or any emotional tone. It is accuracy that is important here.

Even more is called for in a good subjective description, because it must be *both* accurate and imaginative. The fiction writer is confronted with this challenge whenever he sits down to write. Although you may not ever expect to create fiction, you can share the fiction writer's experience and gain valuable insights and practice in writing by carrying out one or both of the assignments below:

1. A *negative* description, involving a moment when you experienced great fear or anger.
2. A *positive* description of a very specific place where you love to be.

1. ***Negative description.*** What can make or has made you very angry or very much afraid? It is easiest if you can *remember* such an occasion rather than try to imagine it, because then you can almost reexperience the feelings you had. If you cannot recall such a moment, can you imagine how you would feel if . . . ? Can you describe the physical symptoms and sensations you have felt at such times—in your head, your back, your hands and feet, your skin, and inside your body?

Make this description a paragraph of seven or eight sentences. Do not take time to narrate what happened except for what you can say in one brief, introductory sentence, such as:

> When the teacher told me she saw me cheating, I was so furious that. . . .
> We were going at least 65 miles an hour when I saw the oncoming car coming straight toward us—driving in our lane. . . .

2. ***Positive description.*** Where would you love to go right now if you could, just to *be* there? Is it a place outdoors or inside a special room, a place you know well or a place you imagine—or some of both? Can you write about it so that your reader feels as though he or she were *there,* seeing with your eyes, hearing with your ears, experiencing it through your senses?

Begin your paragraph with an introductory sentence that gives the reader an indication of where you are:

I am just waking up, early in the morning in my own bed at home. . . .

The rock where I am sitting is warm from the sun, as the cool water of the brook ripples over my feet. . . .

As a child, I loved most to be in the swing my grandfather had made that was fastened to a branch of a great oak tree. . . .

Katherine Anne Porter (1890–1980)

Katherine Anne Porter has been acclaimed as one of America's most significant writers of short fiction. Born in Texas of an old Southern family, she was educated in convent and private schools and was expected to be content with a very conventional, home-centered life. Instead, she went off to Denver, Colorado, as a young woman and worked on a newspaper for three years. It may have been this journalistic experience, where words must not be wasted, that encouraged her to develop her economical writing style, so well suited to short stories.

For most of her life, Miss Porter traveled extensively abroad, spending many years in Mexico and Europe. A Mexican setting is featured in her book Hacienda *(1934), and in a few of the stories appearing in* Flowering Judas *(1930), from which "Rope" is taken. Yet some of her most successful work, such as* Noon Wine *(1937) and* Pale Horse, Pale Rider *(1939), returns to the Southern setting so familiar to her.*

For twenty years she worked to perfect her monumental, allegorical novel, Ship of Fools *(1962), in which the passengers on a ship represent the hopeless entanglement of good with evil. On the whole, however, Katherine Anne Porter will probably be remembered most for her psychological penetration of her characters' mixed motives and her amazingly accurate portrayal of human behavior in simple, everyday situations.*

XI

Rope

Story Setting: *A plain, country farmhouse typical of many rural homes in America a few years ago (and some even now), where there are no close neighbors and often none of the amenities or conveniences such as electricity and running water.*

In the Story: *A young married couple have a quarrel over a very trivial matter, as lovers often do. What happens, however, is of less importance than the way it is told. There is no direct dialogue; yet the story consists almost entirely of conversation between the husband and wife, expressed indirectly but in accurate detail.*

A Special Note Concerning this Story: *The best stories ask something of the reader. They invite one to think, to figure out subtle implications, and to use one's imagination. In responding to the author's challenge, the reader is, in a sense, bringing the story to life—helping to create it anew. It is a very exciting and special kind of reading.*

"Rope" has few long or complicated words, but it can be difficult for a nonnative speaker because it is loaded with many of the colloquial expressions and clichés that abound in American speech. These expressions have little or no definable meaning and therefore are labeled here as "indefinite" (indef). They are worthless additions to most writing except in portraying ordinary conversation, where there is a very human tendency to use them to avoid unpleasant confrontations.

In a story like this, then, the careful reader will want to watch closely in order to be aware of what is really going on. You will often find the speakers' meaning obscure, their words exaggerated, and their reasoning foggy and illogical—but listen to their tone!

Note also that although the author's text has been left in its exact, original form, two variations have been made in the format in order to aid you in your reading and in your study activities. First, certain passages are in italics: these passages are the only parts of the story that are not conversation. *Second, the story has been arbitrarily divided into ten sections, or scenes, to make it easier to find the answers to the study questions, and then to prepare the way for the Special Group Project to follow.*

I

On the third day after they moved to the country he came walking back from the village carrying a basket of groceries and a twenty-four-yard coil of rope. She came out to meet him, wiping her hands on her green smock. Her hair was tumbled, her nose scarlet with sunburn; he told her that already she looked like a born country woman. *His gray flannel shirt stuck to him, his heavy shoes were dusty.* She assured him he looked like a rural character in a play.

Had he brought the coffee? She had been waiting all day long for coffee. They had forgot it when they ordered at the store the first day.

Gosh, no, he hadn't. Lord, now he'd have to go back. Yes, he would if it killed him. He thought, though, he had everything else. She reminded him it was only because he didn't drink coffee himself. If he did he would remember it quick enough. Suppose they ran out of cigarettes? *Then she saw the rope.* What was that for? Well, he thought it might do to hang clothes on, or something. Naturally she asked him if he thought they were going to run a laundry? They already had a fifty-foot line hanging right before his eyes. Why, hadn't he noticed it, really? It was a blot on the landscape to her.

II

He thought there were a lot of things a rope might come in handy for. She wanted to know what, for instance. *He thought for a few seconds, but nothing occurred.* They could wait and see, couldn't they? You need all sorts of strange odds and ends around a place in the country. She said, yes, that was so; but she thought just at that time, when every penny counted, it seemed funny to buy more rope. That was all. She hadn't meant anything else. She hadn't just seen, not at first, why he felt it was necessary.

GLOSSARY

2 **coil of rope:** rope that has been wound in loose circles, for easier handling.
3 **smock:** a loose garment worn over clothes to protect them.
3 **tumbled:** mussed up.
4 **a born country woman:** one who has always lived on a farm.
13 **run a laundry:** manage a business based on washing people's clothes.

INFORMAL SPEECH

8 **Gosh . . . Lord:** mild forms of swearing.
8 **would if it killed him:** exaggeration to show he really meant what he said.
11 **ran out of:** used up the supply.
11 **it might do:** might serve the need of something (usually said in a doubtful, unenthusiastic way).
14 **blot on the landscape** (cliché): an ugly object that spoils the scenery, an "eyesore."
15 **might come in handy for:** might have an unexpected usefulness.
16 **wait and see** (indef): perhaps later (a way of stalling or avoiding the issue).
17 **odds and ends:** assorted things with no particular use or relation to other things.
18 **when every penny counted** (cliché): when money was very scarce.

STANDARD VOCABULARY

3 **scarlet:** bright red.
5 ***assured:** told him very confidently.
9 ***reminded:** caused (him) to remember.

Well, thunder, he had bought it because he wanted to, and that was all there was to it. She thought that was reason enough, and couldn't understand why he hadn't said so, at first. Undoubtedly it would be useful, twenty-four yards of rope, there were hundreds of

GLOSSARY

INFORMAL SPEECH

21 **Well, thunder:** an expression of annoyance.
21 **all there was to it** (stress word is *to*): usually has a double meaning: to indicate the matter is simple—no hidden meanings—but also to hint very strongly that one doesn't want to talk about it any more.

STANDARD VOCABULARY

things, she couldn't think of any at the moment, but it would come in. Of course. As he had said, things always did in the country.

But she was a little disappointed about the coffee, and oh, look, look, look at the eggs! Oh, my, they're all running! What had he put on top of them? Hadn't he known eggs mustn't be squeezed? Squeezed, who had squeezed them, he wanted to know. What a silly thing to say. He had simply brought them along in the basket with the other things. If they got broke it was the grocer's fault. He should know better than to put heavy things on top of eggs.

III

She believed it was the rope. That was the heaviest thing in the pack; she saw him plainly when he came in from the road, the rope was a big package on top of everything. He desired the whole wide world to witness that this was not a fact. He had carried the rope in one hand and the basket in the other, and what was the use of her having eyes if that was the best they could do for her?

Well, anyhow, she could see one thing plain: no eggs for breakfast. They'd have to scramble them now, for supper. It was too damned bad. She had planned to have steak for supper. No ice, meat wouldn't keep. He wanted to know why she couldn't finish breaking the eggs in a bowl and set them in a cool place.

Cool place! If he could find one for her, she'd be glad to set them there. Well, then, it seemed to him they might very well cook the meat at the same time they cooked the eggs and then warm up the meat for tomorrow. The idea simply choked her. Warmed-over meat, when they might as well have had it fresh. Second-best and scraps and makeshifts,

GLOSSARY

27 **they're all running:** the shells are broken and the insides are leaking out.

INFORMAL SPEECH

24 **it would come in:** short for "it might come in handy."
28 **silly:** foolish.
29 **simply:** only, merely (often spoken in defense of oneself).
34 **desired the whole wide world to witness** (cliché): an exaggerated effort to emphasize his innocence (He would probably answer: "I'll tell the world it wasn't!")
35 **what was the use of** . . . a disparaging put-down expression that she was half-blind or was too stupid to see something obvious.
38 **too damned bad:** the swear-word adds emphasis to show her annoyance.
39 **wouldn't keep:** would not stay fresh, would spoil.
43 **warm up:** reheat.
43 **warmed-over:** reheated.
44 **makeshifts:** temporary substitutes.

STANDARD VOCABULARY

26 ***disappointed:** a little sad because of failed expectations.
28 **squeezed:** held tightly together.
43 **choked:** (lit) strangled or killed by blocking the throat.
44 **scraps:** bits and pieces, good for nothing.

even to the meat! *He rubbed her shoulder a little.* It doesn't really matter so much, does it, darling? *Sometimes when they were playful, he would rub her shoulder and she would arch and purr. This time she hissed and almost clawed. He was getting ready to say that they could surely manage somehow when she turned on him and said,* if he told her they could manage somehow she would certainly slap his face.

IV

He swallowed the words red hot, his face burned. He picked up the rope and started to put it on the top shelf. She would not have it on the top shelf, the jars and tins belonged there; positively she would not have the top shelf cluttered up with a lot of rope. She had borne all the clutter she meant to bear in the flat in town, there was space here at least and she meant to keep things in order.

Well, in that case, he wanted to know what the hammer and nails were doing up there? And why had she put them there when she knew very well he needed that hammer and those nails upstairs to fix the window sashes? She simply slowed down everything and made double work on the place with her insane habit of changing things around and hiding them.

She was sure she begged his pardon and if she had had any reason to believe he was going to fix the sashes this summer she would have left the hammer and nails right where he put them: in the middle of the bedroom floor where they could step on them in the dark. And now if he didn't clear the whole mess out of there she would throw them down the well.

Oh, all right, all right—could he put them in the closet? Naturally not, there were brooms and mops and dustpans in the closet, and why couldn't he find a place for his rope

GLOSSARY

46 **arch and purr:** behave like a cat when it's happy.
47 **hissed . . . clawed:** behaved like an angry cat.
50 **swallowed the words red hot:** stopped short, without speaking. The analogy suggests suddenly having to swallow very hot food.
51 **jars and tins:** canned goods and other preserved food.
53 **flat:** an apartment.
55 **in that case:** then, accordingly.
57 **window sashes:** wooden frames that hold the glass at the bottom of windows.
60 **She was sure she begged his pardon:** exaggerated formality, deliberately meant to sound sarcastic.
64 **well:** a deep hole dug in the ground used as a source for drinking water in the country.

INFORMAL SPEECH

47 **surely manage somehow** (cliché): certainly find a way to cope with their problems (usually said when one has no solutions to propose but is trying to sound hopeful).
48 **turned on him:** angrily faced him and spoke sharply.
52 **cluttered up:** filled with in a messy, disorderly way.
55 **what . . . were doing:** why they were there (usually implies something should *not* be there.)
57 **simply:** Note that, when he used this earlier (line 29, p. 186), he was defending his own action. What is he doing here?
63 **the whole mess:** all that worthless junk.

STANDARD VOCABULARY

51 ***belonged:** were properly situated or placed, were meant to be.
52 **positively:** emphatically.
52 ***had borne:** (*past participle of* **to bear**) had endured, put up with.
58 **insane:** mentally deranged, crazy.

outside her kitchen? Had he stopped to consider there were seven rooms in the house and only one kitchen?

V

He wanted to know what of it? And did she realize she was making a complete fool of herself? And what did she take him for, a three-year-old idiot? The whole trouble with her was she needed something weaker than she was to heckle and tyrannize over. He wished now they had a couple of children she could take it out on. Maybe he'd get some rest.

Her face changed at this, she reminded him he had forgot the coffee and had bought a worthless piece of rope. And when she thought of all the things they actually needed to make the place even decently fit to live in, well, she would cry, that was all. *She looked so forlorn, so lost and despairing* he couldn't believe it was only a piece of rope that was causing all the racket. What was the matter?

Oh, would he please hush and go away, and stay away, if he could, for five minutes. By all means, yes, he would. He'd stay away indefinitely if she wished. Lord, yes, there was nothing he'd like better than to clear out and never come back. She couldn't for the life of her see what was holding him, then. It was a swell time. Here she was, stuck, miles from a railroad, with a half-empty house on her hands, and not a penny in her pocket, and everything on earth to do; it seemed the moment for him to get out from under. She was surprised he hadn't stayed in town as it was until she had come out and done the work and got things straightened out. It was his usual trick.

GLOSSARY

70 **idiot:** a silly fool (lit, a feeble-minded person).
75 **decently fit to live in** (indef): She is hinting that their home needs to be made much more convenient and attractive.
79 **by all means:** a rather archaic, formal way of saying "Certainly," "Of course."
82 **not a penny in her pocket** (cliché): with no money.
83 **everything on earth to do** (exag): all the housework to do.
84 **as it was** (cliché): in any case, after all.
85 **his usual trick:** implying that he would try any kind of scheme to avoid helping with the work.

INFORMAL SPEECH

69 **what of it?:** (the *of* is stressed) What does *that* matter?
70 **What did she take him for?** (stress on *take*): What did she think he was?
72 **take it out on:** express negative behavior toward someone who cannot retaliate, or do the same in return.
77 **racket:** confused noise, din.
78 **please hush:** please be quiet.
79 **Lord:** mild swearing.
80 **clear out:** leave for good, taking all one's possessions.
80 **couldn't for the life of her** (cliché): an exaggeration to sound sarcastic.
81 **what was holding him:** what was keeping him at home (sarc).
81 **swell** (sl): fine, wonderful, "great" (sarc).
81 **stuck:** unable to move.
83 **to get out from under:** to escape (all the work that had to be done).
85 **got things straightened out:** (cliché): put everything in good order.

STANDARD VOCABULARY

71 **heckle:** harass or annoy with questions and demands; badger.
71 ***tyrannize over:** rule oppressively, as a dictator would.
76 ***forlorn:** deserted, wretched, miserable.
76 ***despairing:** completely hopeless.
79 **indefinitely:** for an unspecified length of time, perhaps forever.

VI

It appeared to him that this was going a little far. Just a touch out of bounds, if she didn't mind his saying so. Why had he stayed in town the summer before? To do a half-dozen extra jobs to get the money he had sent her. That was it. She knew perfectly well they couldn't have done it otherwise. She had agreed with him at the time. And that was the only time, so help him, he had ever left her to do anything by herself.

Oh, he could tell that to his great-grandmother. She had her notion of what had kept him in town. Considerably more than a notion, if he wanted to know. So, she was going to bring all that up again, was she? Well, she could just think what she pleased. He was tired of explaining. It may have looked funny but he had simply got hooked in, and what could he do? It was impossible to believe that she was going to take it seriously. Yes, yes, she knew how it was with a man: if he was left by himself a minute, some woman was certain to kidnap him. And naturally he couldn't hurt her feelings by refusing!

Well, what was she raving about? Did she forget she had told him those two weeks alone in the country were the happiest she had known for four years? And how long had they been married when she said that? All right, shut up! If she thought that hadn't stuck in his craw.

She hadn't meant she was happy because she was away from him. She meant she was happy getting the devilish house nice and ready for him. That was what she meant, and now look! Bringing up something she had said a year ago simply to justify himself for

GLOSSARY

91 **he could tell that to. . . .** (cliché): really means that she did not believe him.
93 **just think what she pleased:** a defiant way of saying that he didn't care what she thought.
94 **simply got hooked in:** (lit) was caught like a fish, or was quite helpless and unable to get away.
100 **stuck in his craw** (cliché): made him angry so that he had not forgotten it.

INFORMAL SPEECH

86 **going a little far:** (indef): meaning that he thought she was exaggerating and he resented what she said.
86 **if she didn't mind his saying so** (cliché): an exaggerated effort to sound polite.
88 **perfectly well:** very well indeed.
90 **so help him:** a short form of the solemn vow or oath, "So help me God." Meant to sound sincere.
93 **bring . . . up again:** start once more to blame him for something long past.
94 **looked funny:** seemed odd or strange.
95 **take it seriously:** consider it really important.
97 **hurt her feelings:** offend her deeply.
98 **raving about:** talking wildly or angrily, like a mad person.
100 **shut up:**rude slang for "Be quiet!"
103 **devilish** (sw): to emphasize anger and frustration.

STANDARD VOCABULARY

91 **notion:** idea, opinion.
92 ***considerably:** in large degree.
104 ***justify:** show oneself to be free of any blame.

forgetting her coffee and breaking the eggs and buying a wretched piece of rope they couldn't afford.

VII

She really thought it was time to drop the subject, and now she wanted only two things in the world. She wanted him to get that rope from underfoot, and go back to the village and get her coffee, and if he could remember it, he might bring a metal mitt for the skillets, and two more curtain rods, and if there were any rubber gloves in the village, her hands were simply raw, and a bottle of milk of magnesia from the drugstore.

He looked out at the dark blue afternoon sweltering on the slopes, and mopped his forehead and sighed heavily and said, if only she could wait a minute for *anything,* he was going back. He had said so, hadn't he, the very instant they found he had overlooked it?

Oh, yes, well . . . run along. She was going to wash windows. The country was so beautiful. She doubted they'd have a moment to enjoy it. He meant to go, but he could not until he had said that if she wasn't such a hopeless melancholiac she might see that this was only for a few days. Couldn't she remember anything pleasant about the other summers. Hadn't they ever had any fun? She hadn't time to talk about it, and now would he please not leave that rope lying around for her to trip on? *He picked it up, somehow it had toppled off the table, and walked out with it under his arm.*

Was he going this minute? He certainly was. She thought so. Sometimes it seemed to her he had second sight about the precisely perfect moment to leave her ditched. She had meant to put the mattresses out to sun, if they put them out this minute they would get at least three hours, he must have heard her say that morning she meant to put them out. So of course he would walk off and leave her to do it. She supposed he thought the exercise would do her good.

VIII

Well, he was merely going to get her coffee. A four-mile walk for two pounds of coffee was ridiculous, but he was perfectly willing to do it. The habit was making a wreck of her,

GLOSSARY

109 **metal mitt for the skillets:** a potholder for protection from the hot frying pans.
112 **slopes:** hillsides.
117 **hopeless melancholiac:** someone who is incurably depressed.
121 **toppled off the table:** became unbalanced (top-heavy) and had fallen off.
123 **second sight:** the ability to "see" the future before it happens (clairvoyance).
124 **put the mattresses out to sun:** carry out all the bedding to get fresh air and sunshine.

INFORMAL SPEECH

107 **drop the subject:** talk about something else.
108 **from underfoot:** from where it was in her way and thus annoying to her.
111 **simply raw:** chapped, or chafed and sore.
115 **run along:** usually said to a small child who is being a nuisance or a bother to an adult.
123 **ditched** (sl): deserted, abandoned.
129 **making a wreck of her** (cliché): ruining her health.

STANDARD VOCABULARY

106 **couldn't afford:** could scarcely manage to pay for.
112 **sweltering:** steaming with heat.
114 ***overlooked:** failed to notice.
116 ***doubted:** did not believe.
120 **trip on:** to catch one's foot and possibly fall.
123 ***precisely:** exactly.
129 ***ridiculous:** absurd.

but if she wanted to wreck herself there was nothing he could do about it. If he thought it was coffee that was making a wreck of her, she congratulated him: he must have an easy conscience.

Conscience or no conscience, he didn't see why the mattresses couldn't very well wait until tomorrow. And, anyhow, were they living *in the house,* or were they going to let the house ride them to death? *She paled at this, her face grew livid about the mouth, she looked quite dangerous,* and reminded him that housekeeping was no more her work than it was his: she had other work to do as well, and when did he think she was going to find time to do it at this rate?

Was she going to start on that again? She knew as well as he did that his work brought in the regular money, hers was only occasional, if they depended on what she made—and she might as well get straight on this question once for all!

That was positively not the point. The question was, when both of them were working on their own time, was there going to be a division of the housework, or wasn't there? She merely wanted to know, she had to make her plans. Why, he thought that was all arranged. It was understood that he was to help. Hadn't he always, in summer?

Hadn't he, though? Oh, just hadn't he? And when, and where, and doing what? Lord, what an uproarious joke.

IX

It was such a very uproarious joke that her face turned slightly purple, and she screamed with laughter. She laughed so hard she had to sit down, and finally a rush of tears spurted from her eyes and poured down into the lifted corners of her mouth. He dashed toward her and dragged her up to her feet and tried to pour water on her head. The dipper hung by a string on a nail and he broke it loose. Then he tried to pump water with one hand while she struggled in the other. So he gave it up and shook her instead.

GLOSSARY

131 **she congratulated him** (sarc): wished him joy and success.
133 **conscience . . . conscience** (indef): never mind talking about conscience.
141 **once for all:** without ever mentioning it again. (Similar expressions: "Enough of that!" and "That's that!")
146 **Oh, just hadn't he?:** Repetition for its sarcastic effect.
147 **uproarious joke:** something howlingly funny (iron)
149 **rush of tears spurted:** a sudden, hysterical switch from laughing to crying.
151 **dipper:** a tin cup with a long handle.

INFORMAL SPEECH

131 **easy conscience:** a feeling of being free of any guilt or responsibility.
135 **ride them to death:** harass and annoy them all the time.
137 **at this rate:** under such difficult conditions as these.
141 **get straight:** understand the real facts.
152 **gave it up:** stopped trying.

STANDARD VOCABULARY

135 **paled:** lost color in her face.
135 **livid:** unnaturally white (usually a sign of great anger).
142 **point:** the issue being discussed.
152 **pump:** vigorously move a handle (lever) to bring up water from a well.

She wrenched away, crying for him to take his rope and get out, she had simply given him up; *and ran. He heard her high-heeled bedroom slippers clattering and stumbling on the stairs.*

He went out around the house and into the lane; he suddenly realized he had a blister on his heel and his shirt felt as if it were on fire. Things broke so suddenly you didn't know where you were. She could work herself into a fury about simply nothing. She was terrible, not an ounce of reason. You might as well talk to a sieve as that woman when she got going. Darned if he'd spend his life humoring her! Well, what to do now? He would take back the rope and exchange it for something else. Things accumulated, things were mountainous, you couldn't move them, or sort them out or get rid of them. They just lay and rotted around. He'd take it back. Why should he? He wanted it. What was it anyhow? A piece of rope. Imagine anybody caring more about a piece of rope than about a man's feelings. What earthly right had she to say a word about it? He remembered all the useless, meaningless things she bought for herself: Why? because I wanted it, that's why! *He stopped and selected a large stone by the road.* He would put the rope behind it. He would put it in the toolbox when he got back. He'd heard enough about it to last him a lifetime.

X

When he came back she was leaning against the post box beside the road waiting. It was pretty late, the smell of broiled steak floated nose high in the cooling air. Her face was young and smooth and fresh-looking. Her unmanageable funny black hair was all on end. She waved to him from a distance, and he speeded up. She called out that supper was ready and waiting, was he starved?

You bet he was starved. Here was the coffee. He waved it at her. *She looked at his other hand.* What was that he had there?

Well, it was the rope again. *He stopped short.* He had meant to exchange it but forgot. She wanted to know why he should exchange it, if it was something he really wanted. Wasn't the air sweet now, and wasn't it fine to be here?

She walked beside him with one hand hooked into his leather belt. She pulled and jostled him a little as he walked, and leaned against him. He put his arm clear around her and patted her stomach.

GLOSSARY

154 **simply given him up** (cliché): considered him impossible to understand or communicate with.
156 **blister:** a sore place on the skin from the shoe's rubbing it.
158 **work . . . fury:** become very angry and excited.
159 **you might . . . sieve as. . . .:** talking was utterly useless in this situation.
165 **earthly** (indef): simply added for emphasis.

INFORMAL SPEECH

157 **things broke:** circumstances suddenly seemed to change.
158 **not an ounce of reason:** no intelligent thinking.
159 **got going:** became very upset.
160 **darned if:** a euphemism for a swear word.
171 **all on end:** sticking straight up or out.
172 **Was he starved?:** Did he have a good appetite?
173 **You bet:** a cheerful and emphatic "yes."
175 **stopped short:** stopped abruptly or suddenly.

STANDARD VOCABULARY

154 **wrenched away:** violently pulled away.
155 **clattering** (onomat): making a sharp sound.
155 **stumbling:** half falling as one walks or runs.
160 ***humoring:** giving someone whatever he or she wanted. (Note that this usage as a verb has a different meaning from the noun, "humor," as we have used it earlier.)
161 ***accumulated:** kept adding up and increasing.
178 **jostled** (*him*): bumped against him gently.

They exchanged wary smiles. Coffee, coffee for the Ootsum-Wootums! *He felt as if he were bringing her a beautiful present.*

He was in love, she firmly believed, and if she had had her coffee in the morning, she wouldn't have behaved so funny. . . . There was a whippoorwill still coming back, imagine, clear out of season, sitting in the crab-apple tree calling all by himself. Maybe his girl stood him up. Maybe she did. She hoped to hear him once more, she loved whippoorwills . . . He knew how she was didn't he?

Sure, he knew how she was.

GLOSSARY

180 **the Ootsum-Wootums:** a pet name for a small infant. (Lovers often like to use baby talk to each other.)
183 **behaved so funny:** acted oddly, not like her usual self.
183 **whippoorwill:** a night bird whose name comes from its song.

INFORMAL SPEECH

182 **firmly believed:** was absolutely certain (pretending she had just discovered the fact).
184 **clear out of season:** completely off-season, or much later than usual.
185 **stood him up:** left him for another lover.

STANDARD VOCABULARY

180 **wary:** very cautious or careful.

1. STUDY QUESTIONS

DISCOVERING THE STORY THROUGH OBSERVATION AND INFERENCE

Scene I

1. ***Observation:*** The first paragraph is short, but if you look closely you can obtain a lot of information. What specific details can you find there?
   Inference: Based on the information so far, what do you think the man needs at this point, and what is he expecting as he arrives? How are the woman's needs and expectations different from his?
2. ***Observation:*** What reason does the woman suggest for his forgetting the coffee? What is her reaction to his bringing home the rope? Is there any connection between the two comments?
   Inference: In the third paragraph, between the sentence ending with ". . . his eyes" and the one beginning "Why, hadn't . . . ," the man probably answers something. What comment from him is implied? What sort of connotation would you associate with her expression, "blot on the landscape"? Can you explain why she feels as she does about it?

Scene II

3. ***Observation:*** In the first paragraph of Scene II, the woman sounds rather accusing, while the man sounds defensive. In the next paragraph, beginning with "Well, thunder. . . ," what *changes in tone* take place?
   Inference: When she makes that long speech, "She thought that was reason enough . . .", do you think she really *believes* all she is saying? Why does she say it?
4. ***Observation:*** Who gets blamed for the broken eggs? Who does the blaming?
   Inference: Why do both the woman and the man make such a "big deal" of it?

Scene III

5. ***Observation:*** Do we know, really, *how* or *where* he carried the rope on the way home? (Look very closely and be sure.)
   Inference: Why is the rope causing so much trouble between them?
6. ***Observation:*** Beginning with the second paragraph in Scene III, what complaints is the woman making about their living situation in the country?
   Inference: What makes her so angry at the thought of his telling her that "they could manage somehow"?

Scene IV

7. ***Observation:*** How do the hammer and nails get into the argument? (Where are they now, and where have they been?)

Inference: Who is talking in the sentence, "She simply slowed . . ." and in the sentence, "And now if he . . ."? How is the first comment *irrelevant?* How is the second one *intemperate?* Why do they talk this way?

8. ***Observation:*** In what room is the argument taking place? What is it that the man wants to put into the closet?
Inference: Why does the woman talk about "his" rope and "her" kitchen? Do you think she feels satisfied with the role she is assigning to herself? (Give reasons for your opinion.)

Scene V

9. ***Observation:*** What are the effects on the woman of those last comments made by her husband?
Inference: Is it true that "only a piece of rope" is causing all the trouble, or are other things also to blame? Why do they both mention the rope so much?
10. ***Observation:*** The woman's sudden outburst, beginning with "Oh, would he please hush . . . ," tells us a lot about what is on her mind. Mention four or five grievances that are bothering her.
Inference: Which of these grievances would *you* call serious, and which do you think are just annoying or inconvenient? What do you think bothers the *woman* most?

Scene VI

11. ***Observation:*** Which of her complaints does her husband try to answer? Exactly what is *he* responding to in the sentence that begins, "Why had he . . ."?
Inference: Does his answer satisfy her? Can you figure out from that paragraph beginning, "Oh, he could tell that . . . ," what had probably happened last summer?
12. ***Observation:*** The two make their strongest charges against each other in the last part of Scene VI, beginning with the woman's, "Yes, yes, she knew how it was. . . ." What is she accusing him of, and how does he answer her?
Inference: Why do you think she interrupts him with "All right, shut up"?

Scene VII

13. ***Observation:*** This is the only scene that begins in the middle of someone's speech. What change in the woman's line of argument is taking place at this point? Would you say that her attitude is hardening or softening toward him?
Inference: Even rather innocent-looking objects can take on emotional meaning when a couple is having an argument. What is she implying by asking him to bring the metal mitt and the curtain rods? How about the rubber gloves and the milk of magnesia?

14. ***Observation:*** What is the weather like, and how does it affect the two of them differently?
 Inference: How do you think the man's wife is trying to make him feel in those two paragraphs beginning with "Oh, yes, well . . ."? Is she succeeding?

Scene VIII

15. ***Observation:*** What sort of attitude is the man showing toward his wife when he brings up her coffee-drinking? Can you find more examples in Scene VIII of his taking this position toward her?
 Inference: Only a short while before, he asked her sadly if they hadn't "ever had any fun." What has been happening to make him change from the way he was talking then?
16. ***Observation:*** How do they divide up the housework between them? What contrasts do you see in their viewpoints toward housework? Do you think this is representative of most couples' feelings?
 Inference: What do you think the woman might really be trying to say to him? Why is she dissatisfied with his reponse?

Scene IX

17. ***Observation:*** The beginning of this scene contains the most action of the whole story. In your own words, explain what is happening here.
 Inference: Why is the man acting so frantic (wildly excited)?
18. ***Observation and Inference:*** The long paragraph in Scene IX is presented as an interior monologue—as if a person were talking to himself or thinking aloud. Here the man is talking to himself as he starts off to the store.

 From the list of words below, choose those that seem to express the man's state of mind as he says (or thinks) each of the following statements. More than one of the words can be applied to some of the statements. Be ready to explain your choices. (Look up the words you don't know). Some of the words may not be needed.

accusation	boredom	exasperation	grief
amusement	contentment	fault-finding	hostility
anger	determination	forgiveness	obstinacy
bewilderment	discouragement	frustration	self-righteousness

"Things broke so suddenly you didn't know where you were." ______________

"She was terrible, not an ounce of reason." ______________

"Well, what to do now?" ______________

"Things accumulated, things were mountainous. . . ." ______________

"Imagine anyone caring more about a piece of rope than about a man's feelings." ______________

"Why? Because I wanted it, that's why!" ______________

Scene X

19. ***Observation:*** Compare the man's second homecoming with the one in the first paragraph of the story. Which details are similar, and which ones different?
    Inference: What inferences might we draw from the odd little passage: "He put his arm around her . . . for the Ootsum-Wootums"?
20. ***Observation:*** Where and how in this scene does she try to "apologize" for her behavior earlier? Does he accept her apology? How do you know?
    Inference: Do you think that this young couple love each other? What might be some of the reasons behind their quarrel?

2. GRAMMAR: REPORTED SPEECH

WHAT DID GEORGE SAY?

In the story "Going Home," we noted Saroyan's unconventional punctuation of dialogue (omitting the quotation marks), and in Activity 3 of the same chapter we supplied the needed capitals and punctuation for some short passages of direct speech or dialogue.

In the first two exercises you are going to extend your control over the language by converting *direct* speech into *indirect* (reported) speech. In these exercises, instead of using anyone's exact words, as in a direct quotation, you will make a statement *telling* us what was said. Exercise C asks you to do the opposite: to read an *indirect* or reported quotation and figure out the *exact words* of the speaker.

You can readily see that the conversion of direct to indirect speech or of indirect to direct speech actually requires you to manage several different language processes at once. You will need to:

- Read carefully in order to understand the meaning;
- Keep the point of view consistent with the meaning;
- Make the pronouns and the verbs consistent with the change;
- Take special care with contractions ("it's" may become *it was*);
- Make the time signals consistent ("now" may become *then* and "this" become *that*);
- In questions, decide what connecting word should follow *asked* (where, if, who, when, whether, etc).

All this may sound complicated, but you will find that a little practice will make it much easier. If you would like to have a more detailed review of how to convert direct speech into reported speech, see Chapter I, Activity 6: "The Historical Present."

Practice A: Use the Quotations as a Basis for Completing the Statements

All of the direct quotations below come from the stories. Rewrite each one as an *indirect quotation* by completing the statement that has been started for you.

Example: "You look like a baby to me, Countess."
He said that she looked like a baby to him ________.

1. "I am quitting this Company for a different job."

   Juan Garcia said that ________.

2. "Oh, I don't think it's *that*," Mrs. Ericson began. (Omit the "Oh.")

   Mrs. Ericson began to say that ________.

3. "You have been my *only* son," she said.

   She said that ________.

4. "No," he said, "I'm not dressed for it. You come on home with me."
   He told me no, that ________

   and asked me ________.

5. "I will be great," he said. "So I climb unroped where other climbers will not follow."
   He said that ________

   ________.

6. "Well, I'll make it even easier," said Mr. Parkhill lightly. "Where did your boats *land*?"
   Mr. Parkhill said that________

   and asked________.

7. "I'm glad we're going away from it."

   The boy told them that ________.

8. "What belongs to history belongs to all men. You want to go back to the Middle Ages?"
   Mr. Abramovitch said that ________,
   and asked her ________.

9. "Don't climb without a rope, Mr. Hawsmoot," she said.
   The girl urged ________.

10. "Don't you want to come along?" the inspector asked. "Mandy and I don't mind the company."

The inspector asked Mrs. Ericson ______________________________
and said that ____________________________________.

Practice B: Change the Direct Quotations to Indirect or Reported Speech

Rewrite each of the direct quotations below as *indirect* or *reported* speech. Use the same subject for the sentence (usually it will be the speaker, although not always). Keep the verbs and pronouns consistent with the new point of view. Remember, you do not need quotation marks or question marks in an *indirect* statement.

Example: "Your younger brother is coming to study in the States, too," my father told me.

My father told me that my younger brother was coming to study in the States, too.

1. "I have a new dress!" said Chen Lee's little sister.

   ____

2. "Do happily married people ever quarrel?" asked the young bride.

   ____

3. "The visitors' bell's ringing. It's time for us to go," said Vladim.

   ____

4. "I'll meet you at the bus station," I told Andrea.

   ____

5. "Have you had your dinner yet?" John's mother asked him.

   ____

6. "Speak a little louder," the old lady told her grandson, "and don't talk so fast."

   ____

7. The teacher held up a book and said, "This book was left on my desk. Whose book is it?"

   ____

8. "Wait for me!" we heard Lucille call out to her brother Ricardo.

   ____

9. Peter's Aunt Margaret said, "I've brought a surprise for you!"

   ____

10. "My parents like you very much, Nick," said Helen. "I hope you will come to see me again."

    ____

Practice C: Convert Reported Speech into Direct Quotations

This exercise will be a little harder because it requires you to do two extra things: Use your imagination to *figure out the speaker's exact words* and *punctuate your quoted speech correctly*. (You might find it helpful first to review the exercise on punctuating direct quotations found in Chapter VII, "Going Home," Activity 3.)

Example 1: He said he'd walk to the bus with her.
"I'll walk to the bus with you," he said.

Example 2: The climber asked the guide if he thought it was going to snow.
"Do you think it's going to snow?" the climber asked the guide.

1. Rafael promised that he would be there to meet her.

   ____

2. The clerk told me that the scarf was pure silk and cost thirty-five dollars.

   ____

3. My father advised me not to try to date American girls.

   ____

4. Linda said that she couldn't come to my party because she had to stay home and babysit.

   ____

5. My biology teacher asked why I was late getting to class for the exam.

   ____

6. The man told Henry to take a left turn when he came to the traffic light.

   ____

7. The Dean asked my roommate if she had plagiarized any of the material in her term paper.

   ____

8. Svetlana said that she was going to be a research chemist, just like her mother.

   ____

9. The train conductor picked up my coat and asked whose coat this was.

   ____

10. After a delicious dinner, Steve told Bill's mother that she was almost as good a cook as his own mother.

    ____

3. LANGUAGE CONVERSION: A SPECIAL GROUP PROJECT

HOW YOU CAN CHANGE THE STORY "ROPE" INTO A PLAY

A. Introduction and General Plan

Having read the story and considered how you would answer some of the questions, you have probably noticed that "Rope" consists almost entirely of dialogue, or conversation between the two characters. We are never given the exact words of the man and the woman in this story, but from the information the author "reports" to us, we can figure out their exact words by ourselves. All we have to do is to change the indirect speech into direct speech.

In this project, which can mostly be done right in class, you will be working together in pairs or small groups. For the sake of convenience, the story has been divided into ten short scenes, as in a one-act play. Each pair or group can be responsible for rewriting one or two scenes, converting the indirect speech into the *exact words* of each character. Your instructor will give guidance and help, as needed, and each group's rewritten section, or "scene," will constitute the writing part of this project.

The final part will be each group's oral presentation to the class of their portion of the play. Members of the group will be the players and will read their parts in front of the class. Of course, this will be much more effective if you practice in advance reading your part aloud several times. Your instructor can help you get the intonations so that your part sounds natural and real.

B. Directions for Carrying Out the Project

1. Here are a few points to remember about converting the indirect speech of this story into direct dialogue:

   - Everything is said as though the two people were talking *now;*
   - Each one speaks from the *first person* point of view (I) and refers to the other one as "you." (What will you substitute for "they," as in line 7, p. 184?);
   - Except for the "interior monologue" on p. 192 (see also Study Question 18), no third person pronouns (he or she) will be needed.

2. Since you are rewriting the story as a play, you will not need to use quotation marks or speaker tags (she said, he said, etc.). Instead, follow the form used in a drama:

   MAN: Oh, all right, all right—can I put them in the closet?
   WOMAN: Naturally not, there are brooms and mops and dustpans in the closet.

(The italicized passages in the story are *not* dialogue, so they will not need to be changed at all.)

3. Be sure to watch the vocabulary lists closely for idioms and colloquial usage, some of which you may not understand without some help. Work with your partner or your group to make *every* speech sound as idiomatic and as natural as possible. (Try reading them aloud as you write them.)
4. When you are rewriting your passages, *do not omit anything that anyone says!* It is very important to keep your play as close to the author's own original story as possible.
5. When you meet with your partner or your group the first time, make some decisions together to save time:
   a. Decide how you can best divide and share the work of conversion of the text from indirect to direct speech;
   b. Decide who is to read each part;
   c. Plan when you can practice together at least once (several times is better) before the final performance in class.
6. In the few places of the story where there is action but no speech, the instructor will fill in as the narrator in the class presentation. Remember, if any of the narrator's lines are in *your* scene, be sure to include them (in parentheses) when you write your dialogue. Then when you read your parts in class, allow time for the instructor to read the narrator's parts in between.
7. After your story-to-play conversion is written and checked by the instructor, someone should be responsible for typing or handcopying the script very neatly, double-spaced. Every member of the group should sign it because all (or both partners) share the credit for the production.
8. Make sufficient copies so that every member of the group has a script to read from. Hand in the original copy to the instructor after the performance of the play in class.
9. Questions for discussion after performing the play:
   a. Which scene or scenes did you enjoy the most? Why?
   b. What did you feel that you gained from hearing others read the scenes that you had read for yourself earlier?
   c. How did you feel about reading your own part or parts?

   (Further discussion of some of the meanings and implications of the story can be carried out in Activity 4, in questions dealing with the literary terms.)

4. LITERARY TERMS: A. DISCUSSION

DISCUSSION WRAP-UP FOR "ROPE"

"Rope" is another one of those stories that lend themselves to a study of the basic literary terms and their application to short fiction. Now that you are feeling quite familiar with the whole story, you can easily see some of the meanings and implications that those terms might suggest:

1. ***Setting***
   a. How important to this story is its setting?
   b. Why couldn't the story have taken place in a typical suburban neighborhood, or in a city apartment?
2. ***Characters***
   a. Is the woman in "Rope" just a nagging wife—in other words, a "flat" character? Check out each of the five qualities for "round" characters, and see how many of these aspects you can recognize in her.
   b. Follow the same procedure for the man in the story.
3. ***Plot and Motivation***
   a. Of the two characters, the woman is the one who seems to "want" something especially, the coffee being the most obvious thing. But what is it that she *really* wants, or why does she keep on nagging him so much?
   b. Is the important thing in this story whether she actually gets what she wants or whether she *thinks* she gets it? When and what would you say is the climax, or resolution, of the plot?
   c. There seems to be at least one underlying fear motivating them both. What *sort* of fear (or fears) could there be in each of them?
4. ***Symbolism***
   a. It is clear that the man is the only one who cares about the rope. What do you think is its real meaning or significance?
   b. If you trace what happens to the rope throughout the story, what does that say about *him?*
   c. What does the expression mean, "to give someone enough rope"? How does this idea apply to the story and to the relationship of the husband and wife?
5. ***Theme and Style***
   a. What ideas do you think the author is trying to suggest by both the content and the unusual style?
   b. Much of the dialogue in the story, like conversation in real life, consists of meaningless clichés. There seems to be very little real communication going on. Why is this?

4. LITERARY TERMS: COMPOSITION

B. WRITING A LITERARY ANALYSIS

Write an analytical essay of the story from one of the five literary angles discussed above. You may develop your essay according to the following plan, which is the same pattern used for the model essay, "Outsiders or Insiders?," in Chapter II, Activity 5.

Introduction: Begin with a paragraph that gives the title and the author's full name, along with two or three sentences about what happens in "Rope." End your introductory paragraph with a statement of your thesis—your particular angle to be taken in this essay.

Body, or Main Part: Use the questions under the section of your choice to give you leads to the main ideas that you want to develop. This section should be three to five paragraphs in length. Each of the paragraphs would discuss in some detail one of the points concerning your interpretation of that particular literary term and its relation to the story.

Conclusion: Before formulating your conclusion, thoughtfully read back over what you have written so far. Here is where you may feel free to express your personal views—of one or both characters, of the situation or setting and its effect on them, of their quarrel and its implications, etc. You may even bring in personal experience or observation, if you like. Be sure, however, that you wrap up your points and do not leave your reader hanging.

5. TWO POEMS FOR INTERPRETATION AND COMPARISON

A. A WOMAN'S VIEWPOINT

HIS SECRET GARDEN

Blanche McNamara

He locks me out, but begs me stay
and view his garden through the gate;
I find I cannot go away.

I'm sure he bars my sight of weeds—
illegal growth he can't control—
that grew from wild and wind-blown seeds.

Alone he can't eradicate
the guilty plants behind his wall
And I can't climb the sharp-spiked gate.

For love I'd soak up 2, 4–D
and, if he'd let me in, bleed death
upon the weeds and make him free.

But I lose strength; the night is late
and very soon those tangled vines
will hide the narrow entrance gate.

bars (*verb*): places barriers in the way.
weeds: unwanted plants in a garden.
eradicate: uproot, get rid of entirely.
guilty: at fault for committing a sin or an offense.
spiked: pointed iron bars set up to prevent anyone's climbing over.
2, 4–D: a substance for killing weeds, but harmless to other living things.
tangled: twisted and snarled.

1. The whole poem, including the title, is an extended metaphor, or figure of speech. What is the "secret garden" that this person is talking about? In the first stanza, what symbolic meaning is there in the words "lock" and "gate"?
2. In each of the other stanzas, underline words that you think are symbols or metaphors, and be prepared to explain what is meant by them.
3. What tone, or feeling, do you sense in the last stanza? Why does the poet feel this way?

B. A MAN'S VIEWPOINT

A PLEA

John Ciardi

I said to her tears: "I am fallible and hungry,
and refusal is no correction and anger no meal,
Feed me mercies from the first-bread of your heart.

I have invented no part of the error it is
to be human. The least law could jail me
and be upheld; the least theology, damn me

and be proved. But when, ever, have I come to you
to be judged? Set me straight to your last breath,
and mine, and feed me most what I need not deserve

—or starve yourself, and starve me, and be right."

1. What sort of person might be the speaker in this poem? To whom is the poem addressed and why?
2. Both this poem and the one before it seem to be about difficulties in communicating with someone; yet the viewpoints are different. Explain how and why they are different.
3. What do these two poems have in common with the story, "Rope"? How are the speakers in these poems *different* from the man and the woman in "Rope"?

fallible: capable of making mistakes.
refusal: showing unwillingness, rejection.
mercies: expressions of kindness and forgiveness.
first-bread: newly baked bread; an allusion to the "first-fruits," an ancient Hebrew ritual in which people offered to God the first part of the harvest as a way of giving thanks.
invented: created, thought up as an original idea.
jail (*verb*): have a person put into prison.
upheld: supported by authority.
damn: to condemn or punish (in this usage).
set me straight: correct or reform me
deserve: to merit, or receive the just results of one's deeds.

Ernest Hemingway (1899–1961)

Ernest Hemingway is probably one of the most widely admired and imitated of modern authors. From his early career as a journalist and foreign correspondent, Hemingway developed a style known for its direct, narrative approach and its natural-sounding conversation. His words tend to be few and uncomplicated, but they hint of vigorous action that is charged with dynamic feeling.

As a volunteer ambulance driver in World War I, Hemingway was severely wounded and was later awarded the Croce di Guerra. The terrors of the experience permanently affected his outlook by forcing him to recognize his own fear of death and annihilation, a feeling intensified by his father's suicide. His many stories of violence (bullfighting, boxing, big-game hunting, war) represent his efforts to overcome those fears by confronting death again and again through the characters he created.

The first of Hemingway's postwar novels, The Sun Also Rises *(1926), about "the lost generation" and the disillusionment of the 1920s, has been called his outstanding work.* A Farewell to Arms *(1940) deals with World War I,* For Whom the Bell Tolls *(1940) with the Spanish Civil War, and* Across the River and Under the Trees *(1950) with World War II. His well-known and popular novella,* The Old Man and the Sea *(1952), does not contain his best writing, although it was awarded the Nobel Prize.*

His finest short stories are found in Men Without Women *(1927), but also of interest is his collection of short fiction,* In Our Time *(1924), with its autobiographical leading character, Nick Adams. Other stories featuring Nick Adams, appearing from time to time in Hemingway's later work, have been collected and arranged in chronological order by Philip Young as* The Nick Adams Stories *(1972). Even though these stories are primarily fiction, Hemingway's portrayal of the same character, who develops from childhood in Indian territory through adolescence, wartime experience, and adult years as a writer and parent, can be seen as closely parallel to his own life.*

In the story "Soldier's Home," the turmoil that goes on in the mind of Harold Krebs suggests Hemingway's youthful struggle within himself, both men being on the threshold of manhood. Even amidst the horrors of war, the ideal behavior, to Hemingway, was neither to panic nor to resort to vicious brutality oneself, but rather to do "the one thing for a man to do, easily and naturally, when he might have done something else."

XII

Soldier's Home

Story Setting: *A small town in Oklahoma, near the center of the Midwest and of the United States. The period is soon after World War I (WWI), in which American soldiers, along with their British and French allies, fought against Germany (1914–1918) and won the war.*

In the Story: *After serving overseas, a young soldier returns home to find everything just about the same—except that he cannot fit into the life there as he once did and as his family expects him to.*

Krebs went to the war from a Methodist college in Kansas. There is a picture which shows him among his fraternity brothers, all of them wearing exactly the same height and style

GLOSSARY

1 **Methodist:** one of the larger Christian (Protestant) denominations, emphasizing simple faith, hard work, and moral living.
2 **fraternity brothers:** members of a college social club for men, joined by invitation only. Also called Greek letter societies.

INFORMAL SPEECH

STANDARD VOCABULARY

collar. He enlisted in the Marines in 1917 and did not return to the United States until the second division returned from the Rhine in the summer of 1919.

There is a picture which shows him on the Rhine with two German girls and another corporal. Krebs and the corporal look too big for their uniforms. The German girls are not beautiful. The Rhine does not show in the picture.

By the time Krebs returned to his town in Oklahoma the greeting of heroes was over. He came back much too late. The men from the town who had been drafted had all been welcomed elaborately on their return. There had been a great deal of hysteria. Now the reaction had set in. People seemed to think it was rather ridiculous for Krebs to be getting back so late, years after the war was over.

At first Krebs, who had been at Belleau Wood, Soissons, the Champagne, St. Michiel and in the Argonne did not want to talk about the war at all. Later he felt the need to talk but no one wanted to hear about it. His town had heard too many atrocity stories to be thrilled by actualities. Krebs found that to be listened to at all he had to lie, and after he had done this twice, he, too, had a reaction against the war and against talking about it. A distaste for everything that had happened to him in the war set in because of the lies he had told. All of the times that had been able to make him feel cool and clear inside himself when he thought of them; the times so long back when he had done the one thing, the only thing for a man to do, easily and naturally, when he might have done something else, now lost their cool, valuable quality and then were lost themselves.

His lies were quite unimportant lies and consisted in attributing to himself things other men had seen, done or heard of, and stating as facts certain apocryphal incidents

GLOSSARY

3 **Marines:** soldiers highly trained for service on warships and on land.
4 **division:** (used here as an army term) a large, self-contained section of armed forces.
4 **on the Rhine:** beside Germany's most famous river.
6 **corporal:** a higher rank than private, but below the rank of sergeant.
10 **hysteria:** irrational, emotional outbursts, sometimes experienced by a large group of people together.
13 **Belleau Wood,** etc.: battle scenes in World War I.
24 **apocryphal:** (special term) referring to ancient books of doubtful authorship, thus not included in the Bible. Fig. use is a euphemism for "untruthful."

INFORMAL SPEECH

11 **had set in:** had started and seemed likely to continue.
19 **cool and clear inside:** without any feeling of shame or regret; with no need to blame himself.

STANDARD VOCABULARY

3 ***enlisted:** signed up, entered the (armed) service. (Done voluntarily; thus those who enlist are often called "volunteers.")
8 **heroes:** men admired for their brave deeds.
9 **drafted:** required to serve (in the armed services).
10 ***elaborately:** with much care and attention to details.
11 ***reaction:** emotional response against something.
11 **ridiculous:** absurd, strange and silly.
15 ***atrocity:** a horrible act.
16 **thrilled:** excited, usually pleasantly.
16 ***actualities:** real events.
18 **distaste:** dislike.
23 ***consisted in:** were made up of.
23 ***attributing:** regarding or assigning as a cause. (Note usage of both verb and noun.)
24 ***incidents:** small events or happenings.

familiar to all soldiers. Even his lies were not sensational at the pool room. His acquaintances, who had heard detailed accounts of German women found chained to machine guns in the Argonne forest and who could not comprehend, or were barred by their patriotism from interest in, any German machine gunners who were not chained, were not thrilled by his stories.

Krebs acquired the nausea in regard to experience that is the result of untruth or exaggeration, and when he occasionally met another man who had really been a soldier and they talked a few minutes in the dressing room at a dance he fell into the easy pose of the old soldier among other soldiers: that he had been badly, sickeningly frightened all the time. In this way he lost everything.

During this time, it was late summer, he was sleeping late in bed, getting up to walk down town to the library to get a book, eating lunch at home, reading on the front porch until he became bored and then walking down through the town to spend the hottest hours of the day in the cool dark of the pool room. He loved to play pool.

In the evening he practised on his clarinet, strolled down town, read and went to bed. He was still a hero to his two young sisters. His mother would have given him breakfast in bed if he had wanted it. She often came in when he was in bed and asked him to tell her about the war, but her attention always wandered. His father was noncommittal.

Before Krebs went away to the war he had never been allowed to drive the family motor car. His father was in the real estate business and always wanted the car to be at his command when he required it to take clients out into the country to show them a piece of farm property. The car always stood outside the First National Bank Building where his father had an office on the second floor. Now, after the war, it was still the same car.

Nothing was changed in the town except that the young girls had grown up. But they lived in such a complicated world of already defined alliances and shifting feuds that Krebs did not feel the energy or the courage to break into it. He liked to look at them, though.

GLOSSARY

25 **pool room:** a public room where men play pool, a game in which balls are rolled on a table and knocked into small pockets by means of a long cue stick.
26 **chained:** fastened securely with heavy metal links.
30 **nausea:** an upset or sick stomach.
44 **real estate business:** selling and renting homes and other properties.
49 **defined alliances:** connections and loyalties between people that were clearly understood.
49 **shifting feuds:** old arguments or quarrels with issues and circumstances that were constantly changing.

INFORMAL SPEECH

32 **fell into the easy pose:** put on a kind of familiar behavior, trying to do the expected thing and yet seem natural and sincere.
39 **strolled:** walked in a slow way, taking plenty of time.
45 **out into the country:** along roads outside the town, where houses are separated by broad fields and wooded areas.

STANDARD VOCABULARY

25 **sensational:** causing an excited reaction.
26 **detailed:** marked by careful treatment that includes many small particulars.
27 ***comprehend:** understand.
27 **barred:** prevented (from).
28 **patriotism:** love for and loyalty to one's own country.
30 ***acquired:** gained by experience, or in other ways.
42 **wandered:** drifted along, in no particular direction.
42 **noncommittal:** not definite.
45 **command:** order (at his command).
45 **clients:** customers.
49 **complicated:** made of many parts, complex, confusing.

There were so many good-looking young girls. Most of them had their hair cut short. When he went away only little girls wore their hair like that or girls that were fast. They all wore sweaters and shirt waists with round Dutch collars. It was a pattern. He liked to look at them from the front porch as they walked on the other side of the street. He liked to watch them walking under the shade of the trees. He liked the round Dutch collars above their sweaters. He liked their silk stockings and flat shoes. He liked their bobbed hair and the way they walked.

When he was in town their appeal to him was not very strong. He did not like them when he saw them in the Greek's ice cream parlor. He did not want them themselves really. They were too complicated. There was something else. Vaguely he wanted a girl but he did not want to have to work to get her. He would have liked to have a girl but he did not want to have to spend a long time getting her. He did not want to get into the intrigue and the politics. He did not want to have to do any courting. He did not want to tell any more lies. It wasn't worth it.

He did not want any consequences. He did not want any consequences ever again. He wanted to live along without consequences. Besides he did not really need a girl. The army had taught him that. It was all right to pose as though you had to have a girl. Nearly everybody did that. But it wasn't true. You did not need a girl. That was the funny thing. First a fellow boasted how girls mean nothing to him, that he never thought of them, that they could not touch him. Then a fellow boasted that he could not get along without girls, that he had to have them all the time, that he could not go to sleep without them.

That was all a lie. It was all a lie both ways. You did not need a girl unless you thought about them. He learned that in the army. Then sooner or later you always got one. When you were really ripe for a girl you always got one. You did not have to think about it. Sooner or later it would come. He had learned that in the army.

Now he would have liked a girl if she had come to him and not wanted to talk. But here at home it was all too complicated. He knew he could never get through it all again. It was not worth the trouble. That was the thing about French girls and German girls. There was not all this talking. You couldn't talk much and you did not need to talk. It was simple and you were friends. He thought about France and then he began to think about Ger-

GLOSSARY

53 **shirt waists:** (OD) blouses.
53 **round Dutch collars:** very plain little white collars.
54 **front porch:** an open platform with a roof, attached to the front of a house, used for sitting outside in good weather.
63 **politics:** (lit) the art or science of government; more generally, the activities involved in getting what one wants from other people.

INFORMAL SPEECH

52 **fast:** (OD sl) daringly unconventional in sexual behavior (used of women).
64 **It wasn't worth it:** There was too little satisfaction for so much effort.
66 **live along:** just exist, without any particular effort or struggle.
68 **funny thing:** something hard to understand.
69 **a fellow:** a guy.
70 **could not touch him:** could not get him excited or interested.
78 **not worth the trouble:** too hard to bother with.
78 **the thing about:** the important thing, the thing that mattered.

STANDARD VOCABULARY

53 ***pattern:** a model that is copied.
58 ***appeal:** attraction.
60 **vaguely:** not clearly defined or understood.
62 **intrigue:** secret plans made with other people to accomplish one's purpose.
63 **courting:** pursuing with serious intent to marry.
65 ***consequences:** the results of actions.
67 ***pose:** (fig) put on an act, (lit) sit to be photographed or painted.
69 **boasted:** praised oneself or one's acts or belongings, bragged.
74 **ripe:** ready, mature.

many. On the whole he had liked Germany better. He did not want to leave Germany. He did not want to come home. Still, he had come home. He sat on the front porch.

He liked the girls that were walking along the other side of the street. He liked the look of them much better than the French girls or the German girls. But the world they were in was not the world he was in. He would like to have one of them. But it was not worth it. They were such a nice pattern. He liked the pattern. It was exciting. But he would not go through all the talking. He did not want one badly enough. He liked to look at them all, though. It was not worth it. Not now when things were getting good again.

He sat there on the porch reading a book on the war. It was a history and he was reading about all the engagements he had been in. The most interesting reading he had ever done. He wished there were more maps. He looked forward with a good feeling to

GLOSSARY

84 **the world they were in:** their whole outlook and their expectations in life.
90 **engagements:** (special term) military confrontations.

INFORMAL SPEECH

STANDARD VOCABULARY

91 **maps:** charts or diagrams showing details of a geographical area, in this case, showing battle maneuvers.

reading all the really good histories when they would come out with good detail maps. Now he was really learning about the war. He had been a good soldier. That made a difference.

One morning after he had been home about a month his mother came into his bedroom and sat on the bed. She smoothed her apron.

"I had a talk with your father last night, Harold," she said, "and he is willing for you to take the car out in the evenings."

"Yeah?" said Krebs, who was not fully awake. "Take the car out? Yeah?"

"Yes. Your father has felt for some time that you should be able to take the car out in the evenings whenever you wished but we only talked it over last night."

"I'll bet you made him," Krebs said.

"No. It was your father's suggestion that we talk the matter over."

"Yeah. I'll bet you made him." Krebs sat up in bed.

"Will you come down to breakfast, Harold?" his mother said.

"As soon as I get my clothes on," Krebs said.

His mother went out of the room and he could hear her frying something downstairs while he washed, shaved and dressed to go down into the dining room for breakfast. While he was eating breakfast his sister brought in the mail.

"Well, Hare," she said. "You old sleepy-head. What do you ever get up for?"

Krebs looked at her. He liked her. She was his best sister.

"Have you got the paper?" he asked.

She handed him *The Kansas Star* and he shucked off its brown wrapper and opened it to the sporting page. He folded *The Star* open and propped it against the water pitcher with his cereal dish to steady it, so he could read while he ate.

"Harold," his mother stood in the kitchen doorway, "Harold, please don't muss up the paper. Your father can't read his *Star* if it's been mussed."

GLOSSARY

96 **smoothed:** passed a hand over, stroked to remove the creases.
107 **frying:** cooking in fat or oil on top of the stove.
113 **shucked** (off): (generally used of husking corn) removed the wrapping or outside covering.

INFORMAL SPEECH

93 **that made a difference:** If that had not been true he would not have felt the same way.
99 **Yeah?:** Yes? Is that so? (Indicates surprise.)
100 **for some time:** a vague length of time, suggesting a long while.
101 **talked it over:** discussed it.
102 **I'll bet:** I think, I suspect.
102 **you made him:** you influenced him strongly, you put pressure on him.
106 **get . . . clothes on:** get dressed.
110 **Hare:** short form for "Harold" (a nickname).
110 **you old sleepy-head:** affectionate, noncriticizing term.
116 **muss up:** disarrange, destroy neatness and order.

STANDARD VOCABULARY

96 **apron:** a garment worn over the front of one's clothes to protect them (often worn by a woman while doing housework).
103 **suggestion:** mention of an idea.
114 **propped:** set up.
115 **steady:** make it firm and stable.

"I won't muss it," Krebs said.

His sister sat down at the table and watched him while he read.

"We're playing indoor over at school this afternoon," she said. "I'm going to pitch."

"Good," said Krebs. "How's the old wing?"

"I can pitch better than lots of the boys. I tell them all you taught me. The other girls aren't much good."

"Yeah?" said Krebs.

"I tell them all you're my beau. Aren't you my beau, Hare?"

"You bet."

"Couldn't your brother really be your beau just because he's your brother?"

"I don't know."

"Sure you know. Couldn't you be my beau, Hare, if I was old enough and if you wanted to?"

"Sure. You're my girl now."

"Am I really your girl?"

"Sure."

"Do you love me?"

"Uh, huh."

"Will you love me always?"

"Sure."

"Will you come over and watch me play indoor?"

"Maybe."

"Aw, Hare, you don't love me. If you loved me, you'd want to come over and watch me play indoor."

Krebs' mother came into the dining room from the kitchen. She carried a plate with two fried eggs and some crisp bacon on it and a plate of buckwheat cakes.

"You run along, Helen," she said. "I want to talk to Harold."

She put the eggs and bacon down in front of him and brought in a jug of maple syrup for the buckwheat cakes. Then she sat down across the table from Krebs.

GLOSSARY

120 **playing indoor:** (pronounced INdoor) a softball game with the same rules as baseball played on a field outdoors, not inside.
120 **pitch:** throw the ball to the player "up at bat," or ready to bat it.
125 **beau:** (OD) boyfriend.
143 **buckwheat cakes:** hot pancakes served with sweet syrup (often considered a breakfast treat).
145 **maple syrup:** a rather thick (viscous) liquid, very sweet and tasty, made by boiling down the sap from maple trees. (Note: All these "goodies" would be considered a very hearty, delicious, and "homey" meal.)

INFORMAL SPEECH

121 **the old wing:** arm.
123 **aren't much good:** are almost useless.
126 **you bet:** (sl) an expression of strong agreement.
135 **uh, huh:** a rather noncommittal "yes."
137 **sure:** intended to sound like a stronger "yes."
144 **run along:** go away. (Usually said to children, thus meant as a friendly put-down.)

STANDARD VOCABULARY

143 **crisp:** pleasantly brittle, rather than soft or soggy.
145 **jug:** an earthenware container with a handle.

"I wish you'd put down the paper a minute, Harold," she said.

Krebs took down the paper and folded it.

"Have you decided what you are going to do yet, Harold?" his mother said, taking off her glasses.

"No," said Krebs.

"Don't you think it's about time?" His mother did not say this in a mean way. She seemed worried.

"I hadn't thought about it," Krebs said.

"God has some work for everyone to do," his mother said. "There can be no idle hands in His Kingdom."

"I'm not in His Kingdom," Krebs said.

"We are all of us in His Kingdom."

Krebs felt embarrassed and resentful as always.

"I've worried about you so much, Harold," his mother went on. "I know the temptations you must have been exposed to. I know how weak men are. I know what your own dear grandfather, my own father, told us about the Civil War and I have prayed for you. I pray for you all day long, Harold."

Krebs looked at the bacon fat hardening on his plate.

"Your father is worried, too," his mother went on. "He thinks you have lost your ambition, that you haven't got a definite aim in life. Charley Simmons, who is just your age, has a good job and is going to be married. The boys are all settling down; they're all determined to get somewhere; you can see that boys like Charley Simmons are on their way to being really a credit to the community."

Krebs said nothing.

"Don't look that way, Harold," his mother said. "You know we love you and I want to tell you for your own good how matters stand. Your father does not want to hamper your freedom. He thinks you should be allowed to drive the car. If you want to take some of the nice girls out riding with you, we are only too pleased. We want you to enjoy yourself. But you are going to have to settle down to work, Harold. Your father doesn't care what you start in at. All work is honorable as he says. But you've got to make a start at

GLOSSARY

149 **going to do:** planning to do with his life, what kind of job he would look for.
155 **no idle hands:** based on the old saying, mistakenly thought to be from the Bible, that Satan (the devil) "finds mischief for idle hands to do." According to the Puritan ethic, people who don't work get into trouble.
156 **His Kingdom:** reference to the lordship of God and Jesus Christ on earth.
174 **we are only too pleased:** we would be relieved and happy.

INFORMAL SPEECH

152 **about time:** a euphemism for "it's a little late," or "it's high time."
167 **settling down:** finding jobs, wives, and a respectable lifestyle.
168 **get somewhere:** succeed, get ahead in life.
169 **being . . . a credit to:** making someone proud of them.
172 **for your own good:** to help you (often said as a form of reproof).
172 **how matters stand:** a vague way of saying what we think.

STANDARD VOCABULARY

152 **mean:** unkind.
159 **embarrassed:** self-conscious and uncomfortable.
159 ***resentful:** inwardly angry.
160 ***temptations:** attractions to draw one to commit sinful acts.
161 **exposed to:** subjected to, influenced by.
166 ***ambition:** desire and drive to succeed.
168 ***determined:** firmly resolved.
169 **community:** town or local neighborhood.
172 **hamper:** get in the way of.
176 **honorable:** proper and respectable.

something. He asked me to speak to you this morning and then you can stop in and see him at his office."

"Is that all?" Krebs said.

"Yes. Don't you love your mother, dear boy?"

"No," Krebs said.

His mother looked at him across the table. Her eyes were shiny. She started crying.

"I don't love anybody," Krebs said.

It wasn't any good. He couldn't tell her, he couldn't make her see it. It was silly to have said it. He had only hurt her. He went over and took hold of her arm. She was crying with her head in her hands.

"I didn't mean it," he said. "I was just angry at something. I didn't mean I didn't love you."

His mother went on crying. Krebs put his arm on her shoulder.

"Can't you believe me, mother?"

His mother shook her head.

"Please, please, mother. Please believe me."

"All right," his mother said chokily. She looked up at him, "I believe you, Harold."

Krebs kissed her hair. She put her face up to him.

"I'm your mother," she said. "I held you next to my heart when you were a tiny baby.

Krebs felt sick and vaguely nauseated.

"I know, Mummy," he said. "I'll try and be a good boy for you."

"Would you kneel and pray with me, Harold?" his mother asked.

They knelt down beside the dining room table and Krebs' mother prayed.

"Now, you pray, Harold," she said.

"I can't," Krebs said.

"Try, Harold."

"I can't."

"Do you want me to pray for you?"

"Yes."

So his mother prayed for him and they stood up and Krebs kissed his mother and went out of the house. He had tried so to keep his life from being complicated. Still, none of it had touched him. He had felt sorry for his mother and she had made him lie. He would go to Kansas City and get a job and she would feel all right about it. There would be one

GLOSSARY

193 **chokily:** unable to talk well because of crying.
200 **knelt down . . . table:** Among certain religious groups it was a custom after breakfast or dinner to have family prayers. First, the father would read a passage from the Bible; then all the members of the family knelt beside their chairs and took turns praying aloud.

INFORMAL SPEECH

178 **speak to you:** tell you politely what you have to do ("lay it on the line").
184 **wasn't any good:** was not working out as he had hoped or intended.
198 **Mummy:** a small child's name for "mother."
198 **try and be:** try to be.
208 **tried so to:** tried so very hard to.

STANDARD VOCABULARY

182 **shiny:** glistening (with tears).
185 **hurt:** made (her) feel sad and rejected.
197 ***nauseated:** physically sick or upset.
199 **kneel** (past tense: knelt): get down on one's knees.
209 **touched:** see Informal Speech p. 210.

more scene maybe before he got away. He would not go down to his father's office. He would miss that one. He wanted his life to go smoothly. It had just gotten going that way. Well, that was all over now, anyway. He would go over to the schoolyard and watch Helen play indoor baseball.

GLOSSARY

INFORMAL SPEECH

211 **got away:** escaped, left the house, or left home.
212 **miss that one:** avoid getting caught in that particular situation.
212 **just gotten going:** "just nicely started," had only recently begun.

STANDARD VOCABULARY

211 **scene:** an unpleasant emotional incident.
212 **smoothly:** (lit) without wrinkles or ripples; thus, without difficult encounters.

1. STUDY QUESTIONS

DISCOVERING THE STORY THROUGH OBSERVATION AND INFERENCE

1. ***Observation:*** What do we learn about Harold Krebs from the two pictures in which he appears, one taken in 1917 and one in 1919?
Inference: The Armistice ending the War was signed on November 11, 1918. What ironies are implied by the hometown people's attitudes toward returning soldiers and to Krebs in particular (in the third paragraph)? Why does he tell them lies?
2. ***Observation:*** What are the two kinds of lies he tells that cause Krebs to feel a sense of nausea? Is there any part of his wartime experience that he feels he can be proud of?
Inference: When Hemingway says, "In this way he lost everything" (p. 209, line 34), what does he mean?
3. ***Observation:*** Harold Krebs is a soldier home from the war. How does he spend his time, and what do we learn about his family's attitudes toward him?
Inference: What double meaning and irony can you see in the title of the story? (Try looking up the term "soldiers' home" in an unabridged dictionary such as *Webster's Third International* or *The American Heritage Dictionary.*)
4. ***Observation:*** What are the things he likes about the young girls in his home town?
Inference: What does he mean by their being "complicated" and by not wanting "any consequences"? Why do you think this is so important to him?
5. ***Observation:*** What sort of experience has Krebs had with girls when he was in the Marines in Europe? Where can you find some contradictions or inconsistencies in his attitude toward girls?
Inference: Look carefully over the "stream of consciousness" passage beginning on p. 209, line 48 ("Nothing was changed. . . .") and continuing on to p. 210, line 93 ("That made a difference"). How can you tell, by Hemingway's style, that he is portraying what Harold Krebs is thinking? Point out places that seem especially true to life or natural.
6. ***Observation:*** What is Harold Krebs's reaction to his mother's offer of the family car? Why?
Inference: Some of the time the main character is referred to by his surname only (Krebs), and sometimes he is called "Harold" or "Hare." How would you explain this?
7. ***Observation:*** The conversation between Krebs and his sister could be called typical Hemingway dialogue. Point out some characteristics that you notice about it. (You might try comparing it with one or two of the conversations from other stories.) Do people really talk this way?
Inference: What do you learn about Helen herself from the conversation? Why does Harold answer her as he does?

8. ***Observation:*** What is it that his mother wants him to do? What points or arguments does she use to try to persuade him?
   Inference: Would you say she is trying to influence or to manipulate him when she:

   Offers him the family car?
   Cooks him a nice breakfast before talking to him?
   Begins "crying with her head in her hands"?

   Why are these called "feminine tactics" or methods, and why don't men use them?
9. ***Observation:*** How is Harold Krebs's response to his mother's question about his loving her (p. 215, line 181) different from his answers to Helen's similar question?
   Inference: Why does he contradict his first reply to his mother? Which of his answers do you believe, and why?
10. ***Observation:*** At what different points does Harold's mother bring religion into her conversation with him? What effect does this have on Krebs?
    Inference: Why do you think he responds with "I can't" when she asks him to pray with her? How would you describe his mother's kind of religion?
11. ***Observation:*** In what ways or areas has Krebs's relationship with his mother been shown to be basically simple? Does Krebs think it is simple or complicated?
    Inference: What is the meaning of the short passage beginning, "It wasn't any good . . ." on p. 215, line 184? Has Krebs believed that lies made things *more* complicated or less so? What do *you* think?
12. ***Observation:*** In the final paragraph we are told once more that Krebs has "tried so to keep his life from being complicated." How has he been able to do this, up until now?
    Inference: What sort of future is implied for Krebs by the last paragraph, including the final sentence? Do you think he can continue to avoid complications?

2. VOCABULARY: A. ACCURATE MEANINGS

WHAT DOES THE WORD MEAN?

Each of the starred words from the Standard Vocabulary list appears in a sentence below in a form other than it has in the text. This sentence is followed by an uncompleted statement beginning: "This means. . . ." You are to decide which of the four words or phrases comes the closest to the meaning of the vocabulary word as used in the sentence.

Often when you are reading a passage you can guess at the meaning of a word from the context clues of the sentence itself, but few context clues are provided this time. Moreover, as we have seen before (in Chapter XI, Vocabulary Study), new meanings sometimes arise when the *form* of the word has been changed.

For these reasons, you may want to try the exercise with the aid of your English dictionary. In order to make it easier for you to look them up, the words have been used here in alphabetical order.

1. Our rich neighbor, Mr. Panterra, has been buying thousands of acres of land, but the more he has, the more **acquisitive** he becomes. This means that Mr. Panterra is becoming more
   a. anxious
   b. greedy
   c. wealthy
   d. curious
2. The woman told the doctor that her broken arm was caused by her falling downstairs, although it **actually** came from a fight with her husband. This means that the fight with her husband
   a. may have caused it
   b. probably caused it
   c. never caused it
   d. really caused it
3. The backstage was crowded with eager little girls and their **ambitious** mothers. This means that the mothers were
   a. anxious for them to succeed
   b. impatient to go home
   c. proud of their little daughters
   d. sorry they had come
4. Even though I thought the black kitten was the most **appealing,** I decided to take the yellow one with white paws. This means that the black kitten was the
   a. best-looking
   b. friendliest
   c. most charming
   d. most valuable
5. One of the guards was known for his **atrocious** treatment of all the prisoners. This means his treatment of them was
   a. unfair
   b. generous
   c. strict
   d. brutal
6. Before buying a small car, it is wise to find out all you can about the **attributes** of compacts and subcompacts. This means you should learn about their
   a. qualities
   b. miles per gallon
   c. costs
   d. transmissions

7. Each of the graduate students passed a **comprehensive** examination in his or her major field. This means the examination was
   a. very long
   b. very complete
   c. very difficult
   d. very important
8. Max Ferrari was caught driving at 85 miles per hour while drunk, and **consequently** his license was suspended. This means his license was temporarily taken away
   a. as a warning
   b. as a punishment
   c. as a result
   d. as a safety precaution
9. My recipe says to beat the frosting until it is the right **consistency** to spread on the cake. This means to beat it until it is
   a. the right degree of thickness
   b. the same color as the cake
   c. the right temperature
   d. in the best condition
10. The refugees who came by boat were people of courage and **determination.** This meant that they
    a. had great endurance
    b. believed in fate
    c. were desperate people
    d. were strong in resolution
11. His sister **elaborated** on the plans for her wedding. This means she
    a. exaggerated their importance
    b. began to work on them
    c. described all the details
    d. explained how much they would cost
12. The success of the fund drive came about because of the mayor's success in **enlisting** many citizens to help raise money. This means the mayor
    a. paid the citizens out of the treasury
    b. got people to agree to help
    c. made a list of all the citizens
    d. made a list of people who owed taxes
13. When Dianne **incidentally** remarked to her husband that Saks was having its annual sale of fur coats, she was surprised when he suddenly got angry. This means that Dianne
    a. made the remark by mistake
    b. had a reason for her remark
    c. hurt his feelings by her remark
    d. made the remark by chance
14. Julio **patterned** himself after his older brother, who played soccer, rugby, and hockey. This means Julio
    a. wanted to be like his brother

b. wanted to be different from his brother
c. could not keep up with his brother
d. tried to get ahead of his brother

15. The CIA agent was able to break up a large drug-smuggling operation by **posing** as a drug dealer. This means the CIA agent
    a. spied on one of the drug dealers
    b. acted like one of the drug smugglers
    c. testified against the drug smugglers
    d. sent a drug dealer to jail
16. When the Democrats controlled Congress they were called progressive; when the more conservative Republicans took over, they were called **reactionary.** This means Republican policies were considered to be
    a. dominated by young radicals
    b. old-fashioned and out of date
    c. unfriendly to foreign governments
    d. against the U.S. government
17. Every time his roommate came in late, Song-Nien's **resentment** increased. This means Song-Nien felt more
    a. tired from lack of sleep
    b. worried about his roommate's habits
    c. annoyed or angry with his roommate
    d. curious about where his roommate had been
18. I usually don't eat dessert, but your lemon meringue pie certainly is **tempting.** This means the pie
    a. is full of calories
    b. was baked by a good cook
    c. is probably fattening
    d. is hard to stay away from

2. VOCABULARY: B. DISCUSSION: AN ARTIST'S SPECIAL EFFECTS

A GENIUS WITH SIMPLE WORDS

Hemingway was a master in the art of using simple and direct language that packs a lot of meaning. Sometimes also, as in "Soldier's Home," he achieves especially memorable effects by the repetition of a word used in a variety of ways or with double meanings. Hemingway's skill in the manipulation of words deserves a second look.

The five words that we'll examine are: *cool, pattern, good, nausea,* and *touch.* All of them appear two or three times except the word *good,* which is repeated several more times. Use the two study questions below as your guide in looking for some of the more subtle, but interesting, variations of meaning in these very ordinary words.

Questions to Ask Yourself About the Word

a. What does the word *mean* here? (Is it part of an idiom, or is it used literally?) Does the word have a favorable or unfavorable connotation?
b. What does the word, as used here, contribute to the story? (Does it help to reveal someone's character, emphasize a theme, add to the naturalness or realism, or suggest a symbolic meaning?) What is the effect of its repetition?

Cool

1. "All of the times that had been able to *make him feel cool and clear inside himself. . . .*" (p. 208)
2. ". . . the times so long back when he had done the one thing, . . . now lost *their cool, valuable quality. . . .*" (p. 208)
3. ". . . to spend the hottest hours of the day in the *cool dark of the pool room.* He loved to play pool." (p. 209)

Pattern

4. "They all wore sweaters and shirt waists with round Dutch collars. *It was a pattern.*" (p. 210)
5. "They were such *a nice pattern. He liked the pattern.* It was exciting." (p. 211)

Good

6. "There were so many *good-looking young girls.*" (p. 210)
7. "Not now when *things were getting good again.*" (p. 211)
8. "He looked forward *with a good feeling* to reading all the *really good histories* when they would come out with *good detail maps.*" (pp. 211–12)
9. "He had been *a good soldier.* That made a difference." (p. 212)
10. "'*Good,' said Krebs.* 'How's the old wing?'" (p. 213)
11. "The other girls *aren't much good.*" (p. 213)
12. "Charley Simmons, who is just your age, *has a good job. . . .*" (p. 214)
13. "You know we love you and I want to tell you *for your own good* how matters stand." (p. 214)
14. "It *wasn't any good.* He couldn't tell her. . . ." (p. 215)

Nausea

15. "Krebs acquired *the nausea in regard to experience* that is the result of untruth or exaggeration. . . ." (p. 209)
16. "Krebs felt sick and *vaguely nauseated.*" (p. 215)

Touch

17. "First a fellow boasted how girls mean nothing to him, . . . that they *could not touch him.*" (p. 210)
18. "He had tried so to keep his life from being complicated. Still, none of it *had touched him.*" (p. 215)

3. STYLE: A WRITING EXPERIMENT

LET YOUR WRITING FOLLOW YOUR THOUGHTS

In two stories, "Rope" and "Soldier's Home," there are stream-of-consciousness passages in which a main character seems to be thinking aloud. The ideas are expressed in a disjointed, rather illogical way, some of them seem to contradict each other, and certain phrases or words keep recurring in a repetitive fashion.

The effect of this sort of writing is extraordinarily like a person thinking aloud, then reconsidering his own thoughts as though arguing with himself. Like most things that look simple, it is actually quite hard to do well.

But even though you may not be a master craftsman like Hemingway or Porter, you can try your hand at stream-of-consciousness writing. One approach is to do some free-writing, or simply to write as quickly as you can whatever comes into your head. Remember, this time you don't need a main idea or a thesis. The writing is meant to be *without focus;* it doesn't have to go anywhere in particular but can just wander wherever your next thought happens to lead.

This kind of exercise has a twofold purpose, both immediate and potential. Freestyle writing, done occasionally like this, is a way to loosen up your writing and let you simply put words on paper, without worrying about making mistakes. (No one will care how many you make.)

There can be a long-range benefit to such writing also. Done on a regular basis, as you might in a journal or a diary, free-writing is the best way to help you to develop your own style or "voice." The more you write, the more satisfying and exciting it becomes as you begin to sharpen your own powers of observation, discover your true feelings and beliefs, and even find yourself creating new and original ideas. Writing can, in fact, be both an emotional release and a stimulus.

Our writing experiment will be in two parts, the first part in stream-of-consciousness style and the second slightly focused, as an interior monologue.

A. Free-Writing

Directions

This will be *timed* writing. You will be allowed exactly ten minutes to write. (The exercise can be repeated as many times as there is time for or as the instructor wishes.)

1. Begin with a single statement such as you might say to yourself right now: _______ will be waiting for me after class, and we'll go get something to eat. I wonder if I can catch the bus and get to the bank before it closes.

This is a silly assignment, and I don't know what to write about.
If I could smoke in class I'd enjoy it better.

2. After writing your statement, just keep on putting down whatever comes into your head. Don't even worry about sentences or punctuation. JUST WRITE.
3. When time is called, stop immediately. Read back over what you have written. Does any of it remind you of either one of the passages where the man in "Rope" or Harold Krebs seemed to be thinking aloud?
4. *Optional:* Some people might like to read their free-writing passages aloud. If so, note how the writing represents that person's own special point of view and way of thinking. This is where each one's individual *style* comes from.
5. If possible, repeat the exercise.

B. Focused Writing

Directions

In this exercise, which will require more time than the first one, you will try to create an interior monologue. This is like a conversation with yourself, although it is still written in continuous, paragraph style like a stream-of-consciousness passage.

1. Imagine a very ordinary, uncomplicated decision that you must make. It is best to pick a decision in which you sometimes have trouble making up your mind, even though the issue is a rather trivial one such as:

   Whether to wear your blue shirt (or blouse) with a sweater or your white turtleneck pullover;
   Whether to make your lunch or to buy it;
   Whether to study in the library, the student center, the cafeteria, or some other place;
   Whether to buy the main dish or a hamburger for lunch;
   Whether or not to call home tonight.

   You can think of many other choices that you have to make every day.
2. Think of *one* such situation in which you have to decide which of two or more alternatives to choose. Begin by asking yourself the question: "Shall I ____________ or shall I _______?"
3. Then begin to *answer* your question, taking first one point of view and then the other, as though discussing both sides of the question. Remember that the matter does not have to be very important, yet it can still start you on a rather lengthy discussion with yourself. (For instance, do you ever stand and stare at your clothes hanging in the closet and wonder what to wear, or gaze glassy-eyed into the open refrigerator trying to think what you want to prepare for supper?)
4. After you have written your interior monologue, read it over and then compare it with the train-of-thought passage of the man in "Rope" after he has

quarreled with his wife. Do you see in yours any similar pattern of taking first one side, then the other?

In Conclusion: Writing can be approached in a variety of ways and can serve a number of different functions. The most effective and artistic results come by way of calculated purpose combined with training, experience, and much skillful rewriting. However, one does not need to be a good writer to enjoy the pleasures and the therapeutic benefits of simply writing freely, whatever and as much as one chooses to write.

In short, *anyone* can write.

4. GRAMMAR REVIEW: RELATIVE CLAUSES

USE THEM SPARINGLY—BUT *USE* THEM

Hemingway's work is not noted for its smooth, flowing style or its long, descriptive passages. He is much better known for his short, clipped sentences like those in the conversational passages of "Soldier's Home." Nevertheless, Hemingway does occasionally employ a slower, more expository style similar to what you see in nonfiction books and magazines.

You will find examples of this more deliberate style in the first six paragraphs of "Soldier's Home," which cover the two-year background prior to the beginning of the story. The author's method here employs relative clauses to combine ideas and information. We'll examine where and how he did this; then we'll use this same method to combine short sentences by means of well-connected relative clauses.

A. See How Hemingway Did It

Relatives are words that *relate* one part of a sentence to another. A relative is a *pronoun;* it refers to (or substitutes for) a particular noun. The entire relative clause functions as an *adjective* modifying that same noun, known as the *antecedent.* (For additional information on relatives, consult your own grammar or composition reference textbook.)

How many relative clauses and their antecedents can you find in the first six paragraphs of Hemingway's story?

1. In paragraphs 1 and 2, find two examples of "which." Give the antecedent in each case.
2. In paragraphs 3 and 4, find two examples of "who." Give the antecedent for each one.

3. In paragraph 4, give two examples of "that" used as a relative. Give the antecedent each time.
4. In paragraph 6, give one example of "that" used as a relative and one example of "that" used as a conjunction. Explain how you know the difference.
5. In paragraphs 5 and 6, find four examples of the use of "who." Find the antecedent for each one.

B. Make Relative Clauses Work for You, Too

You can see that relatives are useful for joining two related ideas, especially when separate sentences would seem too short or too choppy. For example:

Harold Krebs had two little sisters. They thought of him as a hero.
Harold Krebs had two little sisters, who thought of him as a hero.

Relative clauses are not hard to write, but they can be a bit tricky.

Here are some tips to help you avoid some common mistakes:

a. Use *who/whom* only for a person; use *which* only when *not* referring to a person.
b. Do not add an extra pronoun where none is needed.

   Wrong: The handsome blue Persian cat, which we had hoped *it* would win, only got honorable mention.
   Right: The handsome blue Persian cat, which we had hoped would win, only got honorable mention.
   Wrong: Mr. Gregorian found an excellent business consultant, whose advice he was careful to follow *it*.
   Right: Mr. Gregorian found an excellent business consultant, whose advice he was careful to follow.

c. Know when to set off your relative clause with commas: If it is *simply descriptive* (nonrestrictive), DO add commas. If it is needed to complete the meaning (restrictive), DO NOT add commas. When *that* is the relative, omit the commas.
d. A final reminder: Since a relative clause is an *adjective* clause, be sure to put it in the place where it belongs—*directly following the noun or antecedent it modifies.*

Combine Using Which:

1. Krebs felt it necessary to tell many lies.
   They made him feel like a phony.
2. His mother made him a delicious breakfast.
   It was supposed to put him in a good mood.

Combine Using Who:

3. Harold Krebs had been a soldier in World War I.
   He returned home in the summer of 1919.
4. The townspeople had heard many atrocity stories.
   They expected Krebs to tell them some more.
5. His father was in the real estate business.
   He always wanted the car to be at his command.

Combine Using That:

6. Krebs's mother told him some things.
   His father had said these things to her earlier.
7. Some relationships were complicated.
   Krebs did not like such relationships.
8. There was a book about the War.
   Harold Krebs liked this book the best.

Combine Using Whom

9. Pretty young girls strolled by the house every day.
   Harold Krebs had known them when they were children.
10. The German and French girls were not complicated.
    Krebs had met them in the War.

Combine Using Whose:

11. Krebs seemed to care about his sister Helen.
    Her influence in his life was stronger than his father's.
12. Harold Krebs's dream had been to avoid complications.
    He finally found that he had to begin to accept responsibility.

5. ESSAY EXAMINATIONS: A. TIPS ON HOW TO TAKE THEM

FOLLOW THE METHODS THAT "A" STUDENTS USE

In the first chapter you were introduced to the study of short fiction and given some suggestions for making use of the vocabulary lists and activities. In this last section, the guidelines offered for taking a final examination can help you to decrease your exam anxiety while you substantially *increase* your grade. After you have studied the exam tips in Part A and the key word clues in Part B, try your hand at answering the sample questions in Part C.

Survey the scene.
Plan your attack.

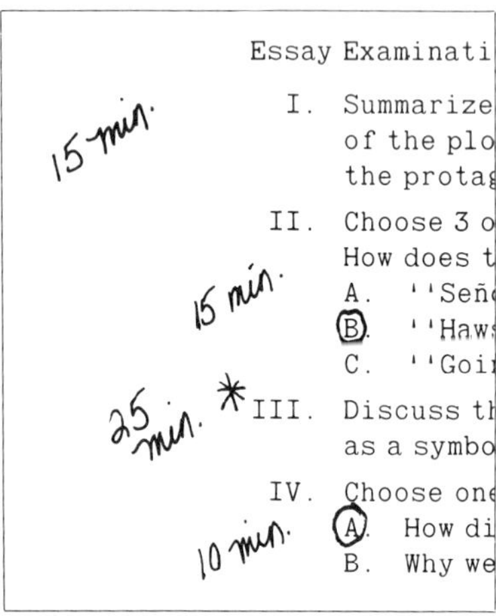

Approach

1. Make a quick, five-minute survey of what you will have to do, which questions can be handled most quickly, and which ones will take more thought. Estimate how much time to allow to write each answer.
2. If you are given a choice of questions, take care to follow instructions, and *do the required questions first.* When you are told to choose one out of three, for instance, write on *only one,* and do it just as well as you can. Remember that a teacher or grader is looking for one well-developed answer, not three that are incomplete.

Procedure

Watch the time!

1. Keep careful track of the time. If possible, *pace* your answers (work more slowly or quickly) according to the value of the question. Try, however, to give the most time to the questions you know the most about.

Label your answers.

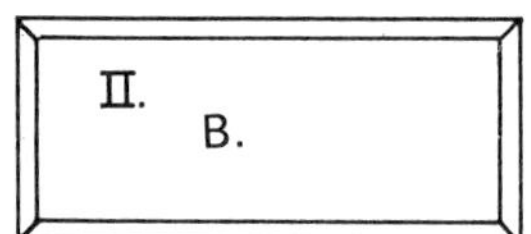

2. Make it very obvious *which* question you are dealing with. Allow enough space so that your answers are easy to read and not crowded. Try to keep them in the same order as the questions, but if you must write an answer out of order, *mark* it plainly to match the question.

Oops!

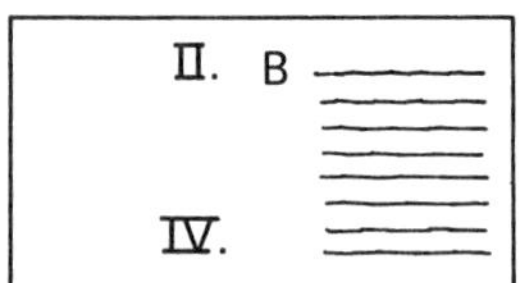

3. Never walk away from an exam without checking to make sure you have answered all the questions. Nothing is more frustrating than to discover later that you lost 20 points because you overlooked a question—and you knew the answer!

Exposition

Read the question twice

1. Read each question an extra time, to make certain that you understand what it means and what it asks you to do. Watch out for any special instruction that might have been added or "tacked on," like ". . . and why?" or ". . . and explain the difference."

Answer first with a thesis statement

2. Before you write, take a moment to *think* what you want to say. Then begin by stating your answer as though it were the *thesis for an essay or composition.* You will then be able to develop your thesis statement by using specific details, reasons, and examples.

Support your thesis with facts

3. Back up your thesis statement with definite facts, ideas, steps in a process, points in your argument, or whatever will best support it. Keep asking yourself the questions: How? Where? When? Who? How often? Why?

Before you actually take an essay examination, it is important to become familiar with the type of wording used and what it means. Part B will list some of the terms that frequently appear in essay questions and will give you some examples of their use.

5. ESSAY EXAMINATIONS: B. KEY WORD CLUES TO FOLLOW

WHAT IS THE QUESTION ASKING FOR?

You have studied your textbook from cover to cover, and you feel confident that you *know* the subject. But wait a minute: All your knowledge will gain you no points if you *fail to answer the question that is asked.* All too often, students give the wrong answer simply because they misread or misunderstand the wording of the question.

Certain words or terms can provide the clue to what the instructor is asking for and expects to find in a "good" answer. Be wise—*familiarize* yourself with these terms before you even get to the exam. What *are* those words, and what do they mean? Most of them can be classified under two general headings:

1. Instructions that ask you to *provide information* about the subject;
2. Directives that ask you to *deal with or work with information.* The first type of question involves content only. If you are familiar with the material, you will find questions of this sort relatively simple to answer.

Questions Requiring You to Provide Information May Want You To:

Paraphrase: State the meaning in your own words.
Example: Paraphrase the man's defense of himself in John Ciardi's poem "A Plea."

Summarize: Cover the *main points* or events in a few sentences.
Example: Summarize what happened in the story "The Loudest Voice."

Describe: Tell about it in detail, as though making a verbal picture.
Example: Describe the kind of life Harold Krebs was living during the first summer after he came home from the war in Europe, or describe the young German climber in "Hawsmoot."

Trace: Follow the course of development over a given period of time.
Example: In the story "Rope" trace the times that the rope appears or is mentioned throughout the story.

Characterize: Mention the person's distinguishing qualities.
Example: Characterize each of the following: The businessman in "On the Outside"; the inspector in "The Test"; and the mother in "Soldier's Home."

Identify: Show that you recognize and understand what or who it is.
Example: Identify the literary term "narrator" and give two examples from the stories.

Explain: Make something clear and understandable, such as a meaning, process, or purpose.
Example: Explain why Hawsmoot continued to climb the Giraffe without using a rope.

Analyze: Tell what the *parts* are and how they are related to each other.
Example: Analyze the literary term "round character" by showing how it applies to one of the following characters: Marian in "The Test"; the young man in "Going Home"; Shirley in "The Loudest Voice."

The second type of question is more difficult, because it makes two requirements of you: You have to *know the material well,* and you must be able to *think logically and critically about it* in relation to other knowledge that you have.

Questions Requiring You to Deal With Or To Use Information May Want You To:

Discuss: Write your ideas about the subject in a thoughtful and purposeful way.
Example: Discuss the importance of *work* as a theme in two of the stories we read.

Evaluate: Give your considered opinion of the worth, importance, or value.
Example: Evaluate Mr. Parkhill's effectiveness as a teacher in "Mr. Kaplan and Vocabulary."

Compare/contrast: Show how two or more things (or persons) are similar or not, *in the particular areas designated.* (Be careful here not to just describe one, then the other, without clearly stating *how* they are alike or different.)
Example: Compare the mothers in "The Loudest Voice" and in "Soldier's Home" on the following points: Personality or character; influence or effect on the main character; and importance to the story.

As a final point, essay questions very often ask you to do a combination of several things in the same question. If you take the time first to *read* each one carefully and make sure that you understand what you are expected to do, you can begin your answer with a simple, direct statement—a thesis. From there on, you can develop your supporting points into a clear and organized presentation—one of the essential features of an "A" paper.

5. ESSAY EXAMINATIONS: C. ESSAY QUESTIONS FOR PRACTICE

AS ZERO HOUR APPROACHES

If you have regularly done the required work in a course, your preparation for the final examination is already well established. If you have put off studying until the last minute, you may be able to cram enough information into your head to get by with a passing grade, but it is unlikely that you will remember much of it beyond the exam itself.

The attitude you have toward an approaching examination can strongly affect your ability to function at your best when the time comes. Although overconfidence is not recommended, your ability to think and to recall information may actually be damaged by excessive anxiety and panic.

Remember that a final examination serves *you* as well as your instructor: It stimulates you to make a thorough and comprehensive review of all you have learned in the course. As a result, the disconnected material that you have struggled to master bit by bit suddenly has meaning for you. The overall subject becomes clearer; you can see the relationship of the parts to the whole. And often it becomes apparent *why* the instructor put so much emphasis on things that had seemed unimportant at the time.

If you think of the coming exam as a puzzle ("What will he or she ask us about ________?"), it becomes a challenge to you to demonstrate how much you have learned and what you can do with it all. One way to raise your confidence level and also to strengthen your preparation for an examination is to anticipate the questions you are likely to be asked and search out the answers in advance.

Following are questions of the type that might appear in a final exam on the stories in this book. Since the questions employ most of the terms given in Part B, they will give you a chance to practice your test-taking skills.

Short-Answer Questions

I. Ten special qualities of character or personality are given below. For each one, mention one person (from a story in this collection) you would CHARACTERIZE in that way. Explain *why* you have named this person.

1. A person of determination
2. A hopeful or optimistic person
3. A hard worker
4. A person who spends money generously
5. A self-confident person

6. A person who is discouraged or depressed
7. A person of courage
8. A lonely person
9. A person who wants to succeed
10. A kindly or considerate person

II. Each of the following passages is a quotation from one of the stories in the book. IDENTIFY which story it is from, and EXPLAIN the circumstances or the context in which it appeared. Write on ______ only. (Your teacher will fill in how many you are to write about.)

1. "Now, Mistress Mandy," the inspector said, "remember your degree."
2. He saw the house from a distance of about a block, and his heart began to jump.
3. "Does it hurt Shirley to learn to speak up? It does not. So maybe she won't live between the kitchen and the shop."
4. "Riots and disturbances," murmured the first student. . . . "Hunger is a crime against society."
5. "Mistake by Mitnick! Ha! Mit *enimals* she is painting chairs? Ha!"
6. "Aw, Hare, you don't love me. If you loved me, you'd want to come over and watch me play indoor."
7. I said, "Little Bits, you're a game kiddie. I admire your spunk."
8. "I'm not as fast as I once was," he said, "but I'm a careful man, a good workman yet."
9. He was exhausted. But he forced his arms to work until slowly by inches his head was level with his hands.
10. Had he brought the coffee? She had been waiting all day long for coffee.
11. "I am quitting this company for a different job. You pay me now?"

III. EVALUATE the *importance of the setting* in three of the following stories:

"Señor Payroll"
"Rope"
"Hawsmoot"
"Going Home"
"The Test"

Questions Requiring Short Essays

IV. A famous American writer, Thomas Wolfe, wrote a novel entitled *You Can't Go Home Again.* Two of the stories we read were about young men who return home after being away for two years.

A. Give the title and author of each of the stories.

B. COMPARE (or contrast) the homecoming experiences of the two young men, and EXPLAIN how you think Wolfe's theme could apply to either or both of them.

V. DESCRIBE *three characteristics* that seem to you to represent an "outsider." Then mention *three examples* of people from the stories whom you would call "typical outsiders." (EXPLAIN why you chose each one.)

VI. Titles are not part of a story; yet they actually play an important part in arousing the reader's interest or curiosity, hinting of the story's content, and suggesting an important theme.

For *only three* of the titles given below, EXPLAIN the *specific meaning* of the title for that story; then DISCUSS the title's relationship to an *important theme* of the story.

"The Loudest Voice" "Hawsmoot" "Going Home"
"The Test" "On the Outside" "Rope"

VII. For *one* of the stories mentioned below, ANALYZE the plot by means of the following steps:

A. TRACE the main episodes, or SUMMARIZE what happens in the story.
B. IDENTIFY the protagonist and what he or she particularly wants.
C. DESCRIBE the way the story turns out—whether he or she *gets* that wish or not.
D. EXPLAIN what decision or choice by the protagonist was involved in the result, and tell what effect it has had on the final outcome.

"The Test" "The Loudest Voice"
"On the Outside" "Going Home"
"Hawsmoot"